David Lean

DAVID LEAN

HOWARD MAXFORD

BATSFORD

For the dream ticket:
David Lean, Freddie Young and Maurice Jarre

And for my workmates at the Ashcroft Theatre in Croydon: Jeremy,
Anne, Tony, Phil, Jim and the crew (remember, it'll soon be Panto!)

A catalogue record for this book is available from the British Library.

ISBN 0 7134 8680 5

Printed in Great Britain by Redwood Books, Trowbridge

Volume © B T Batsford 2000

First published in 2000 by B T Batsford
A member of the Chrysalis Group plc

9 Blenheim Court
Brewery Road
London N7 9NT

CONTENTS

'He was the most extraordinary man I ever knew.'

From Robert Bolt's screenplay of *Lawrence of Arabia*, as spoken by Colonel Brighton

One

~m~

CROYDON DAYS

The town of Croydon, just south of London, has had some bad press down the decades. It may not be the most glamorous of places, probably being home to more accountants and insurance brokers than almost anywhere else in the Britain. Yet it's also the birthplace of many a celebrity from the world of entertainment, among them actor manager Sir Donald Wolfit, character actress Dame Margaret Rutherford, comedy star Arthur Lowe, stage legend Henry Irving, screen star Dennis Price, actress Sylvia Syms, music hall comedian Roy Hudd and actress Dame Peggy Ashcroft, after whom the local theatre is named.

Croydon's most famous son, Oscar-winning film director David Lean, at first seemed destined to follow many of the town's inhabitants into the dusty world of finance. Born at the family home, 38 Blenheim Crescent in South Croydon on Wednesday 25 March 1908, Lean's father, Francis William Le Blount Lean, was himself not only a chartered accountant but a Quaker too, so the last thing anyone expected of the young Lean was that he would become a film director. Indeed, David and his brother Edward, younger by three years, were forbidden to go to the cinema as children by their mother, Helena Annie Lean, for fear of the corrupting influence it might have on them.

By the time Edward was on the scene, the family had moved some miles down the road to Merstham, which is where they were when the First World War broke out in 1914. However, it wasn't the declaration of war, nor Francis Lean's conscientious objections to being a part of it, a by-product of the family's religion, that prompted their return to Croydon for the duration. It was the inability to get David admitted to the local school, a Church of England establishment, that caused the upset. Despite the return to Croydon for David's schooling, he proved far from being an apt pupil. In fact, David was soon slipping behind his younger brother Edward as far as academic achievement was concerned, all of which proved frustrating not only to his parents, but to the increasingly introspective David.

By the time the war was over, while David was at prep school, The Limes, his parents not only resigned from their Quaker meeting house, but also split up; David's father met another woman with whom he wished to spend his life. This came as a devastating blow to Helena and her two sons, especially given the stigma that separation carried in at the time. Francis Lean stayed a part of his children's lives after this split, yet the fact that his new partner, with whom he eventually moved to Hove to live (unwed), had a young son of her own, must have made the sense of abandonment even greater to the Lean boys. It was at this darkest hour of his parents' split that David saw his first film, director Maurice Elvey's version of *The Hound of the Baskervilles*. The year was 1921 and Lean was already 13 years old.

Lean had developed a keen interest in still photography by this time, having been given a Kodak Box

Brownie camera for his 11th birthday by an uncle. This interest in photography would later become a passion. At this stage, his experiences with cinema had all been second hand, via reports from friends, classmates and his parents' char lady, a Mrs Egerton, who regaled the fascinated Lean with the antics of Charlie Chaplin. That first screening of *The Hound of the Baskervilles* must therefore have been quite a revelation, even if today much of Elvey's prolific output (over 300 films) is critically reviled. To Lean, however, untutored as he was in the ways of even the simplest films, Elvey's productions such as *The Elusive Pimpernel* and *Dick Turpin's Ride to York*, accompanied by a live orchestra, must have been irresistible, especially given his burgeoning interest in adventure stories. Little did he then know but Lean would gain a foothold in the film industry as Elvey's camera assistant some years later.

During the next few years, Lean devoured everything the cinema had to offer, even taking trips up to London's West End where he found himself enthralled by such films as *The Big Parade* and *The Gold Rush*. One director in particular greatly impressed him. This was the American Rex Ingram, a former actor and screenwriter who, in the early Twenties, took to making spectacular productions of such popular books as *The Four Horsemen of the Apocalypse*, *The Prisoner of Zenda* and *Mare Nostrum*. The visual power of these movies apparently came as something as a revelation to Lean, for it was while watching them that he gradually came to realise that there were actually people behind the film cameras, shaping what he was watching on the big screen, just as he carefully composed the increasingly ambitious stills he took with his own Box Brownie.

In 1922, despite his lack of academic achievement, Lean was enrolled at Leighton Park Public School in Reading to continue his education. A progressive school in which the Quaker religion took a comparative backseat, it must have seemed like a breath of fresh air to Lean after his stifling experiences in education so far. Still, Lean's academic standing continued on a very average path during his time at the school, although his outside interests – film, photography and a love of natural history – continued to develop.

When Lean left the school at the age of 18, there was still the question of what he would do for a career. Astonishingly, farming was the first occupation given serious consideration, although eventually David went to work as a junior at the accounting firm of Viney, Price and Goodyear in the City, which is where his father worked. Lean, with his poor grasp of maths, found the work tortuous and dull. Thus, in his spare time, his fascination with photography continued as a form of escape, even branching out into amateur home movies at one stage. Like many others of his generation, he also had a passion for radio, having a crystal set in his room at home.

Meanwhile, as if to push home the message that David was an underachiever, it was his younger brother Edward who, having also been sent to Leighton Park during David's last couple of years there, was chosen by their father to be sent to Oxford to continue his education. It wasn't long after this that David decided a career in accounting definitely wasn't for him, but that perhaps a life in film-making was. The question was how to get that all-important first introduction? Surprisingly, the answer lay with his father.

In the director's chair. David Lean observes the action during the making of Madeleine *in 1949.*

Two

~~~

FIRST STEPS

Somewhat conveniently for David Lean, it transpired that his father Francis knew the accountants who dealt with the books for the Gaumont studios at Lime Grove. After much cajoling, David finally got his father to arrange an introduction for him at the studio, which resulted in his being interviewed by one of the studio's executives, one Harold Boxall, who then passed him over to Gareth Gundrey, the studio's production manager, who himself also occasionally wrote and directed films. David's enthusiasm earned him a probationary period – unpaid – at the studio, working as a runner.

The year was 1927 and the Gaumont studios were expanding; there was plenty of work to keep technicians busy. Thus, in addition to making the tea and running errands, Lean also found himself working as a clapper boy on a film called *The Quinneys* being directed by Maurice Elvey. A silent production starring Alma Taylor and John Longdon, *The Quinneys*, which concerns the sale of some fake Chippendale chairs, was made in the established 'silent' manner, with Elvey shouting instructions to the actors as they worked through the various scenes, with a small orchestra always on hand in the background to provide suitable mood music. It is fascinating to think that there may be off-cuts of film somewhere showing the young Lean snapping his clapperboard in front of the camera before a take (a few frames do exist of Lean working on a film, as do several rare behind-the-scenes stills).

Following a difficult period, things were picking up in the British film industry, especially after the introduction of The Cinematograph Films Act in early 1928. This attempted to address America's stranglehold on the film industry by guaranteeing that a quota of films shown in British cinemas were British in origin, thus securing employment for many actors and technicians. This had the less desired effect of heralding the 'quota quickie', in which studios churned out low-budget, low-interest support films simply to fulfil the quota. Nevertheless, some interesting talent emerged from the set-up, most notably director Michael Powell, who cut his teeth at the helm of a number of quota quickies in the early Thirties, treating the experience as equivalent to education in a modern day film school.

Gaumont may not have concentrated too heavily on quota film-making but it did give Lean the grounding he needed if he was going to make anything of himself in the film business. He also

In the late Twenties, Lean began to make a name for himself as an editor. By the time he came to make Doctor Zhivago *he was a master of the craft. Here, he supervises the work of Norman Savage, who would go on to win an Oscar for his editing on* Doctor Zhivago.

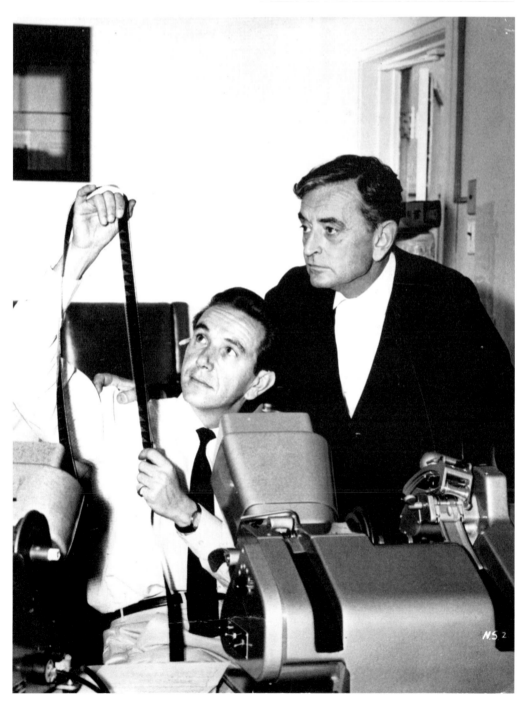

learned a little about film criticism at the time from one of the studio's camera assistants, Henry Hasslacher who, using the pen name Oswell Blakeston, wrote for the highbrow magazine *Close Up*. Just as Herbert Pocket pretentiously re-Christened Pip as Handl in Dickens' *Great Expectations*, Hasslacher decided to change David's name to Douglas, which later caused some mild confusion when Lean decided to revert to his real name. This affectation aside, Hasslacher did show Lean that countries other than America and Britain successfully produced films, and although they seldom were shown outside their country of origin, except at film societies, they were often of a higher artistic value than those churned out by British directors such as Maurice Elvey.

There was a lot for Lean to observe and take in during the following months, including the practicalities of cinematography, editing, film development, set construction and lighting. Such was his enthusiasm, however, that he absorbed everything, although his interest was most keenly taken by editing. When the opportunity arose, he jumped at the chance to watch Maurice Elvey cut *The Quinneys*, proving to be a useful assistant to the director. He also observed Will Kellino direct *Sailors Don't Care*, on which he assisted cinematographer Baron Ventimiglia, a role he continued on *The Physician*, which was produced by Maurice Elvey and directed by German George Jacoby. Lean also remained under the watchful eye of Elvey for the director's next film, a thriller entitled *Palais de Danse*, on which Lean again assisted the director in various capacities.

By late 1928, Lean was a familiar face at Gaumont and, having gained confidence with Elvey, was also proving a valuable assistant to other directors, among them Edwin Greenwood, for whom Lean assisted with the camera on *What Money Can't Buy*. He was also persuaded to appear in front of the lens, too, in a brief walk-on role, sharing a few frames with the film's star, Madeleine Carroll. Unfortunately, a blunder by Lean in the dark room lost some valuable footage which subsequently had to be re-shot. As a consequence he was taken off *What Money Can't Buy* and was demoted to wardrobe 'mistress' for his next assignment. A lavish re-enactment of the Charge of the Light Brigade, it went by the title *Balaclava* and was directed by Maurice Elvey. A major production of its day, it proved to be a big success for the studio. Nevertheless, Lean hated his time on the film, on which his duties involved handing out, retrieving and maintaining the hundreds of British and Russian uniforms needed for the production. It's hard to imagine Lean sitting, needle and thread in hand, sewing on a button or doing a quick bit of repair work!

By the time *Balaclava* was released, technology had marched on apace. In America sound was now all the rage thanks to the pioneering success of *Don Juan* and *The Jazz Singer*, both of which had been made by Warner Brothers using the Vitaphone process. Released in 1926 and 1927, respectively, these two films, along with a number of Vitaphone novelty shorts, helped to revolutionise the industry. Britain quickly jumped on the bandwagon, with Alfred Hitchcock re-shooting much of his 1929 film *Blackmail*, originally made as a silent, to take advantage of the new medium. Made for British International Pictures (BIP), the film proved an instant hit. Gaumont wasn't far behind, re-issuing *Balaclava* with a music and effects soundtrack. The studio also put into production a futuristic fantasy entitled *High Treason*. Directed by Maurice Elvey and based on a play by Noel Pemberton-Billing, the film, set in 1950, is a pacifist tract in which women unite to prevent the outbreak of a second world war. Seemingly forgiven for his dark room gaffe on *What Money Can't Buy*, Lean was back as Elvey's assistant on the film, which was also released as a silent, owing to the slow changeover to sound in the cinemas of Britain's smaller towns and villages.

The coming of sound proved to be the making of Lean, for after assisting on *High Treason*, he went on to help director Sewell Collins in the cutting room with a musical short called *The Night Porter*. Unfortunately, Collins couldn't master the craft of sound cutting. Lean, however, learning from newsreel editor John Seabourne, quickly took in the basic rudiments of synchronisation and proved valuable to Collins in the editing of the picture. This did much for Lean's standing at Gaumont, so much so that following the departure of John Seabourne to another company – plus a costly editorial blunder by his replacement, Roy Drew – Lean was given the job of editing the Gaumont Sound News. Lean had come a long way in his few years at Gaumont, and all by the age of 21.

Three

CUTTING EDGE

Lean quickly proved his worth in the Gaumont News cutting rooms, handling with speed and efficiency breaking stories such as the crash of the R101 airship in France. News of the crash came on the morning of Sunday 5 October 1930; by that evening Lean had cobbled together a report on the disaster which was subsequently played in cinemas, complete with a commentary by Lean himself.

Closer to home, developments were also taking place in Lean's personal life. An affair with his first cousin Isabel resulted in her getting pregnant during a trip to Paris. Isabel and David saw no option but to get married, which they did on Saturday 28 June 1930. The birth of their son, Peter David Tangye Lean, followed on Thursday 2 October the same year. With his busy workload, Lean was barely around at the home that he shared with Isabel and the baby in London's Holland Park, which was perhaps just as well, for although proud to be the father of a healthy son, Lean wasn't the ideal candidate for the job of parenting. Rather than family and home, his life centred around work. Changing nappies and digging over the garden were just not his forte. Lean thrived in the cutting rooms, and with EVH Emmett taking over from Lean as commentator, Gaumont Sound News quickly established itself as a staple programme with cinema audiences.

In 1931, Lean was offered a job at British Movietone News. His duties would be more or less the same as they had been at Gaumont, but the pay would be better. Given his domestic situation, Lean quickly agreed to take the job. It was also in that year that Lean edited his first feature film. A light society comedy starring Nora Swinburne and Godfrey Tearle entitled *These Charming People*, it was directed by Swiss-born Louis Mercanton. He was best known for co-directing (with Henri Desfontaines) the highly successful and influential 1912 film *Queen Elizabeth* (aka *Les Amours de la Reine Elisabeth*), starring the legendary stage tragedienne Sarah Bernhardt. Unfortunately, Lean was carried away by his enthusiasm and, having cut just one reel of the film, was demoted to assistant editor. There was a lot of difference between editing a newsreel and a feature, and Lean still had much to learn. The demotion must have hurt his pride considerably but it was back to the newsreels. *These Charming People* is all but forgotten today, although it has one interesting footnote: Lean's future wife, Ann Todd, had a small role in it.

Undeterred by his setback, Lean was determined to master the art of feature cutting. Consequently, when not tied up with newsreels, he became a familiar face in the studio's other editing suites, often assisting the cutters with their work, simply to gain experience. His efforts eventually paid off, for he was asked to go to Paris to edit a Foreign Legion picture entitled *Insult*, which had been directed by an American Harry Lachman. Set in North Africa, it stars the young

John Gielgud, Elizabeth Allan and Sam Livesey. Like *These Charming People*, it is forgotten today. Nevertheless, it was an important stepping stone for Lean, for it provided him with his first official feature credit. However, his lengthy absence and increased workload put an unbearable strain on his marriage, which Lean decided to end in mid-1932, leaving Isabel and his young son to fend for themselves.

Lean's next feature assignment was *Money for Speed* for the British and Dominion (B&D) studio, starring John Loder, Cyril McLaglen and a young Ida Lupino. A low-budget quota quickie, it marked the directorial debut of the German-born Bernard Vorhaus, who had been working in America as a writer before this assignment. Although a routine production, Vorhaus and Lean got on well together, so much so that after cutting *Matinee Idol* for director George King, Lean went on to edit Vorhaus's next film, the equally low-budget *Ghost Camera*, starring Henry Kendall. The plot concerns Kendall as a chemist who, while on holiday, inadvertently picks up someone else's camera and decides to develop the film inside to see if he can trace the owner through it: his investigations uncover foul play. Despite this promising scenario, the film, based on a novel by Jefferson Farjeon, is scuppered by its low budget, Vorhaus's stilted handling and some fairly stiff performances from Kendall, Ida Lupino, George Merritt and John Mills; no amount of clever cutting on Lean's part could salvage it.

Nevertheless, Lean was gaining experience as an editor by leaps and bounds, and he learned some useful tips from B&D's editor-in-chief, an American named Merrill White, who had cut innovative Hollywood films such as *The Love Parade* for Ernst Lubitsch and *Love Me Tonight* for Rouben Mamoulian, each of which are notable for their stylish and pioneering use of sound and music. Consequently, despite having just edited newsreels and a handful of unimpressive B movies, Lean's reputation was growing, even to the point that other editors at both his own and other studios would ask for his help and advice when they ran into problems. In 1933, in addition to the three features he'd already cut (*Money for Speed*, *Matinee Idol* and *The Ghost Camera*), his newsreel work and his unaccredited work as a trouble-shooter, he cut a further two features. The first of these, *Tiger Bay*, stars Henry Victor and Anna May Wong and was directed by designer–director J Elder Wills for Ealing. The second, *Song of the Plough*, stars Rosalinde Fuller and Stewart Rome, and was directed for B&D by John Baxter, later known for such social dramas as *Love on the Dole*.

The heavy workload continued into 1934 with *Dangerous Ground*, a thriller starring Joyce Kennedy and Malcolm Keen, directed by Norman Walker for B&D. This was followed by the more interesting *Secret of the Loch*. Directed by Milton Rosmer for Ealing, it centres round a diver's belief that he has encountered the fabled monster in Loch Ness' murky depths. Starring Seymour Hicks, Nancy O'Neill, Gibson Gowland and Rosamund John, the film exploited a resurgence in interest in the Loch Ness myth (complete with a magnified lizard), and proved mildly popular, despite being a pretty shoddy piece of work.

Assisting Merrill White, Lean next tackled the Anna Neagle vehicle *Nell Gwyn*, which had been directed by Herbert Wilcox and photographed by Freddie Young, then B&D's cinematographer-in-chief. *Nell Gwyn* marked the first of several close encounters between the future director and

the established cinematographer, although their partnership wouldn't become a reality for another 25 years.

In the meantime, Lean kept slogging away in the cutting rooms with Merrill White, his next job being an adaptation of George Barr McCutcheon's oft-filmed comedy *Brewster's Millions*, which had been tailored for debonair song and dance man Jack Buchanan. A lively production, it was the first British film from the American director Thornton Freeland, then best known for the Eddie Cantor musical *Whoopee*, and Fred Astair and Ginger Rogers' breakthrough hit *Flying Down to Rio*. Again, among the *Brewster's Millions'* credits could be found one of Lean's future collaborators. This time it was Anthony Havelock-Allan, who would go on to produce many of Lean's films, although at this stage Havelock-Allan was a casting director.

In addition to his official work for B&D, 1934 also saw Lean work on *Java Head* with editor and future director Thorold Dickinson over at ATP for producer Basil Dean. Like *Brewster's Millions*, *Java Head*, a period romantic drama about a Bristol shipbuilder, marked the British debut of another American, J Walter Ruben who, before his work here, had directed a number of unambitious productions in Hollywood at both RKO and MGM, among them *Where Sinners Meet*, *Public Hero Number One* and *Riff Raff*, the latter of which, a con-man comedy, had at least been enlivened by the performances of Jean Harlow and Spencer Tracy. Ruben's work on *Java Head* was equally unambitious, and despite an interesting cast that included Anna May Wong, John Loder, Edmund Gwenn, Elizabeth Allan and Ralph Richardson (later to appear in Lean's *The Sound Barrier* and *Doctor Zhivago*), the film needed all of Dickinson's and Lean's talents to bring it to life.

The year of 1935 brought a better prospect in the form of *Turn of the Tide*, a would-be prestige production about two fishing families who feud, like Montague and Capulet, until their arguments are quelled by a romance and marriage. Produced by John Corfield for British National, the film remains important for the fact that it was the first production financed by the Methodist flour magnate J Arthur Rank, who entered the industry in a bid to promote religion, but ended up heading the largest and perhaps most influential and prolific production company in British film history. He was responsible for such subsidiary outfits as The Archers, Two Cities and Cineguid, the latter was co-founded by Lean, Ronald Neame and Anthony Havelock-Allan, through which they would make *This Happy Breed*, *Blithe Spirit* and *Oliver Twist*.

Directed by Norman Walker (*Tommy Atkins*, *The Middle Watch*), *Turn of the Tide*, based on *Three Fevers* by Leo Walmsley and starring Geraldine Fitzgerald (making her film debut), John Garrick, Niall MacGinnis, Wilfred Lawson and Moore Marriott, was photographed by the German-born Franz Planer (who'd go on to photograph Hollywood spectaculars such as *20,000 Leagues Under the Sea*, *The Pride and the Passion* and *The Nun's Story*). As with *Java Head*, Lean worked unaccredited on the film, which went on to surprise everybody by earning some very respectable reviews, although

Studio portrait of producer/director Herbert Wilcox, for whom Lean edited several films in the early to mid-Thirties. Among them was Nell Gwyn *in 1933, photographed by Freddie Young, who would photograph Lean's* Lawrence of Arabia *over 25 years later.*

the American trade paper *Variety* pointed out that the 80-minute production would have benefited from being, 'Cut to an hour,' to, 'make an acceptable second feature.'

It was back to B&D for the even more prestigious *Escape Me Never* starring German refugee Elisabeth Bergner as Gemma Jones, a waif who marries a composer to provide a name for her illegitimate child, only to discover that the musician loves another. Despite the scenario (based on the play by Margaret Kennedy in which Bergner had appeared in both London and New York), the film was lavishly produced by Herbert Wilcox (including location work in Venice and The Dolomites), with director Paul Czinner (another refugee from Hitler's Germany and also Bergner's lover and future husband) bringing out the best qualities in the star, who went on to earn an Oscar nomination for her performance. Although Bergner would ultimately lose the award to Bette Davis for *Dangerous*, the nomination at least helped to raise the film's profile in America, where *Variety* commented that, 'Its able presentation commands attention.'

For Lean to have been chosen to edit the film for the highly respected Czinner (*Der Traumende Mund*, *Catherine the Great*, both starring Bergner) was a major coup, and he learned much from observing the director at work filming the interiors at the B&D studios. Lean would go on to edit a further two films for Czinner. However, before that came another move (or perhaps Lean was 'poached' after the success of *Escape Me Never*), this time to Elstree, where his first assignment was *Ball at the Savoy* for producer and occasional director John Stafford. Little seen today, the film, a romance starring Conrad Nagel, Marta Labarr, Lu-Anne Meredith and Esther Kiss, was directed by Victor Hanbury (*Admirals All*, *The Crouching Beast*).

Ball at the Savoy may have been something of a non-event, but Lean's private life was becoming increasingly busy with a string of romances and affairs, among them *Ball at the Savoy* starlet Lu-Anne Meredith, all of which culminated in Lean's bid for true freedom by asking Isabel for a divorce, which she finally agreed to in 1935.

Back at work with Paul Czinner, Lean edited an adaptation of *As You Like It*, for which he earned an incredible £60 a week, an industry record at the time for an editor. A major production, *As You Like It* is notable for the talent involved, which includes the Russian-born Hollywood producer Joseph M Schenck, who helped to finance the film through Twentieth Century Fox, of which he was the founder. The screenplay was by *Peter Pan* author JM Barrie and Robert Cullen, the cinematography by American Harold Rosson (already a veteran from *Tarzan of the Apes* and *The Scarlet Pimpernel*, with *The Wizard of Oz* and *Singin' in the Rain* to come), while the music was by William Walton, who'd provided the score for Czinner's *Escape Me Never*. Elisabeth Bergner heads the cast as Rosalind, and she is supported by Laurence Olivier (Orlando), Leon Quartermaine (Jacques), Sophie Stewart and Felix Aylmer, while further down the list can be found Peter Bull and John Laurie.

Despite the best efforts of all concerned (Lean even did a couple of days directing on the picture when Bergner fell ill and Czinner went to her bedside), the film was over-produced, while Czinner's restrained directorial approach resulted in several slow passages, prompting Graham Greene to observe in *The Spectator*, 'Czinner has been too respectful towards stage tradition. He

A stirring performance. Elisabeth Bergner in the 1937 remake of Dreaming Lips. *The film was directed by her husband, Paul Czinner, and edited by David Lean.*

seems to have concluded that all the cinema can offer is more space: more elaborate palace sets and a real wood with room for real animals. How the ubiquitous livestock weary us before the end.' Like many Shakespeare films of the Thirties, such as George Cukor's *Romeo and Juliet* (with its 43-year-old Romeo and its 36-year old Juliet) and Max Reinhardt's *A Midsummer Night's Dream*, *As You Like It* is an over-decorated affair. Graham Greene continued, 'How disastrously the genuine English woodland is spoilt by too much fancy, for when did English trees, in what apparently is late autumn, bear clusters of white flowers?'

Perhaps all (Czinner, Bergner, Lean, William Walton) were more comfortable with their next production, *Dreaming Lips*, a less consciously arty and more typical star vehicle concerning the wife of an invalid musician who commits suicide after having an affair (indeed, Bergner and Czinner had already successfully tackled the subject in Germany in *Der Traumende Mund* in 1932). It went down a storm with female audiences ('How the handkerchiefs flutter at the close,' wrote Graham Greene in *The Spectator*). Based on the play *Melo* by Henry Bernstein, the film was again made by top class talent, among them writer Margaret Kennedy (the author of *The Constant Nymph* and *Escape Me Never*), who penned the screenplay with Lady Cynthia Asquith and the German-born Carl Meyer. The latter was already a Czinner veteran having co-written the screenplays for *Ariane* and *Der Traumende Mund*, although he was perhaps best known for *The Cabinet of Dr Caligari*, *The Last Laugh* and *Sunrise*. Although Meyer would live until 1944, *Dreaming Lips* would be his last screenplay.

Also involved behind the cameras was the noted American cinematographer Lee Garmes, hailed for his work on *Zoo in Budapest*, *Scarface* and *Shanghai Express*, the latter earning him an Oscar for his lighting of Marlene Dietrich, which was no doubt why he was hired to photograph Bergner (although *Dreaming Lips* would be his only British film). The art department was headed by the Russian-born Andrei Andreiev, assisted by Tom Morahan, while the film was financed and produced by a Czechoslovakian Max Schach. The international flavour was also carried over into the cast, with Bergner supported by Mexican Romney Brent and Canadian Raymond Massey, while Joyce Bland, Sydney Fairbrother, Felix Aylmer and Donald Calthrop batted for England.

A glossy production, the film earned some strong notices: *Variety* commented, 'One of the finest productions ever made in England. [Had it been] made in Hollywood, the story would be whitewashed and much of its strength weakened.' Unfortunately, the film wasn't the commercial hit everyone hoped it would be. However, Lean found consolation in another affair he'd started, although this time the relationship would prove longer lasting. The name of the girl, an up-and-coming actress, was Kay Walsh who, having gained experience as a dancer in revue in London's West End, had made her film debut in 1934 in *Get Your Man*, which she had followed with appearances in *How's Chances?*, *The Luck of the Irish* and *The Secret of Stamboul*. Although none of these films left a lasting mark, Walsh would go on to become one of Britain's most-liked female leads – she also ended up becoming the second Mrs David Lean.

Four

—⁂—

LEAN TIMES

After the commercial disappointment of *Dreaming Lips*, Lean was unemployed. Worse still, he had been less than prudent with his money. He had to move from the luxurious apartment he'd been living in at Mount Royal – a haven for the film industry close to Marble Arch – and into the lodgings at which Kay Walsh was living (a bold step given that the couple weren't yet married and cohabiting was taboo at the time).

At least Walsh was working, her appearance in the play *The Melody That Got Lost* having earned her a contract with Ealing Studios, where her first film was the George Formby vehicle *Keep Fit*. Produced by Basil Dean and directed with verve by Anthony Kimmins, it was an immediate hit and did much to help establish Walsh with audiences (certainly more so than the programmers and pot-boilers in which she'd previously appeared). Also among the burgeoning talent involved in the film's making was cinematographer Ronald Neame and art director Wilfred Shingleton, both of whom would later make substantial contributions to Lean's films.

The long period of unemployment for Lean came to an end when he was approached to edit *The Last Adventurers* in 1937. By no means a prestige production in the Czinner manner, the film was a low-budget drama involving the adventures, romantic and otherwise, of the crew of a fishing trawler. But the rent needed paying and the film achieved its modest goals adequately enough. Produced by Henry Fraser Passmore, it marked the directorial debut of respected cinematographer Roy Kellino, while the cast included such familiar faces as Niall MacGinnis, Peter Gawthorne, Linden Travers, Katie Johnson (remembered for her later performance as the kindly old landlady in *The Ladykillers*) and, in a supporting role, Kay Walsh, whose fee no doubt also came in handy for the household bills.

Lean must have been a little more cautious with the money he earned from *The Last Adventurers* because he didn't edit a feature again for almost a year. Work was also a long time coming for Walsh too, who was cast to appear opposite George Formby again, this time in *I See Ice*. Like *Keep Fit*, the film was directed by Anthony Kimmins, with Ronald Neame and Wilfred Shingleton involved again as cinematographer and art director, respectively. Soon after, Walsh also secured a supporting role in another comedy, a minor effort entitled *Meet Mr Penny*, which centres round a clerk's attempts to prevent a property tycoon from building on some local allotments. Directed in a workmanlike fashion by the prolific David MacDonald (*Double Alibi*, *The Lost Curtain*), the film features radio star Richard Goolden (known to millions as Old Ebenezer), Vic Oliver, Hermione Gingold, Fabia Drake and Wilfred-Hyde White. Despite these familiar faces, it was quickly forgotten.

When things were just about as bad as they could get financially, Lean was given the opportunity to edit his most prestigious film yet – an adaptation of George Bernard Shaw's 1913 masterpiece

Pygmalion. Made in 1938, it is rightly regarded as one of the great British films of the Thirties and went on to become the country's biggest money maker in 1939, earning kudos for all involved.

Born in Ireland in 1856, George Bernard Shaw was one of the leading playwrights of his generation (*Saint Joan*, *The Millionairess*, *Major Barbara*, *Man and Superman*). Yet perhaps because his life was almost halfway over before the invention of cinema, he was always wary of the medium, and given the resultant mediocrity of the few plays he'd allowed to be filmed before *Pygmalion*, one can understand why. Among the disappointments had been a half-hour version of *How He Lied to Her Husband* starring Edmund Gwenn (notable chiefly for an early screenplay credit by Frank Launder) and a lacklustre adaptation of *Arms and the Man* with Barry Jones (as Bluntschli), Anne Grey and Angela Baddeley (later known for playing Mrs Bridges in television's *Upstairs Downstairs*). Both of these films were directed (in 1930 and 1932, respectively) with Shaw's blessing, by Cecil Lewis for BIP. There had also been a German version of *Pygmalion* in 1935, plus an attempt by Paul Czinner to film *Saint Joan* with Elisabeth Bergner in 1936. Unfortunately, this proposed production (which would invariably have been edited by Lean) was scuppered by Shaw when Czinner expressed fears about a Catholic boycott.

Enter a silver-tongued Hungarian producer named Gabriel Pascal who, although practically penniless, was determined to produce a series of films in Britain based on Shaw's works, the rights to which he miraculously managed to secure during a meeting with the playwright, who was suitably amused and impressed by Pascal's bravura and sheer effrontery, if not by his bank balance. Before *Pygmalion*, Pascal had made films in Italy (*Populi Morituri*, as both actor and co-director) and Germany (*Friedrike, Unheimliche Geschichten*, which he produced), as well as Britain (*Reasonable Doubt* and *Cafe Mascot*, which he produced, the latter based on a work by Cecil Lewis). Yet despite his contacts in the business, it took Pascal some considerable time to set up the financing for *Pygmalion*. Once secured, the producer put to work Cecil Lewis and WP Lipscomb on adapting the play for the screen, over which Shaw had complete control.

The story revolves around the phonetics teacher, Professor Henry Higgins, who takes up a bet from his friend Colonel Pickering that he can't turn a Cockney flower girl – Eliza Dolittle – into a lady and pass her off in high society. This the Professor successfully does but not without learning a little about humanity along the way. Lewis and Lipscomb's work on the screenplay primarily involved streamlining the play without drastically altering its structure or dialogue. Inevitably, certain expositional scenes, necessary in the theatre but less vital on screen, fell by the wayside in a bid to keep the narrative flowing, while the freedom of film also allowed the creation of several entirely new scenes and exchanges of dialogue, the most important of which was Eliza's triumph at the ball, alluded to but not actually part of the original text. Shaw wrote this lengthy new sequence himself, which involved the creation of an entirely new character, the Hungarian Aristid

A rare still of Pygmalion's *producer, the flamboyant Hungarian Gabriel Pascal, pictured giving instructions to Stanley Holloway and Leo Genn during the making of* Caesar and Cleopatra.

Karpathy, a former pupil of Higgins', now himself a noted phonetician, whose ear for dialect could well expose Eliza for the fraud she is.

By this time Anthony 'Puffin' Asquith, the son of the former Liberal Prime Minister Lord Herbert Asquith, was on board as director. At the time Asquith may have seemed a curious choice, for although he would later distinguish himself with such classics as *The Way to the Stars* and *The Importance of Being Earnest*, and had made a splash with his debut feature *Shooting Stars* back in 1928, his recent career had included some notable failures, among them the Gallipoli-set drama *Tell England* ('Not likely to bring in any money' commented *Variety*) and *Moscow Nights* (the direction of which Graham Greene described as 'puerile' in *The Spectator*).

Perhaps because of this, working alongside Asquith as director, as well as playing Professor Higgins, was the popular romantic lead Leslie Howard, known for successes such as *Of Human Bondage* and *The Scarlet Pimpernel* (although apparently Shaw's preferred choice for Higgins was Charles Laughton). Playing Eliza was Wendy Hiller, whom the film would 'introduce' and whom Shaw himself had apparently 'discovered' in a production of his play *Saint Joan* (despite the fact that Hiller had already starred in a film in 1937 entitled *Lancashire Luck*, a comedy about the effect a pools win has on a poor family). The film also contains the first screen appearance (brief and unaccredited) of future star Anthony Quayle as an Italian wigmaker.

The pedigree of those involved behind the cameras was no less impressive, among them cinematographer Harry Stradling (who would go on to win an Oscar for photographing *My Fair Lady*, the musical version of *Pygmalion*, in 1964), French composer Arthur Honegger (*Napoleon*, *Les Miserables*, *Crime et Chatiment*), art directors John Bryan and Laurence Irving (the latter being the grandson of Sir Henry Irving), sound recordist Alex Fisher (important on a film about phonetics) and, of course, David Lean in the cutting room. Further down the list of technical credits could be found camera operator Jack Hildyard, a cinematographer in waiting who'd go on to photograph four films for Lean, including *Bridge on the River Kwai*, which would earn him an Oscar.

The result of everybody's labours – despite the sometimes counterproductive interferences of Gabriel Pascal – is a triumph of Thirties cinema. From its opening scene amid the bustle of Covent Garden (recreated on a soundstage at Pinewood Studios) through to its subtly hinted happy ending ('Eliza, where are my slippers?'), this is a fluid film, with Harry Stradling's camera making impressively sweeping moves amid the sets and characters, immediately banishing any thoughts that this might be a stuck-in-the-stalls record of the play.

The performances are all superbly realised, most notably Howard as the self-obsessed Higgins, the ultimate Englishman (despite, like Karpathy, being of Hungarian descent), his beautiful voice making the very most of Shaw's delicious dialogue (although it's perhaps fair to say that Rex Harrison did an even better job in *My Fair Lady*). Easily Howard's equal is Wendy Hiller as Eliza, effortlessly accomplishing the difficult task of being believable as both the unrefined 'squashed cabbage leaf' at the beginning of the story and the elegant lady at the end (a feat that sadly eluded Audrey Hepburn in *My Fair Lady*, with only the latter half of her performance ringing true). Also of note are Scott Sunderland as the gentlemanly Colonel Pickering, Marie Lohr as the regal but

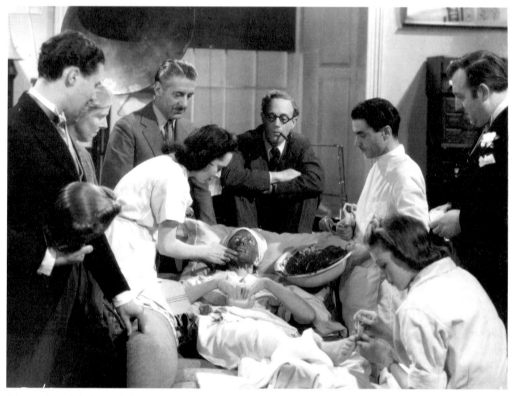

'More mud there!' Professor Higgins (Leslie Howard) and Colonel Pickering (Scott Sunderland) supervise the beautification of Eliza Dolittle (Wendy Hiller) in Pygmalion. *An unaccredited Anthony Quayle (far left) looks on as an Italian wigmaker. Twenty-four years later he would star as Colonel Brighton in Lean's* Lawrence of Arabia.

understanding Mrs Higgins and Wilfred Lawson as Alfred Dolittle, whose foul breath one can almost smell as he wheezes in front of Higgins' shrivelling face. David Tree also manages to infuse some humour into Freddy Eynsford-Hill, an upper class twit of the very first order, while Jean Cadell's Mrs Pearce is not a woman on whose wrong side you'd want to get.

The most discussed aspect of the film at the time was its language, however. Perhaps because it was based on a text that was widely acknowledged to be a classic, the censor allowed a variety of expletives and blasphemies to pass by unchecked, among them several 'blasts', 'pigs' and 'Oh Gods', not to mention more 'damns' than you could shake a stick at (it should be remembered that in Hollywood the following year, producer David O Selznick was fined $5000 for refusing to cut Rhett Butler's exit line, 'Frankly, my dear, I don't give a damn!' from *Gone with the Wind*). Dolittle also intimates that Eliza is illegitimate, another major taboo of the time. All this was small potatoes compared with the film's most notable affronts. The first of these is Alfred Dolittle's two-fingered dismissal of morality. The second is Eliza's response to Freddy's enquiry as to whether she would be walking home through the park after the tea party at Mrs Higgins'. 'Walk?' she replies incredulously. 'Not bloody likely. I'm going in a taxi.' Laughable by today's standards, this line caused uproar at the time, hence the film's advertisement: 'Miss Pygmalion? Not ****** likely!'

So what of Lean's involvement in all this? He certainly made a smooth job of cutting together the acres of chat, keeping the dialogue flowing at a brisk and even pace. His work was practically invisible for much of the film, and rightly so, for ultimately this was a drawing room comedy. Fast cuts and clever segues were not needed. Lean was able to show off his technique during only two montage sequences depicting Higgins teaching Eliza how to speak, inserts for which Lean directed himself. Given his burgeoning ambitions to direct, Lean was regularly on set, making himself useful to Anthony Asquith by suggesting camera angles and placement.

If the film has a fault for present day audiences, then it's the lack of pace in the final reel as the drama comes to a head, although this was by no means Lean's fault. It's attributable to the fact that one can see the ending coming a mile off, yet we still have to endure several more confrontational exchanges between Higgins and Eliza before they too see the light of day. This aside (and perhaps the fact that the film eschewed its period setting in favour of a contemporary one), the film survives remarkably well.

Critics of the day were immediately impressed by the production. 'An excellent, witty and always entertaining picture,' wrote Franz Hoellering in *Nation*, adding, 'Wendy Hiller steals the show.' In *The New Statesman*, Peter Galway enthused that, 'The acting is remarkably good… It is altogether a capital film, with everything handsome about it.' Although Basil Wright in *The Spectator* added, 'Like the bulk of Shaw's work, there is a completely static and stagy feeling to the story; it depends largely on good acting and [the] well-timed interplay of dialogue.'

Whatever its perceived shortcomings, *Pygmalion* was an immediate success both at home and, more importantly for a British film, in America, where it earned four Academy Award nominations: best picture, best actor (Howard), best actress (Hiller) and best screenplay and adaptation (Shaw, Lewis, Lipscombe and Ian Dalrymple). Sadly, it only won the screenplay award, Howard losing out to Spencer Tracy for *Boys' Town* and Hiller to Bette Davis for *Jezebl*, while best picture went to *You Can't Take It with You* (which also beat off *The Adventures of Robin Hood* and *Grand Illusion*, so *Pygmalion* was in good company).

At the end of the day, *Pygmalion* put all those concerned in its making on the map, from producer Pascal down to the most humble technician. Lean now had a bona fide world success on his CV, and from that standpoint, his career prospects could only get better.

Five

A BIT OF FRENCH

Despite being fêted as Britain's top editor, Lean still had to make a living, so while waiting for something prestigious to come along, he took on the job of editing a minor picture called *Spies of the Air*. Based on the play *Official Secrets* by Jeffrey Dell, it centres around a test pilot who turns out to be an enemy agent. Starring Barry K Barnes, Roger Livesey, Basil Radford and Felix Aylmer, it was produced by John Corfield and directed by David MacDonald (who'd directed Barnes in the popular *This Man Is News*, which had been produced by Lean's future partner Anthony Havelock-Allan). All told, the film seems to have been little more than a time filler for all concerned and is now almost totally forgotten.

After the international success of *Pygmalion*, director Anthony Asquith decided to keep many people involved in its making on for his next production, among them Lean, camera operator Jack Hildyard, sound recordist Alex Fisher and actor David Tree. The project was an adaptation of Terence Rattigan's hit West End comedy *French Without Tears*, which followed the adventures of a group of British diplomats in France trying to learn the lingo. However, the men find themselves acting anything but diplomatically when the flirtatious sister of one of their number arrives for a visit.

The first of his plays to be adapted for the screen, *French Without Tears* was scripted by Rattigan, assisted by Anatole de Grunwald, who would go on to adapt and later produce many more of Rattigan's works for the screen (*Quiet Wedding*, *The Winslow Boy* and *The VIPs*). Rattigan would go on to write the screenplay for Lean's *The Sound Barrier*.

The original West End production of *French Without Tears* boasted a number of up-and-coming names in its cast, most notably Rex Harrison (who would later star in Lean's *Blithe Spirit*) and Trevor Howard (who'd work on *Brief Encounter*, *The Passionate Friends* and *Ryan's Daughter*). Unfortunately, at this stage in their careers, neither were deemed sufficient film draws (despite the fact that Harrison had made over 10 films, among them semi-classics such as *Storm in a Teacup* and *St Martin's Lane*, both with Vivien Leigh). Consequently, only Roland Culver made it to the film version, joining Ray Milland (already a stalwart of countless American films, including *Beau Geste*), Ellen Drew, Guy Middleton, David Tree and Janine Darcy – although there was no sign of Marlene Dietrich, for whom Paramount had apparently originally bought the rights!

Made at Shepperton, the film was produced by the American David E Rose (presumably sent over by Paramount to keep an eye on things) and Italian Mario Zampi, while joining them behind the cameras were art director Paul Sheriff, composer Nikolaus Brodsky and cinematographer Bernard Knowles, all of whom would work with director Asquith again many times over in the following years.

Again, as with *Pygmalion*, Lean's task wasn't exactly daunting. *French Without Tears* is a farce with plenty of door slamming and misunderstandings; all Lean had do was keep the pace flowing, which he did again, subtly, without drawing attention to technique. The results were an immediate smash hit, providing a much-needed tonic for a nation that had just declared war on Germany. Even Graham Greene, who'd previously been so dismissive of Anthony Asquith's talents, was among those to admit that the film achieved its aims perfectly. '*French Without Tears* is a triumph for Mr Anthony Asquith,' he wrote in *The Spectator*. 'After the first 10 minutes his witty direction and firm handling of the cast (Mr Ray Milland has never acted so well as this before) conquer the too British sexuality of Mr Rattigan's farce.' With another success under his belt, it was clear that Lean was on a roll.

However, as had been the case after *Pygmalion*, bills still had to be paid, and before Lean was reunited with Pascal and Shaw on their next production, he kept the wolf from his and Kay's door by editing another low-budget film. Produced again by Mario Zampi, who also directed, the film was *Spy for a Day* starring Northern comedian Duggie Wakefield as a gormless farmhand who discovers that he is the double of a spy. Based on a script by Anatole de Grunwald, Hans Wilhelm, Ralph Black and Emeric Pressburger (with whom Lean would soon collaborate on something worthier), the film has the air of a cast-off George Formby vehicle, and like *Spies of the Air*, quickly disappeared from memory, despite the talent involved in its making.

Given the increasingly grave international situation, Lean's next film couldn't have been more fortuitous. It was time for him to go back to Gabriel Pascal and George Bernard Shaw, this time for an adaptation of Shaw's 1905 work *Major Barbara*, the story of a Salvation Army major who resigns her post when her superiors accept a large donation from her father, a munitions millionaire.

This time, not only would Pascal be producing, he'd also be co-writing the screenplay (with Anatole de Grunwald) as well as directing. Given that he hadn't wielded a megaphone since 1928, he was aided in this task by Lean (who mostly handled the camera) and Harold French (who concentrated on the actors). For their efforts, the duo received the credit 'assistants in direction'. For Lean, this was a major opportunity, allowing him to exercise his directorial ambitions, but under the protective arm of Pascal. The assignment was also a major step forward in the career of Harold French who, before this, had directed only three undistinguished low-budget pictures (*Cavalier of the Streets*, *Dead Men Are Dangerous* and *The House of the Arrow*), although it was probably his success in directing the stage version of *French Without Tears* that earned him this particular job. This, in turn, would lead to *Dear Octopus*, *English Without Tears* and *Quartet*, not to mention a stint directing the second unit for Lean's penultimate film, *Ryan's Daughter*.

Also assisting Pascal, this time in production, was Stanley Haynes (future Lean collaborator and director of *Carnival*), while Jack Ellis handled the film's release. All of which adds up to the fact that Pascal's involvement in the film was mostly in a supervisory capacity, somewhat akin to David O Selznick's involvement in *Gone with the Wind*. Luckily, like Selznick, Pascal had chosen the very best talent to bring his adaptation of *Major Barbara* to the screen. Among the technicians involved were cinematographer Ronald Neame, (although he was not the first choice, Harry Stradling, Osmond

Studio portrait of Ronald Neame, who photographed Major Barbara, *here seen during the making of* Meteor, *which he directed in 1979. As well as photographing several of Lean's films in the Forties, Neame would also be his partner in the production company Cineguild.*

Borrodaile and even Freddie Young briefly worked on the film), composer William Walton (who'd previously turned down an offer from Pascal to score *Pygmalion*), costume designer Cecil Beaton, art directors Vincent Korda and John Bryan, and editor Charles Frend (future director of *Scott of the Antarctic* and *The Cruel Sea*). As well as being an assistant in direction, Lean was also credited for being in charge of 'montage', although there's little doubt he also supervised Frend's work in the editing rooms.

Following the credit sequence, which is played over a portrait of Shaw, a hint of the drama to come follows in the form of a hand-written synopsis which we are led to believe has been penned by Shaw, given that a hand is shown signing his name (doubts as to whether this really is Shaw arise when one notices the youthfulness of the hand – Shaw was 84 at the time). Then it's straight into the action, with Rex Harrison's Greek professor Adolphus Cusins falling in love with the beautiful Major Barbara (Wendy Hiller) after having heard her speak at a Salvation Army meeting (Harrison inherited the role after Shaw vetoed Leslie Howard; another actor, Andrew Osborn, had also been deemed unsatisfactory after only a few days' filming). Cusins thus joins the Army in a bid to woo Barbara, during which he is introduced to her family, learning that her father is none other than Andrew Undershaft (Robert Morley), the munitions millionaire.

Circumstances then take a turn for the worse, for Barbara's superior, The General (Sybil Thorndike), accepts a huge donation from Undershaft. Idealistic to the end, Barbara resigns from the Army, only to have her opinion of her father change when she visits his factory, where she learns of his passion for benevolent management over charity and moral uplift, and sees the homes he provides for his grateful employees, who naturally repay him with loyalty and doubled effort in the workplace. So much so that she agrees to marry Cusins, despite the fact that he too has now left the Army and is going to run the factory for her father.

Several subplots are also woven into this narrative, the most important of them involving the reformation of a brutal idler called Bill Walker (Robert Newton), who hits Barbara's assistant Jenny Hill (Deborah Kerr) in the mouth, only to see the error of his ways, reform and find work – at Undershaft's factory, of course – although not before goading Barbara over the Army's all too easy acceptance of Undershaft's money ('What price salvation?').

Even more so than *Pygmalion*, *Major Barbara* is a film in which performances rather than cinematic technique dominate, for although smoothly put together, it is very much a dialogue-driven piece. As Basil Wright commented about *Pygmalion*, 'There is a complete static and stagy feeling to the story,' and this is very much the case with *Major Barbara*. The characters don't so much converse with each other as lecture and pontificate. Yet so sharp and witty is the dialogue, and so strong the performances, it barely seems to matter that Shaw uses the story as a platform for his variably argued Fabian views (as spectacular as Undershaft's futuristic factory and holiday camp-like employee living quarters are, one doesn't quite swallow his idea of an industrial Utopia).

Of the performers, Wendy Hiller is excellent as Major Barbara and is more than ably supported by Rex Harrison as her fiancé. It's interesting to see Harrison – a future Henry Higgins – play opposite Hiller – a former Eliza Dolittle. More so, Harrison also has a brief scene early in the film with a policeman, who is played by none other than Stanley Holloway, who would go on to play Alfred Dolittle in *My Fair Lady* with Harrison on both stage and screen. There's even a sideways reference to *Pygmalion* in the script, for when Major Barbara invites Cusins back to her house, he suggests they take a taxi, to which Barbara responds, 'We don't take taxis in this part of the world. Most of us have never been in one. We'll have to take a bus.'

Other *Pygmalion* veterans in the cast include Marie Lohr, here playing Barbara's mother, Lady Brittomart, and David Tree as Charles Lomax, fiancé to Barbara's sister, Sarah (Penelope Dudley-Ward). Also leaving their mark are Robert Newton, whose Bill Walker is just one of many memorable bullies and braggarts he'd play, while Deborah Kerr (making her film debut) is delightful as the abused Jenny Hill. Of special note is Robert Morley who, although only 32 at the time, is entirely believable as the elderly Undershaft, despite the fact that Hiller, playing his daughter, was 28, while the dowager-like Lohr, his wife, was 50. In supporting roles can be found actor–playwright Emlyn Williams, Kathleen Harrison, Miles Malleson, Felix Aylmer and Joe Gladwyn.

However, the real star is Shaw's dialogue, to which everything else is subservient. The film does occasionally drag its heels, and at just over two hours, the running time is overlong compared with *Pygmalion*'s brisk 96 minutes. William Walton's score, absent where it's most needed and inappropriate where it's included, is also something of a liability. Still, many of the exchanges are quite delicious, while the Pascal–Lean–French triumvirate provides the occasional cinematic flourish to keep things moving, including a spectacular crane shot into the Salvation Army's barracks, all of which were built on a soundstage at Denham, where the film was made under constant threat from the Luftwaffe.

On a technical level, also of note is Lean's superb montage sequence towards the end of the picture showing the production line at Undershaft's factory. A spectacular blend of man, machine and molten metal, it has a real propagandist edge to it, prompting the reviewer in *Documentary Newsletter* to write, 'It is an extremely well-made film, technically comparable to any from any country.' *Variety* was more impressed with the performances, commenting, 'Hiller, lead in *Pygmalion*, delivers an excellent and personable performance throughout, and does much to carry the story along through some rather dull and weighty passages.' The reviewer went on to add, 'Secondary acting honours are shared by Robert Morley as the father, and Robert Newton, a tough Limey whose soul is finally saved.'

Despite the praise, there were no Oscars, nor even any nominations. In fact, so costly was the production, the film failed to make a profit on its first run. But things couldn't have been better for Lean, who capped off a rewarding and productive year by finally marrying Kay Walsh on Saturday 23 November 1940. There was barely enough time to settle into married life before Walsh was called on to perform in *The Second Mr Bush*, while Lean (who, like many film technicians at the time, was granted an artist's deferment from military service) was asked to edit Michael Powell and Emeric Pressburger's latest production, *The 49th Parallel*.

Powell and Pressburger were developing into a major force in British cinema, and although at the time they had collaborated on only two films (*The Spy in Black* and *Contraband*), *The 49th Parallel* would herald the beginning of their classic period, during which they would make *The Life and Death of Colonel Blimp*, *I Know Where I'm Going* (with Wendy Hiller), *Black Narcissus* and, most famously, *The Red Shoes*. With *The 49th Parallel*, they made their contribution to the war effort with a propaganda drama, the aim of which was to encourage America into the Second World War. But with Powell and Pressburger being who they were, this was no ordinary propaganda drama, for it followed the adventures of five Nazis who, having survived the destruction of their submarine by RAF bombers in Canada's Gulf of St Lawrence, attempt to make their way – by fair means and foul – out of Canada and to safety in America, then a neutral country.

Determined on making the film as realistic as possible, Powell and Pressburger received permission and backing of The Ministry of Information to make it on location in Canada, which involved everyone concerned travelling across the Atlantic when the threat from U-boats was all too real. Among those making the trip were director Powell, cinematographer Freddie Young and art director David Rawnsley, along with cast members Eric Portman, Niall MacGinnis, Finlay

Currie, Raymond Lovell and John Chandos, who'd be playing the Germans. Ironically, the only true German among the cast, Anton Walbrook (Powell's favourite and most oft-used actor) would be playing Peter, the leader of a pacifist Hutterite community. Also involved was Leslie Howard as an eccentric novelist, a woefully miscast Laurence Olivier as a French–Canadian trapper (his accent has to be heard to be disbelieved) and Raymond Massey as an AWOL soldier. Elisabeth Bergner was also briefly involved in the project as Anna, Peter's daughter, with whom MacGinnis's character, Vogel, falls in love and wishes to stay. Unfortunately, Bergner decamped to Hollywood in mid-production, where she made another anti-Nazi propaganda piece, *Paris Calling*, with Basil Rathbone. Consequently, after much panic, she was replaced by the young Glynis Johns, who made the role of Anna her own.

David Lean didn't travel to Canada for the location shooting, simply because at that stage in the production he was not yet on board, Powell's original choice of editor being John Seabourne, who cut many of his films during this period. Unfortunately, Seabourne became ill during the production and Lean was called in to save the day. Just the sort of challenge Lean had been hoping for, *The 49th Parallel* made an exciting change from the drawing room-style comedies he'd been cutting for the past couple of years. Here were chases across the great outdoors, explosions and a tense climax, coupled with many vignettes – comic and dramatic – along the way.

Today, at 123 minutes, the film seems somewhat long (the American release, known as *The Invaders*, is almost 20 minutes shorter), yet there is much to enjoy in this celebrated production, especially the performances of Eric Portman as the evil Nazi leader Lieutenant Hirth, and Niall MacGinnis as Vogel, the doubting German who wants nothing more than to settle down in peace with the Hutterites.

'An important and effective propaganda picture,' exclaimed *Variety* of the finished product, to which critic James Agate added, 'The thing that makes this picture remarkable is its extraordinary fairness. To show the Nazis as unalloyed gangsters was never good enough… There is scope in the individual Nazi for loyalty, purpose, tenacity and courage.'

A commercial success on both sides of the Atlantic, *The 49th Parallel* earned several Oscar nominations, including best picture, best screenplay (Emeric Pressburger and Rodney Ackland) and best original story (Pressburger). Lean's editing didn't rate a nomination, although at least Pressburger went on to win the award for best story.

Having made successful pictures with Gabriel Pascal and Anthony Asquith, Lean now found himself associated with another winning team so he remained on board for Powell and Pressburger's next collaboration, *One of Our Aircraft Is Missing*. Another propaganda exercise, the film was almost a mirror image of *The 49th Parallel*. This time instead of Nazis, it was the crew of

Portrait of cinematographer Freddie Young at work on Ryan's Daughter. *Before to his first official collaboration with David Lean on* Lawrence of Arabia *in 1962, Young photographed several films in the Thirties and Forties on which Lean worked as the editor, among them* The 49th Parallel.

an RAF bomber, returning from a raid on Stuttgart, who are on the run. The mission accomplished, the aircraft is hit on the return leg of its journey, and although the pilot attempts to limp the Wellington home, it eventually crashes into a power line in occupied Holland. Having bailed out just before impact, the six crew have make their way back to Britain. Luckily, they're helped along the way by members of the Dutch Resistance.

Based on an original script by Powell and Pressburger (now working as The Archers), the film re-united many of those involved in the making of *The 49th Parallel*, among them Lean, art director David Rawnsley and actor Eric Portman, who this time plays one of the Wellington's crew, Tom Earnshaw. He is joined in his flight across Holland by Godfrey Tearle, Hugh Williams, Bernard Miles, Hugh Burden and Emrys Jones, playing a cross section of British types. Behind the camera was cinematographer Ronald Neame (whose first film this was since photographing *Major Barbara*), while the supporting cast includes such notables as Peter Ustinov, Googie Withers, Pamela Brown, Joyce Redman, Hay Petrie, Robert Helpmann and Roland Culver.

Although not quite as thrilling as *The 49th Parallel*, *One of Our Aircraft Is Missing* remains a watchable wartime morale booster, smartly presented in typical Powell–Pressburger style, and full of the kind of vignettes and amusing character traits for which they'd become famous. 'Script, production, direction and photography are splendid,' enthused *Variety*. The Academy of Motion Pictures Arts and Sciences responded likewise, nominating the film for two Oscars: best original screenplay (Powell and Pressburger) and best special effects (Ronald Neame [photographic] and CC Stevens [sound]). Again, Lean missed out on a nomination, but unbeknownst to him, an even greater reward was just around the corner.

Six

SERVING THE MASTER

The war film *In Which We Serve* brought together some of the most remarkable talents working in the British entertainment industry at the time. The most important was Noel Coward, without whom the film would not have been made. Born in 1899, Coward was very much the boy genius of the West End stage in the Twenties and Thirties, during which he wrote and often acted in such imperishable classics as *The Vortex* (the play that secured his fame in 1924 at the age of just 25), *Hay Fever*, *Cavalcade*, *Bitter Sweet*, *Private Lives* and *Design for Living*.

Many of these plays were adapted for the screen in the early Thirties in both Britain and Hollywood, in particular *Private Lives* (starring Norma Shearer and Robert Montgomery), *Bitter Sweet* (starring Anna Neagle under the direction of Herbert Wilcox) and *Cavalcade* (featuring Clive Brook, Una O'Connor and Diana Wynyard), the latter winning the 1933 best picture Oscar, as well as awards for direction (Frank Lloyd) and art direction (William Darling).

Yet despite the success of these productions, Coward, who held the cinema in disdain, seemed wary of appearing on screen himself. In fact, before writing, producing, co-directing, scoring and acting in *In Which We Serve*, he'd appeared in only two films. The first of these, a 1918 silent called *Hearts of the World*, directed by none other than DW Griffith, was a propaganda piece about the First World War, starring such luminaries as Lillian and Dorothy Gish and Erich Von Stroheim. The 19-year-old Coward appeared in a supporting role. The second, *The Scoundrel*, was made in Hollywood in 1935 after successful appearances on Broadway, and features Coward as a self-centred publicist who discovers that, having been killed in a plane crash, he can only go to heaven if he can find someone to mourn for him. A quirky supernatural comedy written, directed and produced by Ben Hecht and Charles MacArthur (who won an Oscar for the film's original story), it was well received by the critics but considered something of an arty oddity by the movie-going public.

Then, in 1941, came an offer from producers Anthony Havelock-Allan and Filippo del Giudice to make a film of his choosing, over which he would have total artistic control. Unable to resist this carte blanche offer, Coward determined to go ahead with the production, which he decided to base on an actual event that had happened to his close friend Lord Louis Mountbatten. A commander in the Royal Navy, Mountbatten had survived the sinking of his ship, the destroyer HMS Kelly, during the Battle of Crete. Working under the title *White Ensign*, Coward set about creating a story based on this incident, which he used to examine the lives of the ship's crew and captain, all of them stalwart British types determined to see the war through with a stiff upper lip. A story of this nature would make ideal propaganda.

Captain Kinross (Noel Coward) assures his family before returning to HMS Torrin *in a scene from* In Which We Serve. *Also pictured are son Bobby (Daniel Massey, Coward's godson), daughter Lavinia (Ann Stephens) and wife Alix (Celia Johnson).*

Although perfectly at ease with writing the script, Coward had reservations about directing a feature film, and so began to enquire who might be the ideal technician to help him bring his idea to the screen. After several people suggested David Lean for the job (among them director Carol Reed), a meeting was arranged, during which Coward read Lean his script in progress. Coward's efforts proved somewhat unwieldy, and so with suggestions from Lean and Havelock-Allen, Coward agreed to cut the script, in the process of which he hit on the idea of telling the story via a series of flashbacks following the torpedoing of The Kelly, now renamed The Torrin.

Then came the question of how Lean – who was by now officially on board the production, having been approved by Coward – would be credited. After several suggestions it was agreed that, although the film was unquestionably A Noel Coward Production, Lean and Coward would be credited as having directed the picture together, while Ronald Neame, who Lean insisted on bringing in as cinematographer, was listed below them on the title card as having photographed it.

The film was really beginning to move forward now, and while Lean began work on the shooting script with Ronald Neame, producers Anthony Havelock-Allan and Filippo del Giudice began to secure the finance. Just as it was for Lean, *In Which We Serve* was the producers' shot at the big time, although neither of them was a stranger to success. Havelock-Allan had already had a hit in 1938 with *This Man Is News*, a low-budget *Thin Man*-style comedy thriller starring his then wife Valerie Hobson, Barry K Barnes (whose *Spies of the Air* Lean had edited) and Alastair Sim, while del Giudice had founded Two Cities Films in 1937, through which he had financed and released the modestly budgeted but highly successful *French Without Tears*. Now came the duo's chance to produce a really first-class film. The provisional plan to make *In Which We Serve* for Columbia's British arm had fallen through in its early stages. Thus, del Giudice hawked the film around various studios, most of which seemed reluctant to help back it (for a brief time GFD – General Film Distributors – was involved). Among the concerns raised was the fact that Coward was still not a film draw, while his image as a matinee idol seemed at odds with the fact that he'd be playing a naval officer. Indeed, several of the British tabloids ran editorials voicing such concerns. del Giudice pressed ahead nevertheless, finally securing a deal with British Lion and Rank.

Now green-lit, production in earnest began. At Coward's insistence, his close friend Gladys Calthrop, who'd designed all his theatrical productions since *The Vortex*, was engaged to design the film's civilian interiors, leaving it to David Rawnsley to design and construct The Torrin, which was mocked up on the soundstages of Denham. To ensure that the ship was as authentic as possible, the Navy provided several advisors to the film, among them Terry Lawlor, another survivor of HMS Kelly, who also advised Lean on procedure during armed conflict. The production also made extensive use of the studio's water tank which convincingly doubled for the sea in which the Torrin's survivors find themselves marooned in a Carley float.

Shooting began on Thursday 5 February 1942, by which time auditions and screen tests had been completed and all the roles cast. If the studio had worried that Coward wasn't enough of a star name to carry the film, they may well have balked at some of the other choices, for while many of the actors featured in *In Which We Serve* would go on to become some of the biggest and best-loved names in British film history, at the time, many of them were either just starting out in their careers or coming into their own.

Key among them was John Mills, who would go on to become one of Lean's most frequent leading players. A former chorus boy, Mills had made his London debut in 1927 in *The Five O'Clock Revue*, and had broken into films in 1932 with the Jessie Matthews vehicle *The Midshipmaid*, the same year he appeared on stage in Noel Coward's *Cavalcade*. During the following decade, Mills became an adept support in such films as *Those Were the Days* (opposite the great Will Hay) and *Cottage to Let* (with Alastair Sim and Leslie Banks). He even had a brief role in *The Ghost Camera*, which Lean had edited back in 1933. Yet Mills' one true stab at stardom, *Brown on Resolution* in 1935, in which he plays a seaman who holds an enemy ship at bay with a single rifle in the First World War, wasn't quite the hit everyone expected it to be. However, his performance as Ordinary Seaman Shorty Blake in *In Which We Serve* helped to propel him to stardom in the Forties.

It's through Shorty's eyes that we follow his romance and marriage to Freda Lewis (Kay Walsh), whom he meets on a train. Through him we also get to meet the below decks crew of the Torrin, whose experiences on board we then follow, both through armed conflict and quieter moments, when they reminisce about home life.

Another important cast member was Bernard Miles who plays Chief Petty Officer Walter Harvey. On stage since 1930 and in films from 1933 with *Channel Crossing* (with Max Miller, Constance Cummings and Edmund Gwenn), Miles later became known for his comical portrayal of rustics (most notably in *The Tawny Pipit*, which he also produced, co-wrote and co-directed), as well as for founding The Mermaid Theatre in London in 1959. In the late Thirties and early Forties, he'd become an able support in a handful of films, among them *The Four Feathers*, Hitchcock's *Jamaica Inn* and *One of Our Aircraft Is Missing*, which had been edited by Lean. Like Mills, *In Which We Serve* enabled him truly to shine. Through Harvey we follow the on-board life of a mid-ranking officer, while at home we get to meet his wife Kath (Joyce Carey), who happens to be Freda Lewis's aunt. After her marriage to Shorty, Freda, who is now pregnant, goes to stay with Kath while the two men are at sea. Unfortunately, Kath and her mother, Mrs Lemmon (Dora Gregory) are killed during an air raid. Freda, who has been hiding under the stairs, survives, but the trauma of the explosion forces her into labour, although mother and son come through the ordeal in one piece. Unfortunately, Shorty, to whom Freda has written regarding what's happened, then has the task of breaking the news to Walter that his wife and mother-in-law have been killed, thus perfectly bringing to a climax two of the film's flashbacks.

As Captain 'D' Kinross, Coward carries the rest of the film. Through him we meet not only the higher ranking officers of The Torrin, but also his wife Alix (Celia Johnson) and his two children. A respected stage actress, Johnson had made her stage debut in 1928 in *Major Barbara*. Her subsequent film work had been fleeting: a brief appearance in the Ben Travers farce *Dirty Weekend*, plus two Ministry of Information shorts, *We Serve* and *A Letter from Home*, the latter directed by Carol Reed. However, this didn't prevent her from seeking out Noel Coward at a party and asking for a role in his film venture. Her audacity paid off, and following a screen test she won the role of his wife. Again, this resulted in stardom and led to further collaborations with Lean (*This Happy Breed*, *Brief Encounter*) and Coward (*The Astonished Heart*).

Meanwhile, the film's supporting cast is filled out with such now-familiar names as Richard Attenborough as a young stoker who deserts his post in the midst of battle, James Donald as the ship's doctor, bored until the casualties start piling up, and Kathleen Harrison as Shorty's fussy East End mum. Joining them are Michael Wilding, Wally Patch, Penelope Dudley Ward and Leslie Dwyer, while John Mills' baby daughter Juliette, Coward's godchild, briefly appears as Shorty and Freda's baby boy. The Kinross' children are played by Ann Stephens and Daniel Massey, Massey being the son of actor Raymond Massey and another of Coward's godchildren (in fact, the young Massey would go on to impersonate his godfather in the musical *Star!* in 1968, earning a best supporting actor Oscar for his work).

Survivors from the torpedoed destroyer HMS Torrin cling to a Carley float in the studio tank at Denham during a scene from In Which We Serve.

With Mountbatten on hand to smooth out any problems – the Ministry of Information had strong reservations about the production which he helped to allay – filming switched to high gear, with Coward handling the direction of the performances while Lean handled the camera set-ups. To show his public support of the film, Mountbatten visited the set during filming, bringing along with him King George VI, Queen Elizabeth and their daughters, the Princesses Elizabeth and Margaret.

The MoI's doubts were about a British ship shown being bombed and destroyed in the film. Yet if Coward were realistically to depict the consequences of war, such scenes were absolutely necessary (the whole film's flashback structure was built around the sinking of the Torrin). Also necessary and realistically depicted is the bombing of the Harvey household, which suffers a direct hit. The MoI may have short-sightedly criticised Coward for including such scenes, yet no one could have doubted his patriotism, nor his wish to show the Navy in the best light possible. The film opens with the statement, 'This film is dedicated to The Royal Navy, whereon under the good providence of God, the wealth, safety and strength of the kingdom chiefly depend.'

We're then told, 'This is the story of a ship!' (the brief opening and closing narration is spoken by an unaccredited Leslie Howard), after which follows a montage of the Torrin being built. The shots for this sequence were filmed by a second unit, although there's no doubting Lean's hand in their cutting together (despite Thelma Myers' credit as the film's editor, Lean was wholly in charge of the editing process). We then see the Torrin launched (cheering crowds can be heard on the soundtrack, but the docks clearly lack onlookers) after which we follow her into action, bombing enemy ships (surprisingly good model shots care of effects supervisor Douglas Woolsey and his team) and retaliating against an aerial attack by the Luftwaffe. An exciting sequence to behold, it is again brilliantly edited for maximum impact.

The Torrin's luck eventually runs out when she is bombed and begins to capsize, at which point Captain Kinross orders the crew to abandon ship. Shots of Kinross struggling underwater follow, and it's during this that the screen ripples and we're into the first flashback (could this be Kinross's life literally flashing before his eyes?) The brief sequence that follows shows the Captain unpacking in his cabin during his first day on board the Torrin (Lean even cleverly makes use of the flashback ripple effect in mid-scene to cover a slow bit of action). At the scene's conclusion, we're back in the water with Kinross, who by now has surfaced amid oil and wreckage, only to see the propellers of the capsized Torrin whirring away. Another flashback showing the crew preparing the ship for sea soon after follows, again making expert use of montage.

The film's form having now been established, the flashbacks follow thick and fast, connected by scenes of the surviving crewmembers holding on to the Carley float, although even these connecting threads are not without incident, as the German planes continually fly over, attempting to pick off the crew ('Look out, here come the bastards again!').

Gradually, we're introduced to all the crewmembers and their families, and while one might criticise Coward the writer for sticking to class stereotypes (all the officers are jolly decent chaps while the ordinary seamen are of the gor blimey/salt of the earth variety), he weaves a remarkably complex tapestry of incidents and emotions. Coward himself may not be entirely convincing as the captain of a destroyer (his home life with the wife and kids doesn't exactly ring true, either), yet he and the other actors inhabit their roles so perfectly this hardly seems to matter. John Mills, Bernard Miles, Celia Johnson, Kay Walsh, Joyce Carey and Kathleen Harrison all give warm and textured performances, so that when tragedy or happiness befalls them, one is truly touched, despite the proliferation of stiff upper lips all round.

Coward's score (performed by The London Symphony Orchestra under the direction of the prolific Muir Mathieson) also helps to wrench every last ounce of emotion and patriotic pride from the situations. Clever use is also made of source music. When Richard Attenborough's young stoker, who deserts his post, tries to drown his sorrows while on leave, the pub Pianola he puts money into tauntingly plays *Run, Rabbit, Run*. Later, when Shorty's mother and wife are awaiting to hear if he is alive and well after the torpedoing of the Torrin, a barrel organ can be heard playing outside when the telegram, inevitably misconstrued to mean bad news, arrives. This East End cliché is then successfully turned on its head when Mrs Blake reads the contents of the telegram to Freda, telling

'Run, rabbit, run!' Richard Attenborough as the cowardly stoker makes his film debut in In Which We Serve.

her the good news that Shorty is alive, for the tune being played is *If You Were the Only Boy in the World!*

The film is full of clever details like this — as well as plenty of technical flourishes. Perhaps the most impressive of these comes during one of the action sequences, during which Lean follows the progress of a shell as it makes its way from the stores in the bowels of the ship, up through the various decks to the giant gun, where it is loaded and fired. A remarkable sequence full of urgency and excitement, it is another masterstroke of editing.

The finished film — whose budget came in at a hefty £250,000 — was premiered at the Gaumont cinema in the West End on Sunday 27 September 1942. It was an immediate commercial and critical success. '*In Which We Serve* took a handful of typically British men and women and made from their stories, ordinary enough in themselves, a distillation of national character,' wrote Dilys Powell in *The Sunday Times*. *The Guardian* observed that the film was, 'Like a hymn to human nobility, staunchness, friendship and love,' while in America, *Newsweek* commented, 'One of the screen's proudest achievements at any time and in any country.'

David Lean (standing on camera crane) photographs his wife Kay Walsh (waving by the life preserver) on a mock up of a P&O liner in a scene from This Happy Breed. *The film was Lean's first colour production.*

So impressed with the picture were the Americans, they nominated it for two Oscars: best picture and best screenplay (both of which it lost). Coward also received a special Oscar, 'For his outstanding production achievement in *In Which We Serve*' (Lean wasn't mentioned). The film also won the New York Film Critics' Circle Award for best picture, plus several more international gongs. Coward, who at first had been vilified in the press for playing a naval officer, and Lean, who had been uncertain whether he could pull such a complex production off, had been vindicated.

Even today, despite the class stereotypes and sometimes clipped dialogue (especially between the Torrin's top brass), the film remains a powerful viewing experience. When Kinross bids farewell to the surviving crew of the Torrin in a dockyard warehouse, one can't fail to be emotionally drawn by the scene. Although the end for the Torrin and her crew may not be a happy one, the film concludes on a hopeful note with the launch of a new ship and the declaration, 'God bless our ships and all who sail in her!' Thanks to Coward and Lean, wartime audiences could believe that Britannia really did rule the waves and that one day their country would be victorious.

Suitably impressed by Lean's endeavours during the making of *In Which We Serve*, Noel Coward offered Lean access to all his works for filming, which was not unlike the agreement Gabriel Pascal had with George Bernard Shaw. However, while Pascal lumbered ahead with his elephantine adaptation of *Caesar and Cleopatra*, which would become infamous for being Britain's costliest production when finally released in 1945, Lean aimed for something more modest and closer to home.

The subject chosen was *This Happy Breed*, another slice of propaganda which tells the story of a London family – the Gibbonses – from 1919–39. Based on Coward's 1943 West End hit, the film marked Lean's debut as solo director, although after the technical complexities encountered during the making of *In Which We Serve*, *This Happy Breed* must have been a comparatively easy ride.

To make the film and the other Coward adaptations that followed, Lean, cameraman Ronald Neame and producer Anthony Havelock-Allan formed Cineguild Productions, giving themselves a certain degree of autonomy. Despite being bankrolled by GFD and Filippo del Giudice's Two Cities, the makers of *This Happy Breed* were answerable primarily to themselves. But having already delivered a commercial hit in the form of *In Which We Serve*, one can't imagine there being too much concern over the making of another Coward adaptation in the boardrooms of those financing it.

Perhaps the most surprising thing about *This Happy Breed* is that Lean chose to make it in Technicolor, despite the almost documentary air of the subject matter. Lean had never worked with colour before, not even as an edito. It was a bold move, especially given that for much of the time the colour would be muted, given the drab decor of the Gibbons' Clapham home.

Given the time span of the story, opening with the return of Frank Gibbons, head of the family, from the First World War, and ending just before the outbreak of the Second World War, much use was made of passing events, among them the British Empire Exhibition of 1924, The General Strike of 1928, the arrival of the talkies, the death of George V and the rise of fascism in Germany, all of which either involves or affects the Gibbons in some way.

On stage, Noel Coward had played the almost Cockney Frank Gibbons himself, opposite Celia Johnson as his wife Ethel. Although he had come from a lower middle class background (one can imagine him drawing on his childhood years spent in lodgings in Battersea for the play), Coward was hardly your average audience member's idea of a salty South London type. Consequently, Lean turned to Robert Newton, who'd been so memorable as Bill Walker in *Major Barbara*, to play Frank Gibbons, although he did decide to ask Celia Johnson to recreate her stage role for the screen (but, to be honest, Johnson was a little on the genteel side herself for such a role).

Also cast as Gibbons' family members are Amy Veness as Ethel's ever-moaning mother Mrs Flint, Alison Leggatt as Frank's hypochondriac sister Aunt Sylvia, John Blythe as Frank and Ethel's headstrong son Reg, and Eileen Erskine as their daughter Vi. Of Lean's established rep company of players, Kay Walsh was back as Queenie Gibbons, Frank and Ethel's eldest daughter, who wants nothing more than to rise above her 'common' surroundings, and John Mills as Billy Mitchell, the sailor who lives next door. Playing Billy's father and Frank's old army pal Bob Mitchell is Stanley Holloway, who must have impressed Lean in his brief role as the policeman in *Major Barbara*.

Although this is a Noel Coward–Cineguild Production, Coward's involvement in *This Happy Breed* was mostly peripheral once he'd submitted the screenplay, which was then adapted by Lean, Ronald Neame and Anthony Havelock-Allan. Coward kept an eye on things from a distance, but returned only to score the finished product, which Muir Mathieson conducted, again using the London Symphony Orchestra.

In the film one can see Lean begin to exercise his visual style more confidently. After a brief opening narration spoken by an unaccredited Laurence Olivier, a good friend of Coward, the camera pans across the London skyline, honing in on the back of the Gibbons' new home, 17 Sycamore Road. We then cut to one of the upstairs windows (now in a studio), through which the camera glides, passing through the empty rooms before making its way down the stairs to the front door, just as Frank opens it to let the family inside, closely followed by the removal men and the furniture. This is pure cinema, indicating immediately that what is to follow will be much more than a flat-filmed version of the play.

As the family unpacks their possessions we gradually learn about them and their foibles (Mrs Flint's comical whining is delightfully put over by Amy Veness). However, while much of the drama that follows concentrates on the family's domestic dramas, Lean often opens up the story, bringing the outside world into the lives of the Gibbons. He does this first by having the family watch a parade of soldiers and sailors returning from the war, alongside which the camera smoothly dollies, perfectly capturing the excitement of the music and cheering crowds. This is classic Lean (and a precursor of a similar scene in *Doctor Zhivago* in which crowds cheer troops as they part for action). In a masterstroke, this scene of triumphalism concludes with a sobering shot of a cenotaph, at the corners of which four soldiers stand, their heads bowed. This was, after all, triumph at a great cost.

Lean then cuts to a black and white photograph showing the horrors of the battlefront – all mud and lowering skies – only to reveal that the photo is an advertisement in the shop window of Tickners Travel Agents, where Frank Gibbons now works, selling tours of the battlefields. But the ad for these tours soon transforms into a more colourful one for the British Empire Exhibition of 1924, for which the shop is handling tickets. The war is now but a past memory and times have moved on to happier days (Lean makes use of several transformations such as this seamlessly to move the time scale forward without having to resort to title cards).

Being patriotic Brits, the Gibbons naturally attend the Empire Exhibition in Wembley, although much to Frank's consternation and our amusement, his children and their friends are more interested in doing the funfair rides than touring the educational exhibits. For a single shot in this sequence, a giant Taj Mahal-like structure was erected on the Denham back lot, the scale of which immediately gets across the grandeur of the Exhibition. That Lean doesn't shoot this from every conceivable angle possible to make the most of what is obviously an expensive set shows his restraint as a director, for rather than allow the scene to become stale for the sake of spectacle, he quickly moves the story forward again, this time care of a Christmas card on the Gibbons' mantelpiece which tells us that it is now Christmas 1925.

These are relatively prosperous times, and the family is shown eating, drinking and making merry with their friends and neighbours. During one scene, Queenie (Kay Walsh) spends much of the time stuffing her face with cake, nuts and an orange, which must have been more than some audiences could endure when the film was released in 1944, when rationing was in full force and an orange was a rarity.

After the celebrations — during which neighbour Billy tells a surprised Queenie he loves and wants to marry her — things again move quickly on to take in the General Strike, Vi's marriage to would-be Communist Sam Leadbitter (Guy Verney) and the arrival of the talkies in the guise of *Broadway Melody* ('The all-singing, all-talking, all-dancing marvel of 1929'), a clip of which we're shown ('I don't understand a word they say,' sneers Sam, to which Vi responds, 'But it's marvellous, isn't it?').

Then it's on to the rise of the Fascists in Germany, the marriage of Reg, the absconding of Queenie with a married man (surely an eyebrow-raiser in 1944?) and the arrival of electric lighting at number 17. Tragedy arrives with the death of Reg and his wife Phyllis, who have been killed in a car crash. Vi breaks the news to Mrs Flint and Aunt Sylvia, who are in the living room. What follows is again pure directorial talent. Sylvia takes Mrs Flint upstairs to her room, leaving Vi to go into the garden to tell the news to her parents. However, rather than have the camera follow this action, Lean keeps it in the empty room. Eventually, after a long moment, Frank and Ethel enter the room and silently sit down at the table, completely bereft, as the camera discreetly pulls back and the screen fades to black. And the icing on the cake? All the while the scene is running, a band can be heard playing a noisy, upbeat number on the radio in complete counterpoint to the drama of the scene.

After this it's swiftly on to the 1935 general election, the death of George V (another sobering shot here, this time of the King lying in state as the crowds pass by to pay their respects) and the return of Queenie, now married to Billy and with a child on the way. With the house now empty of their children, Frank and Ethel finally decide to move from number 17 to a flat with a balcony, and although Chamberlain promises 'Peace in our time' (a look-a-like Chamberlain is shown waving to cheering crowds on a Downing Street set), the future doesn't look too good, despite the fact that the film concludes with an instrumental rendition of Coward's *London Pride* (although to tell the truth, without the lyrics, it sounds more like *Deutschland Uber Alles*, more ominous than upbeat). With Frank and Ethel now gone and the house empty again, Lean pulls back his camera through the deserted rooms, out of the back window and up to the London skyline, bringing the film full circle.

The fast-moving patchwork of vignettes works superbly in *This Happy Breed*, with the cast bringing their not always entirely believable characters to vivid life. Robert Newton is remarkably subdued as Frank Gibbons, and is all the better for it, and he is ably supported by Celia Johnson as the often-harried Ethel. Kay Walsh is also noteworthy as the not always likeable Queenie, whose priority is a good time above everything else (in a sequence in which she does The Charleston at a dance she almost jumps off the screen!), while John Mills is as reliable as ever as Billy. Ultimately, this is a film of ordinary lives in which the raison d'être is the observation of everyday detail, be it the chores of the kitchen (with Merle Tottenham giving a delightful comic turn as the Gibbons' skivvy Edie) or the buttering of the cat's paws when the family first move in. This was the kind of thing working class audiences could easily identify with ('Nearly two hours of the pleasure of recognition,' observed Richard Mallet in *Punch*), even if Coward's view of suburban life is a little on the patronising side. When released in June 1944, *This Happy Breed* went on to become the biggest money maker of its year (despite this, the film didn't get released in America until April 1947).

'It is the small detailed life of No. 17 that steals the picture,' commented critic Richard Winnington in his review of the film, going on to add, 'To those who believe fervently in the British cinema, the three young men who made the picture [i.e. Lean, Neame and Havelock-Allan] are a confirmation and a hope.' *The Times* was similarly enthusiastic, adding, 'The film is yet another proof of the excellence of the work British studios are now doing.' The film even went down well north of Watford, with the *Manchester Guardian* commenting, 'Miss Johnson's inarticulate portrait of Mum is extraordinary,' while *Variety* concurred, 'Celia Johnson, as the mother of three grown-up children and the rock around which the family revolves, presents a masterful, poignant portrayal.'

When it came to directing feature films, it was clear that Lean had now finally arrived. Yet *This Happy Breed* was not the only film with which he was involved in 1944. He also had a hand in two documentaries that Cineguild made for the Ministry of Information, for distribution to liberated countries. The first of these was *Failure of a Strategy* which Lean edited (with Peter Tanner) concurrent to *This Happy Breed*. The short film, compiled from existing newsreel footage, was executive produced by Sidney Bernstein (the future producer of Hitchcock's *Rope* and founder of Granada Television, who at the time was working as an adviser to the MoI), and offers a factual account of the war so far, free from German propaganda and lies. *Failure of a Strategy* was followed by a similarly themed piece called *Failure of the Generals*, which also helped to set the record straight for those countries starved of unbiased news. Little more than a footnote to Lean's feature career, these two films are forgotten today, which perhaps isn't surprising given that they were sandwiched by such important works as *This Happy Breed* and Lean's next project, an adaptation of another Noel Coward stage success, the fondly remembered *Blithe Spirit*.

An instant West End hit when it first appeared in 1941, *Blithe Spirit* is a sophisticated comedy in which a successful author, Charles Condomine, arranges to have a seance at his home to help him research his latest book, *The Unseen*. Unfortunately, the seance, conducted by the eccentric Madame Arcati, summons up the playful spirit of Condomine's late first wife Elvira, much to the consternation of his second wife Ruth, who can neither see nor hear the apparition, coming to the conclusion that her husband has gone completely round the bend.

As he had done with *This Happy Breed*, Coward supplied the script for *Blithe Spirit* (adapted by Lean, Neame and Havelock-Allan), which was subsequently made under the established Noel Coward–Cineguild banner, with Lean directing, Neame behind the camera and

Laura Jesson (Celia Johnson) gets some grit in her eye in Brief Encounter. *Myrtle Bagshot (Joyce Carey) and Albert Godby (Stanley Holloway) look on. The film earned Lean his first best director Oscar nomination.*

Havelock-Allan in charge of production. On stage, Cecil Parker had played Charles Condomine, but for the film Rex Harrison was chosen, with Constance Cummings (familiar to film audiences from *Movie Crazy* and *The Foreman Went to France*) as Ruth, replacing Fay Compton who'd played the role on stage. Making the jump from stage to screen was Kay Hammond (who'd appeared in the 1933 film version of Coward's *Bitter Sweet*) as the ghostly Elvira, and Margaret Rutherford as the splendidly dotty Madame Arcati (Rutherford would later go on to star in the popular Miss Marple films of the Sixties, all of which were directed by George Pollack, who was Lean's assistant on *Blithe Spirit* and several other of his early films). In support as the Condomine's guests at the seance are Hugh Wakefield and Joyce Carey as Dr and Mrs Bradman, while Jacqueline Clark plays Edith the maid who, it turns out, has strong supernatural powers herself.

Filmed in Technicolor at Denham on lavish interiors designed by Gladys Calthrop and CP Norman, *Blithe Spirit* sticks closely to Coward's stage original, with few excursions into the outside world (memorable is Madame Arcati's comical journey to the Condomine's on her bicycle, and Charles' trip to Folkstone with Elvira, with Elvira driving the car, much to the consternation of an RAC officer who cannot see her). The only real deviation from the play comes at the conclusion, when Charles has a car accident and joins both his wives as a ghost (by this point Elvira has mistakenly killed Ruth). In other hands all this might have seemed rather ghoulish, especially given that people were being killed on a daily basis in the war, yet this flippant view of death was tactfully handled by all concerned (just as it had been in the similarly themed *Topper* films made in Hollywood).

After the credits, the film opens with a Victorian sampler which reads,

> When we are young,
> We read and believe,
> The most fantastic things.
> When we grow older and wiser,
> We learn, with perhaps a little regret,
> That these things can never be.

Then, on the soundtrack, can be heard an unaccredited Noel Coward exclaiming, 'We are quite, quite wrrrrrong!' as the unfolding story goes on to prove.

Lean was never quite comfortable making *Blithe Spirit*, high comedy not being his forte (Coward later accused him of ruining his best play). Nevertheless, Lean turned in his customary professional job, making sure that the film didn't just look like a photographed play. Given that it's set mostly within the confines of the Condomines' home, this is something of an achievement, but careful camera placement and discreet editing keep things moving along smoothly. Lean exercises his directorial style very little in the film, his one flourish being a sweeping camera move through the Condomine's living room and out into the hallway, the camera catching the living room doors as they magically close behind it in a mirror. Clever stuff.

More than any other of Lean's films, *Blithe Spirit* is a film of performances rather than technique. It is well served in this respect by Rex Harrison and Constance Cummings, who make light work or Coward's bantering dialogue ('If you wish to make an inventory of my sex life I think it only fair to tell you that you've left out several episodes,' Charles informs Ruth during one exchange. 'I shall consult my diary and give you a complete list after lunch'). As Elvira, Kay Hammond is also in spirited form, making the most of her scenes with Charles ('You've absolutely ruined that border by the sundial. It looks like a mixed salad,' she chides him), although one wishes she didn't sound like she had a punnet of plums in her mouth. In many respects, the film is stolen by Margaret Rutherford's turn as the dotty Madame Arcati, all tweed and flamboyant gestures as she goes into her trance, accompanied by Irving Berlin's *Always* on the gramophone. As the bustling maid, Edith (another of Coward's lower class stereotypes), Jacqueline Clark also manages to leave her mark.

One's only regret is that Joyce Carey and Hugh Wakefield's characters aren't involved in the action more – or that Kay Walsh was overlooked entirely for a role this time round (she could have carried off Ruth or Elvira with equal success).

Save for a couple of blue screen sequences, the film has very few special effects in it, all of Elvira's appearances being achieved 'live' on set, with Kay Hammond dressed from head to foot in green hair, make-up and chiffon and followed about by a green light. This proved a challenge for cinematographer Ronald Neame, who had to make sure the green light didn't spill on to the other actors. Everyone was surprised then to learn that the film's effects technician, Tom Howard, later won an Oscar for the film's 'effects'.

Despite Lean's reservations about the film, there is much to enjoy in *Blithe Spirit*, be it the dialogue, the performances or Richard Addinsell's sprightly score (conducted by Muir Mathieson). Nevertheless, it failed to recoup its outlay when first released in April 1945 (September 1945 in America), and earned some lukewarm reviews into the bargain, perhaps the most pertinent of them coming from Dilys Powell writing in *The Sunday Times*: 'Personally I would have liked Mr Coward to start again from scratch and write his astringent joke as a film.' Although *Blithe Spirit* was perhaps a step backwards for Lean in a cinematic sense, it has survived well and while it might not be vintage Lean, it's certainly vintage Coward.

If *Blithe Spirit* failed to stretch Lean artistically, his next – and final – association with Noel Coward would produce one of the milestones of British cinema: *Brief Encounter*. Based on a short 1935 play by Coward titled *Still Life* (originally performed on stage by Coward and Gertrude Lawrence as part of the *Tonight at 8.30* series), its story could not be simpler. A suburban housewife, Laura Jesson, has a series of romantic encounters with a dashing doctor, Alec Harvey, during her Thursday shopping trips to Milford. The affair (in the film) is never consummated, yet Laura who, like Alec, is long married (to the dull but devoted Fred), is wracked with guilt. Thus when Alec is offered a job in South Africa, they decide never to see each other again.

As had been the case with their two previous projects, Coward wrote the screenplay for *Brief Encounter* himself, which was then adapted by Lean, Havelock-Allan and Neame, with Neame now also producing with Coward and Havelock-Allan, leaving the job of photographing the film to Robert Krasker. Born in Perth, Australia, in 1913, Krasker arrived in Britain in 1932, getting a job working for London Films as an operator for Georges Perinal. Later, he worked as Ronald Neame's operator on *One of Our Aircraft Is Missing* (so he was a known quantity), after which he graduated to full director of photography with *The Lamp Still Burns* for director Maurice Elvey, from whom Lean himself had learned so much back in the early Thirties. By the time Krasker came to photograph *Brief Encounter*, he also had *The Gentle Sex*, *The Saint Meets the Tiger* and Olivier's monumental *Henry V* under his belt, so was more than qualified for the task (he went on to photograph many other notable films, such as *Odd Man Out* and *The Third Man* for Carol Reed, the latter winning him an Oscar).

In casting the film, Lean could not have made better choices. 'Noel and Gertie' were luckily out of the question, Coward being away entertaining the troops and Lawrence having decamped to America for a series of successful (and lucrative) appearances on the Broadway stage. Lean turned to Celia Johnson, who had served him so well in *In Which We Serve* and *This Happy Breed*, to play the role of Laura, and so right was she that the line between actress and role became forever blurred. For the role of the doctor, Lean originally wanted Roger Livesey, then best known for Powell and Pressburger's *The Life and Death of Colonel Blimp* and *I Know Where I'm Going* (the latter with Wendy Hiller). However, when Livesey proved unavailable, Lean thought of Trevor Howard, having noticed his brief performance as Squadron Leader Carter in Anthony Asquith's *The Way to the Stars*. At the time, Howard's only other screen credit was in Carol Reed's *The Way Ahead*, before which he'd trained at RADA and made his stage debut in *Revolt in a Reformatory* in 1934. Lean's faith in Howard turned him into a star, and he went on to appear in such classics as *The Third Man*, *Green for Danger* and *Sons and Lovers*, as well as two more for Lean: *The Passionate Friend* and *Ryan's Daughter*. Yet despite these films, it is as Alec Harvey that most remember him.

Perhaps what distinguishes *Brief Encounter* most, however, is the very ordinariness of its settings, photographed in black and white, Technicolor having been given the elbow this time. The most drab of these is the dingy refreshment room on the platform of Milford Junction, which is where Laura and Alec first meet, Laura having some grit in her eye from a passing train. Returning to the refreshment room to get some water with which to bathe it, she finds herself being assisted by the good doctor. As Laura, narrating the story, comments, 'That's how it all began – just through me getting a little piece of grit in my eye.' But this is to jump ahead. Lean and Coward begin the film at the story's end, with Laura and Alec saying goodbye for the last time. Unfortunately, their farewell scene is interrupted by Dolly Messitter, a gossipy friend of Laura's who barges in on the couple, not realising what's going on. Once Alec has departed – a squeeze on the shoulder instead of a kiss now has to do – Dolly accompanies Laura back home on the train to Ketchworth. By this time Laura has taken a turn for the worse, for while Dolly is busy buying chocolate, she runs out onto the platform ('I just wanted to see the express go through,' she explains), and it is while recovering from her 'spell' on the journey back to Ketchworth that she begins to recount, in narration, what has been going on over the previous few weeks.

Entirely innocent at first, Laura and Alec's meetings initially involve their sharing lunch together at the Kardomah (and giggling about the orchestra, one comical-looking member of which is played by an unaccredited Irene Handl) and visiting the cinema to see the 'epoch-making' *Flames of Passion* (where it turns out the organist is also Irene Handl). When the outings progress to boat rides in the park and tea in the boatman's hut, things start to get serious ('You know what's happened, don't you?' Alec asks Laura). Yet when it comes to consummating the affair in a flat Alec has borrowed from his friend Stephen Lynn (an unaccredited Valentine Dyall), Laura can't go through with it, such is her guilt, especially when Stephen returns unexpectedly and she has to skulk out the back way down the tradesmans' staircase. Humiliated and defeated, Laura walks the streets in a daze. Alec eventually catches up with her at the station where he persuades her to meet him one last time the next Thursday. The day flies by all too quickly, and just as the couple are saying their final goodbyes in the refreshment room, along comes Dolly Messitter. This time, however, we see what Laura really does as Dolly is buying her chocolate – she runs outside not to see the express

'That boatman thinks we are dotty, but look how sweet he has been. Tea, milk – even sugar!' trills Laura (Celia Johnson) in a scene from Brief Encounter. *It's not tea that Alec Harvey (Trevor Howard) is after though.*

go by, but to throw herself under it ('I meant to do it, Fred, I really meant to do it'). But sanity prevails and Laura returns home to Fred and the children ('Thank you for coming back to me,' says Fred, somewhat cryptically, on the fadeout).

As the war was still raging, Lean had to find a station to double for Milford Junction far from London, where the arc lights used during the filming of the evening sequences wouldn't attract too much attention. The unit decamped to Carnforth in Lancashire for two weeks to film the location sequences, where Lean made much use of trains thundering through the station (the film opens with an impressive shot of an express tearing through). The station interiors, where Laura has her unfortunate encounter with Dolly, were filmed back at Denham. Unfortunately, the actress cast to play Dolly – Joyce Barbour – got camera fright and was replaced by Everley Gregg, whom Lean no doubt remembered from *Pygmalion* (in which she'd played Mrs Eynsford-Hill).

Also featured in the refreshment room sequences, and adding some much-needed comic relief to the proceedings, is Joyce Carey as Myrtle Bagshot, the uppity proprietor. A long-time friend of Noel Coward's, she had already made telling appearances in *In Which We Serve* (as Kath) and *Blithe Spirit* (as Mrs Bradman), as well as Anthony Asquith's *The Way to the Stars*. As Myrtle she has arguably her best screen part, a marvellous cameo in which her mock-refined accent proves to be the comic highlight of the film (although her come-on surprisingly fools Laura, who comments in the narration, 'I told you about her the other day – the one with the refined voice,'). Joining Carey in these comic moments is Stanley Holloway as station guard Albert Godby, who has his beady eye on the widow Bagshot, and Margaret Barton as the cafe's idle skivvy Beryl Waters ('Go and clean off number three, Beryl, I can see the crumbs on it from here,' admonishes Ma Bagshot at one point). Meanwhile, as Laura's adoring husband Fred, Cyril Raymond (who'd appeared in *Dreaming Lips*) is given the difficult task of appearing as dull as ditch water, while at the same time remaining likeable.

Brief Encounter is very much a film of its period. Had it been made five years earlier or five years later, it would not have been so effective. Its minor imperfections are very much of its period too: the dialogue and accents often seem of another age, as does Laura and Alec's eventual determination to do the decent thing and not consummate their affair. Laura's children, Bobbie and Margaret, irritate more than they endear with their quarrel about how they should celebrate Bobbie's birthday. Says Bobbie, 'Well, Mummy, tomorrow's my birthday and I want to go to the circus, and tomorrow's not Margaret's birthday, and she wants to go to the pantomime, and I don't think it's fair,' to which Margaret replies, 'I don't see why we've got to do everything Bobbie wants, just because it's his silly old birthday. Besides, my birthday is in June, and there aren't any pantomimes in June.' Fred's jovial solution to the dilemma, later proposed over the dinner table, seems quite reasonable: 'We'll thrash them both soundly, lock them in the attic and go to the cinema ourselves.' Perhaps the old boy's not so dull after all.

These are only minor quibbles in an otherwise faultless piece of cinema, in which performances and direction, accompanied by Rachmaninov's Piano Concerto Number Two on the soundtrack (played by Eileen Joyce) combine to create the archetypal Forties romance. Lean's direction is mostly discreet, with the camera almost eavesdropping on Laura and Alec's affair, although when the action calls for it, he provides several flourishes. Among these are Laura's fireside reminiscences, in which the living room cross-fades to a series of flashbacks, while at the same time leaving Laura, sat in her armchair, as part of the scene, almost as if she's watching a film of her romance. The huge close-up of Dolly Messitter's incessantly chatting mouth is also extremely effective, as is the subtle drop of light surrounding Alec and Laura in the refreshment room during their last meeting. The pièce de résistance, however, is the brief scene in which Laura runs out onto the platform to throw herself under the express. Here, Lean tilts the camera to show her distraught state of mind, only to level the camera once the train has gone through the station and Laura's moment of madness has passed. The impact of this effect almost has a physical force to it.

The most fluid of Lean's early films, *Brief Encounter* was a solid box office success when it was released in November 1945 (August 1946 in the States), earning some excellent reviews into the

The shot that says it all.

bargain. 'No praise can be too lavish,' enthused Patrick Kirwan in the *Evening Standard*, adding that he thought the film contained, 'the most polished production and performances of the year.' *The Daily Mail*'s critic was also equally enthusiastic, commenting, 'I found my handkerchief a sodden ball without having noticed that I was crying, because I was too absorbed in what I was seeing.' Across the pond, *Variety* was also full of praise, even if the reviewer did seem under the impression that Coward, and not Lean, had directed the film. '*Brief Encounter* does more for Noel Coward's reputation as a skilled film producer than *In Which We Serve*. His use of express trains thundering through a village station coupled with frantic, last-minute dashes for local trains is only one of the clever touches masking the inherent static quality of the drama.'

The film also did pretty well on the awards circuit, winning the Critics' Prize at the Cannes Film Festival. It was also voted among the best films of 1946 by the DW Griffith Awards (alongside Olivier's *Henry V* and John Ford's *My Darling Clementine*), while Celia Johnson won the best actress gong at the New York Film Critics' Circle Awards. More importantly, the film also earned three Oscar nominations, for best screenplay (Lean, Neame and Havelock-Allan, who lost out to Robert Sherwood for *The Best Years of Our Lives*), best actress (Johnson, who lost out to Olivia de Havilland for *To Each His Own*) and best director (with Lean losing out to William Wyler for *The Best Years of Our Lives*). Although the film failed to win in any of its categories, simply being nominated for best director must have been prize enough for Lean, then making him only the second British director to be nominated (Alfred Hitchcock had already been nominated for *Rebecca*, *Lifeboat* and *Spellbound*, but these films were made in Hollywood, not Britain). The nomination also helped to consolidate Lean's reputation internationally as a director.

Despite its age, *Brief Encounter* remains a powerful viewing experience, while its impact has reverberated down the decades. There have been countless spoofs (most notably a sketch written and performed by Mike Nichols and Elaine May), as well as two remakes. The first of these, which went by the same title, was a 1975 television movie starring Richard Burton as Alec and Sophia Loren as Laura. Directed by James Bridges, it was a disaster of the first order. Slightly better is the New York-set *Falling in Love*, a 1984 variation on the same theme starring Robert De Niro and Meryl Streep, this time as Frank and Molly. A passable romance, adequately directed by Ulu Grosbard, it nevertheless seems from another age, and elicited from *Variety* a delicious putdown: 'The effect of this talented pair acting in such a lightweight vehicle is akin to having Horowitz and Rubinstein improvise a duet on the theme of Chopsticks.' There was even a short film entitled *Flames of Passion*, which told the story from a homosexual point of view, while Lean himself returned to the same territory in 1948 with *The Passionate Friends*, complete with Trevor Howard.

Yet despite the success of *Brief Encounter* and his fruitful association with Coward, without whom he would not have had the chance to direct, Lean felt that their working relationship had by now run its course. Between them, Lean, Coward, Neame and Havelock-Allan had made some of the key British films of the war years. But it was time to move on and explore pastures new. The split between Lean and Coward, such as it was, was totally amicable. The problem facing Lean now, was where to next?

Seven

WHAT LARKS!

J ust as there had been adaptations of Noel Coward's work before David Lean, so too had there been adaptations of Charles Dickens' books. Some of them, such as George Cukor's Hollywood version of *David Copperfield*, with WC Fields' memorable turn as Mr Micawber, had been highly successful. Many, however, failed to exploit the intricate plotting and rich characterisations found in the novels. In Lean, the cherished author found his ideal screen interpreter.

In breaking away from Noel Coward, Lean decided to take on a completely different kind of subject, yet had it not been for a visit to the theatre in 1939, he might never have considered Dickens. The production was an adaptation of *Great Expectations* by an up-and-coming actor called Alec Guinness, with Guinness playing Herbert Pocket and Martita Hunt as Miss Havisham. The play obviously had a great effect on Lean who, after further urging from his wife Kay Walsh, decided to tackle it as his follow up to *Brief Encounter* in 1946. There had been previous screen versions of the book, among them two silents and a 1934 Hollywood production directed by Stuart Walker, starring Phillips Holmes as Pip and Henry Hull as Magwitch. Neither proved memorable and so posed no threat to Lean's proposed version.

The writing process for *Great Expectations* was a lengthy one. Lean and Ronald Neame, who would produce the film through Cineguild, began work on adapting the book before filming *Brief Encounter*. This meant that Lean had already made his mind up about breaking away from Coward long before the Master suspected anything. Lean and Neame's outline was then worked on further by Anthony Havelock-Allan (who would executive produce the film), Cecil McGivern and Kay Walsh, who trimmed Dickens' vast canvas down to the essentials.

As in the book, the story opens on Christmas Eve with the young Philip Pirrip – Pip to all – running across the marshes to lay flowers on his parents' grave. While in the graveyard, Pip encounters an escaped convict called Magwitch, who frightens the boy into bringing him some food and a file from the home he shares with his sister and her husband, the local blacksmith. Afraid of disobeying, Pip carries out the task early the next morning, much to the convict's gratification. Nevertheless, Magwitch is still caught by local soldiers in the evening and sent back to the 'hulks' from whence he came. The incident is soon forgotten, however, when it transpires that the wealthy but eccentric Miss Havisham has requested that Pip go to her crumbling mansion, where time has stood still since she was jilted on her wedding day, to play with her ward, the beautiful Estella. Pip naturally falls in love with Estella, despite the fact that she taunts him for being common and coarse ('He calls knaves Jacks, this boy!'). Pip determines to become a gentleman and one day to marry Estella.

David Lean has a chat with studio head J Arthur Rank during the making of Great Expectations.

The opportunity presents itself on Pip's 20th birthday, when he learns that he has 'great expectations' and that an unknown benefactor (whom he assumes to be Miss Havisham, given that he is told the news by her solicitor Mr Jaggers), is to pay for him to travel to London, where he is to learn how to become a gentleman. This he does with assistance from one Herbert Pocket, whom he encountered many years ago in the grounds of Miss Havisham's house, where they fought each other, much to Estella's amusement. Now Pip and Herbert become firm friends, spending way above their allowances in the process. Mr Jaggers, appointed by the benefactor, is luckily on hand to prevent Pip from getting into too much trouble. However, trouble does indeed come when Magwitch turns up on the scene again, revealing himself to be Pip's benefactor, having made a fortune in sheep farming in Australia, from whence he has illegally returned.

Once over the shock of the revelation, Pip determines on getting Magwitch out of the country by boat, but the attempt ends in tragedy when Pip's rowboat crashes with a packet steamer and Magwitch drowns. But there is a happy ending of sorts, Pip is re-united with Estella, whom he has since discovered is the daughter of Magwitch and Jaggers' housekeeper Molly, having been placed with Miss Havisham as a baby by Mr Jaggers after Magwitch's conviction.

Even in this abridged form, there is an abundance of plot and many characters to cram into the running time, all providing Lean plenty with which to work.

Once production was officially underway, John Bryan was hired to design the film's sets, for which he made good use of forced perspective and low angles. This was perfectly captured by cinematographer Guy Green. Robert Krasker, who'd photographed *Brief Encounter*, was originally on board as the cinematographer. Unfortunately, Lean was less than impressed with Krasker's first few days of work, and so he was replaced by Green, who had operated for Ronald Neame on both *In Which We Serve* and *This Happy Breed*, since when he had photographed *The Way Ahead* (for Carol Reed) and *Carnival* (for Stanley Haynes, who'd been the 'assistant in production' on *Major Barbara*). Other technicians involved in the film familiar to Lean were editor Jack Harris, who'd cut (under Lean's supervision) *This Happy Breed*, *Blithe Spirit* and *Brief Encounter*, sound recordists Stanley Lambourne and Desmond Dew, and assistant director George Pollack.

Familiar faces in the growing Lean repertory company returned to flesh out Dickens' characters: John Mills as the grown-up Pip, Bernard Miles as Pip's blacksmith brother-in-law Joe Gargery and Everley Gregg in a cameo as Sarah Pocket. There were plenty of newcomers this time round too: Alec Guinness as Herbert Pocket, which seemed only fair given that it was his stage adaptation that had inspired Lean to make the film in the first place. Guinness would go on to become one of Lean's most frequently used actors, winning an Oscar for *The Bridge on the River Kwai*, yet at this stage in his career he was an unknown quantity to film audiences. Born in 1914, Guinness had studied acting at the Fay Compton Studio of Dramatic Art and made his stage debut in 1934 in *Libel* – the same year in which he made his first film, appearing as an extra in the Evelyn Laye vehicle *Evensong*. Guinness hated the experience and, save for war service in the Royal Navy, remained on the stage until he received the call from Lean to recreate the role of Herbert Pocket.

Also on board was portly character actor Francis L Sullivan (*Sabotage*, *Pimpernel Smith*, *Caesar and Cleopatra*) who was given the plum role of Mr Jaggers, a part he'd already played on screen in the forgotten 1934 Hollywood version. Joining him as the grown-up Estella (and also, briefly, as Jaggers' scarred housekeeper Molly) was Mrs Havelock-Allan, better known to audiences as Valerie Hobson. While as Magwitch, Lean chose veteran character man Finlay Currie (*The 49th Parallel*, *Major Barbara*). Although 68 at the time, Currie still had another 22 years ahead of him as a screen actor in *The Mudlark*, *Quo Vadis?* and *Billy Liar*. Also returning from the stage production was Martita Hunt, who re-created her role as Miss Havisham, while the younger versions of Pip and Estella were handed to Anthony Wager and Jean Simmons, respectively, the latter having already begun to make a name for herself in *Mr Emmanuel* and Gabriel Pascal's *Caesar and Cleopatra* (with *Black Narcissus*, *Hamlet*, *Elmer Gantry* and *Spartacus* to come). Further down the cast list in supporting roles could be found Ivor Barnard (as Wemmick), Freda Jackson (Mrs Joe Gargery), Eileen Erskine (Biddy), Hay Petrie (Uncle Pumblechook), OB Clarence (Aged P) and Edie Martin (Mrs Whimple).

'Aaaarrrgh!' The young Pip (Anthony Wager) has an unexpected encounter in the graveyard with escaped convict Magwitch (Finlay Currie) in the opening scene in Great Expectations.

Location filming for *Great Expectations* took place on the rivers and marshes around the town of Rochester, where Dickens lived for many years. It was here that John Bryan built the exteriors of Joe's forge and where the capture of Magwitch was filmed, along with his later drowning. For this, a paddle steamer was suitably disguised as the packet boat with which Pip's rowboat collides, although the close-ups of Pip attempting to save Magwitch were filmed in the safety of the studio tank at Pinewood, where a mock-up of the boat's giant paddle was built. The interiors, as well as the faked exteriors, were shot back at Denham. Among the faked exteriors is the graveyard seen during the opening sequence, with its masterful use of forced perspective, the small church in the background being barely six feet high, as careful examination reveals. The creaking graveyard trees,

An original call sheet from Great Expectations. *Fascinating stuff.*

INDEPENDENT PRODUCERS, LTD.

DAILY PRODUCTION AND PROGRESS REPORT

A CINEGUILD PRODUCTION

TIME		SCRIPT REPORT			WHERE WORKING	

DAY	Monday	DATE April 15th, 1946.	REPORT No. 196
PRODUCTION No. 106 I.P.		PRODUCTION "GREAT EXPECTATIONS"	DIRECTOR David Lean
ALLOTTED DAYS 99		ELAPSED DAYS 76 plus Exteriors	STATUS 1 day behind
DATE STARTED 3rd Dec. 1945.		ESTIMATED FINISHING DATE 30th March, 1946	FINISHED DATE

			Number	Minutes	TO-DAY	
COMPANY CALLED	8.00	SCENES IN ORIGINAL SCRIPT	808		Int.	Ext.
TIME STARTED	10.15	SCENES PREVIOUSLY TAKEN	632	120.17	EXT. PADDLE WHEEL.	
LUNCH CALLED	1.00	SCENES TAKEN TO-DAY	3	30	PINEWOOD TANK	
TIME STARTED	2.00	TOTAL TAKEN TO DATE	635	120.47	STAGE 'D'.	
FINISHED	6.45	BALANCE TO BE TAKEN	173			
		ADDED SCENES TAKEN TO-DAY			TO-MORROW	
		ADDED SCENES TAKEN TO DATE			Int.	Ext.
STILLS PREVIOUSLY 635		RETAKE SCENES TAKEN TO-DAY	3	23	EXT. PADDLE WHEEL.	
TO-DAY 3		RETAKE SCENES TAKEN TO DATE	71	12.15	PINEWOOD TANK	
TOTAL 638					STAGE 'D'.	

STAR & LEADS	Worked	Held	Rehearsed	SMALL PART	Worked	Held	Rehearsed	EXTRAS & STAND-INS NUMBER & RATE	Worked	Held
JOHN MILLS	114							Stand-Ins		
FINLAY CURRIE	67½							R. Cantouris £2.17.0d		
GEORGE HAYES	37½							D. Yarrington £2.17.0d		
								W. Hatton £2.13.6d		
B. Simmonds £3.7.8d								4 OARSMEN @ £2.7.3d		

ACTION PROPS Number and Kind	EFFECTS
Crane. Pip's boat Four-oared Galley P.A. System Electric Wind Machine	

	PICTURE FOOTAGE				SOUND FOOTAGE	
	GROSS B. & W.	GROSS COLOUR	PRINT B. & W.	PRINT COLOUR	GROSS	PRINT
PREVIOUS	231115		113010		209215	83116
TO-DAYS	545		355		460	70
TOTAL	231660		113365		209675	83186

No. OF CAMERAS	
TO-DAY	2
TO-MORROW	1

SLATE NUMBERS 845 - 848
SCENE NUMBERS 726 - 728

2nd CAMERA USED TODAY.

KINDLY INDICATE REASON FOR TIME LOST, EXCESSIVE FOOTAGE OR SCENES, ETC.; ALSO INDICATE WHEN STARTING OR FINISHING WITH ANY ARTISTE.
18490' of Picture and 15975' of Sound footage has been used on Tests.
Location No.1 started ...... 10th Sept, 1945
Location No.1 finished ..... 30th Nov. 1945
Total No. of days worked on location 64
SUNDAY 33rd DAY .. MONDAY 34th DAY OF LOCATION NO. 2. AT ROCHESTER.

CORRECT :

Assistant Director

with their claw-like branches, are also worth examining closely, as one of them has an ugly face carved into its trunk. The grounds of Miss Havisham's crumbling home, Satis House, where the young Pip has his punch-up with Herbert, were also created in the studio.

Of the many interiors Bryan created for the film, perhaps the most striking are those of Miss Havisham's mansion, particularly the shadowy staircase leading up to her rooms – especially when lit by Estella's lone candle – and the dining room where her wedding breakfast stills lies, the mouldering cake looking like some grotesque marble statue, covered in cobwebs and mice. Not exactly the sort of place to bring up a young lady like Estella (one wonders why Jaggers placed the child with such an unstable woman in the first place). Jaggers' London office catches the eye too, with its shelves of books and its walls decorated with the death masks of executed convicts. Pip's lodgings with Herbert at Barnard's Inn also have the required look of run-down gentility to them.

From the first shot through to the last, there is no doubt that *Great Expectations* is a designed film. There isn't a shape, shadow or piece of furniture that hasn't been carefully considered. Clever use is even made of the soundtrack. When Pip steals the pie and file for Magwitch, the house seems to compel Mrs Joe to wake up and catch him ('Wake up, Mrs Joe,' a disembodied voice whispers). Even the cows on the marshes look askance at Pip, with the boy imagining that they are accusing him of thieving. The cleverest touch, however, comes in the form of a brief music cue (the score having been composed by the German-born Walter Goehr). When Mrs Joe and Uncle Pumblechook draw up at the forge in his trap, excited at the news that Miss Havisham wants Pip to go and play at her house, instead of Mrs Joe's shouts of, 'Pip! Joe! Pip!' musical screeches and bellows from the brass section issue from her mouth! Other effects that also catch the ear include the sound of Jaggers' quill pen as he scratches away with it in his office, and the brief scene in which a group of convicts is hanged in front of a baying crowd; just before the hangman pulls the lever and they drop to their deaths, a hush descends on the crowd, to the point that birds can be heard twittering, after which comes the drop and the cheer of the mob. (The idea obviously had an effect on writer–director Michael Crichton, as he re-used it in *The First Great Train Robbery*, although here the camera pulls back from the noise and clatter of the Folkstone Express as it is being robbed to a quieter view of the surrounding countryside where the birds can be heard twittering away.)

There are also plenty of directorial embellishments to relish: the panning shot as young Pip runs into Magwitch in the graveyard, which never fails to make audiences jump. The rapid travelling shot along Miss Havisham's wedding breakfast table as the grown-up Pip pulls the cloth off it to extinguish Miss Havisham's dress, which caught fire when a coal rolled on to it from the fireplace, is also highly effective, as is the climactic scene in which Pip pulls down the drapes in Satis House and finally lets the sunlight in (even though in the previous scene it has been dark outside).

The performances, meanwhile, are immaculate. As the young Pip, Anthony Wager is superb, exuding the right amount of ignorance and naïveté without becoming too sentimental (*Great Expectations* proved to be the highlight of his career, after which he appeared in increasingly routine fare such as *The Secret Tunnel*, *The Hi-jackers* and *Blood Beast from Outer Space*). As the young Estella,

The truth revealed. Herbert Pocket (Alec Guinness), Pip (John Mills) and Magwitch (Finlay Currie) in a scene from Great Expectations. *The film was the first of six Guinness made with Lean.*

Jean Simmons is suitably haughty (and beautiful), while as the young Herbert Pocket, John Forrest makes a brief but effective appearance during his bout with Pip.

At the age of 38, John Mills was perhaps a little too old to be playing Pip as a 20-year-old, yet such is his enthusiasm for the role, especially after the revelation that he has 'great expectations,' one hardly seems to notice, especially during the comical dining scene in which Herbert attempts to teach him the rudiments of good table manners. At 32, Alec Guinness was also too old for Herbert Pocket, but again, sheer enthusiasm in the role saves the day. Only slightly less satisfactory is Valerie Hobson's turn as the older Estella, who seems to have lost some of her youthful spark.

In the end, it is the film's eccentrics and grotesques who stay in the mind most. Martita Hunt makes a memorably spectral Miss Havisham, while Francis L Sullivan's robust performance as Jaggers seems at times about to burst from the screen. Finlay Currie as Magwitch, meanwhile, pulls off the clever feat of making us fear him at the beginning of the film, while later he earns our

Oliver (John Howard Davies) receives some advice from Fagin (Alec Guinness) in Oliver Twist. Guinness's make-up produced accusations of anti-Semitism from certain quarters, despite being closely based on Dickens' own description of the character and George Cruikshank's original illustrations.

sympathy. There's no sympathy for the shrewish Mrs Joe, however, in the assured hands of Freda Jackson (complete with swishing 'Tickler'), making one wonder why Bernard Miles' bumbling Joe stays with her. He nevertheless makes an excellent comic foil – 'What larks, Pip, what larks!' – especially when he comes to London to visit Pip dressed in his Sunday best only to make a fool of himself over the tea table when his hat, which he has precariously balanced on the mantelpiece, ends up amid the crockery.

Audiences and critics for once agreed. 'Lean's triumph lies in the manner in which he catches the subtleties both of atmosphere and character and keeps the serial moving on the twin but different levels of excitement and personality,' enthused *The Times*. *The Daily Mail* added, 'It is a complete triumph for all concerned, and a milestone in the progress of British films... There is not much more a motion picture can have and *Great Expectations* has the lot.' There were dissenters, such as *The Observer*'s critic who commented, 'This is not art; this is nonsense,' but mostly they were in the minority, and the film went on to considerable box office success when released in December 1946 (and May 1947 in America).

As had been the case with *Brief Encounter*, Lean found himself nominated for a best director Oscar, although again he lost out, this time to Elia Kazan for *Gentleman's Agreement*. *Great Expectations* was also nominated for best picture (losing to *Gentleman's Agreement*) and best screenplay (Lean, Neame, Havelock-Allan, who also lost, this time to George Seaton for *Miracle on 34th Street*). Guy Green did however win the black and white cinematography award, while John Bryan and his assistant Wilfred Shingleton won for best black and white art direction. As had been the case with *Brief Encounter*, *Great Expectations* was also named as one of the year's 10 best films by the DW Griffith Awards.

Such is the popularity of Dickens' novel, there have been several other versions of *Great Expectations* since Lean's, among them a lavish 1975 television movie (originally intended as a musical) starring Michael York, and a 1998 Florida-set update starring Ethan Hawke and Gwyneth Paltrow, not to mention a handful of television adaptations. However, more than 50 years on, it's the Lean version that survives the best and captures the flavour, atmosphere and drama of the novel.

Despite Lean's public success, his private life during the making of *Great Expectations* was far from rosy. An affair with the film's assistant costume designer Margaret Furse all but ended his marriage with Kay Walsh. However, like many of Lean's affairs, it proved to be a passing fancy, and Lean and Walsh managed to patch things up again in time to collaborate on another Dickens adaptation. This time the subject would be the author's best-known work, *Oliver Twist*.

Again, the result is a classic piece of British cinema, smartly adapted and professionally told. Unfortunately, this time round, one of the main characters, Fagin, raised a certain amount of controversy at the time, given that not only is he Jewish, but is shown, as per the original George Cruikshank illustrations, to be stoop-backed and beak-nosed, and, as per the original Dickens text, manipulative and avaricious. Everything that the Nazi propaganda machine had caricatured Jews to be like. Perhaps it was naïve of Lean and Alec Guinness, who plays the role, to insist on so perfectly re-creating the Fagin described by Dickens. Nevertheless, despite their best intentions (and it was never their object to be purposely anti-Semitic), so soon after the war, sensibilities were quickly, and arguably rightly, aroused. It was to be several years after the film's completion that it received a release in America in anything like an uncut form.

Lean adapted Dickens' book to the screen himself, this time assisted by Stanley Haynes. As with *Great Expectations*, the novel was stripped of all irrelevancies and decoration, and condensed down to the absolute basics. The story opens with a pregnant young woman making her way across a desolate moor during a thunderstorm. Eventually, she sees a light in the distance and makes her way towards it. It turns out to be the local workhouse, which is where she gives birth to a boy. Having taken one loving look at him, she promptly dies. The boy, as named by the Beadle, Mr Bumble, is Oliver Twist, who is brought up in the brutal regime of the workhouse, where children, as well as adults, are worked to the bone, and all for a measly bowl of gruel.

Forever hungry, the workhouse boys decide on a minor revolt, and so draw straws as to who will dare ask for more food come suppertime. Inevitably, young Oliver draws the short straw, and as a consequence of his daring, finds himself farmed out to the local undertaker's – Sowerberry's –

where he is made to work as a skivvy and fed with scraps left for the dog. After an altercation with Noah Claypole, Sowerberry's apprentice, Oliver runs away and makes for London, where he meets a young pickpocket nicknamed The Artful Dodger, who introduces him to Fagin, the ringleader of a band of boy thieves with whom he lives in a squalid attic. Oliver is soon indoctrinated into the ways of the thieves. Unfortunately, on his first trip out, he ends up being arrested outside a bookshop for allegedly attempting to rob a kindly old gentleman, a Mr Brownlow. With the help of the bookshop proprietor, who witnessed the whole scene, Brownlow realises that it was Oliver's accomplices who were really responsible for the attempted robbery, and when Oliver faints in the dock during the subsequent court hearing, Brownlow drops all the charges and takes the boy home with him.

Back at the workhouse, it transpires that Oliver's mother left a locket behind after her death, and that it could lead to the discovery of her identity. This being Dickens, coincidence is part of the narrative and it transpires that Oliver's mother was Mr Brownlow's daughter, thus making Oliver his grandson. However, a happy ending is far from inevitable, as Fagin has sent the evil Bill Sikes and his prostitute girlfriend Nancy in pursuit of Oliver, for fear that the child might give the game away. Nancy proves to be the original 'tart with a heart' and contacts Mr Brownlow about how to get Oliver back. This doesn't go down too well with Bill Sikes who bludgeons Nancy to death. However, Sikes' dog ends up leading the police to his brutal master, now on the run with Oliver, all of which culminates in a rooftop chase, with Sikes killed by a police marksman and Oliver returned to his grandfather. This all could easily have descended into a roller-coaster ride of sheer melodrama. As with *Great Expectations*, Lean turned all these hoary events into a film to cherish.

It took Alec Guinness some effort to convince Lean that, having played the fresh-faced Herbert Pocket in *Great Expectations*, he could now pull off playing the ageing villain with matted hair. Determined on winning the role, Guinness coerced the director into allowing him to make a screen test in full make-up. So convincing was Guinness in the role during these preliminary tests, Lean gave the actor the role without any further hesitation (disguise became something of a trademark for Guinness during the following years, reaching its peak in *Kind Hearts and Coronets*, in which he plays eight members of the D'Ascoyne family).

To flesh out the rest of the cast, Lean again turned to his growing repertory company. Robert Newton was perhaps the inevitable choice to play Bill Sikes, while as his girlfriend Nancy, Lean cast his wife Kay Walsh, who invested the role with a certain degree of warmth. Francis L Sullivan, who'd made such a memorable Jaggers, returned, this time as Mr Bumble, while from *This Happy Breed*, Amy Veness, who'd played the comical Mrs Flint, came back as Mrs Bedwin, Mr Brownlow's housekeeper. Brownlow himself was played by veteran character actor Henry Stephenson, who returned from Hollywood (where he'd appeared in such classics as *The Charge of the Light Brigade* and *The Private Lives of Elizabeth and Essex*) to play the role.

Character portrait of actress Kay Walsh (Mrs Lean number two) as Nancy in Oliver Twist.

Lean directs the workhouse boys in a scene from Oliver Twist. *Anyone want more?*

Also joining the cast was Mary Clare as the Widow Corney, Kathleen Harrison as Mrs Sowerberry, Ivor Barnard as The Chairman of the Workhouse Board, and the young Diana Dors as Charlotte, Noah Claypole's paramour at the undertaker's. To play Oliver, a lengthy search eventually produced John Howard Davies, the son of *Daily Express* film critic Jack Davies, a long-standing acquaintance of Lean's, while the part of The Artful Dodger went to the up-and-coming child star Anthony Newley, who would later blossom into a renowned singer–songwriter–actor, familiar from *Cockleshell Heroes* and *Dr Dolittle* (John Howard Davies became a producer at the BBC). Before appearing in *Oliver Twist*, Newley was working on Peter Ustinov's delightful film adaptation of F Anstey's *Vice-Versa*, starring Roger Livesey and Kay Walsh, through whom he was introduced to Lean. In more minor roles, could be found such soon-to-be-familiar faces as future *Carry On* star Hattie Jacques (as a singer at The Three Cripples public house), Peter Bull (as the

Cripples' landlord), Maurice Denham (as the Chief of Police) and Hammer horror regular Michael Ripper (as Barney).

Lean surrounded himself with familiar talent behind the camera: among the technicians and artists were producer Ronald Neame, cinematographer Guy Green, art director John Bryan, assistant director George Pollack and, now in charge of designing the costumes rather than just assisting, Margaret Furse. New to the team was camera operator Oswald Morris, who not only would go on to become a noted cinematographer himself (winning an Oscar for *Fiddler on the Roof*), but who would also photograph the musical *Oliver!* (*Oliver Twist*'s assistant editor, Clive Donner, would also go on to direct a 1982 television movie starring George C Scott as Fagin). Alec Guinness's make-up was meanwhile placed in the highly capable hands of Stuart Freeborn (here credited as Freebourne), who'd go on to work on such films as *Star Wars* (again with Guinness) and *The Elephant Man*.

Oliver Twist opens spectacularly with a brilliant montage following the painful trek across the moors by Oliver's mother (Josephine Stuart). Like the opening of *Great Expectations*, much use is made of low clouds, while the soundtrack resonates with thunder. A wholly visual sequence, no one actually speaks for almost five minutes. The pain of Oliver's mother, now in labour, is cleverly yet economically conveyed by the shot of a thorny branch bending in the wind, accompanied on the soundtrack by three high-pitched notes from the violin section (the score was penned by Master of the King's Music, Sir Arnold Bax). Lean also makes use of his famous tilt shot from *Brief Encounter* as Oliver's mother, clinging to a tree for support, is wracked by labour pains. Then comes salvation – a light in the distance. Unfortunately, it's the workhouse, and straightaway the newly born Oliver seems doomed to a life of hardship, hunger and poverty.

However, the governors of the workhouse (all of them seemingly corrupt and on the take) clearly fail to recognise the hardship their charges endure, one of them commenting that the poor seem to regard the place as a 'house of entertainment.' On this line, Lean cleverly cuts to the workhouse laundry, all noise and steam, with the workers flogging themselves to death. The inequalities of the workhouse are further pointed out in a scene in which the governors and their cronies stuff their faces at the dining table while a group of hungry boys enviously look on through an overhead window, all of which results in Oliver's plea of 'Please, sir, can I have some more?' (So famous did this line become that it was later spoofed in the 1950 Margaret Rutherford/Alastair Sim comedy *The Happiest Days of Your Life*, in which a young schoolboy, sick of the school's dreadful food, begs, 'Please, sir, I don't want any more!')

The workhouse scenes, with their grimy walls and chiaroscuro shadows (John Bryan again made excellent use of forced perspective), all too quickly pass by, and before long Oliver is at Sowerberry's, enduring taunts from Noah Claypole about his mother, which result in a fight and Oliver being locked in the pantry. When called on to sort out the situation by Mrs Sowerberry, Mr Bumble blames it all on the scraps which Oliver has been fed from the dog's plate ('Meat, ma'am, meat!'). A marvellously comic scene, played to the full by all concerned, this comes as welcome light relief after the intensity of the workhouse sequences.

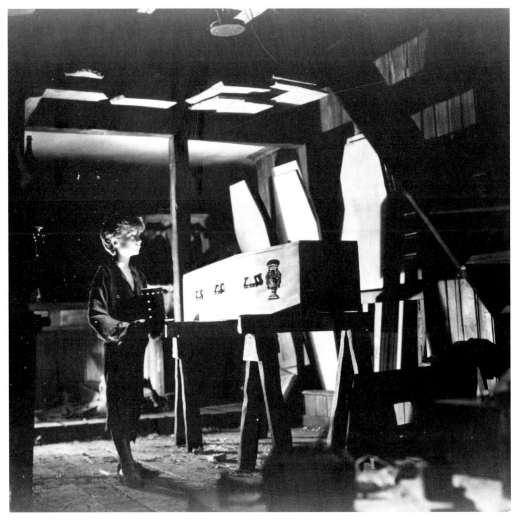

Oliver (John Howard Davies) braves it out in the basement of Sowerberry's funeral parlour.

It's on to London and Fagin's den, with John Bryan and Guy Green making the most of the black brick walls and the rotting timbers overhead. The only relief from such grimy surroundings can be found during the brief scenes in Mr Brownlow's home.

As ever, Lean the director brings plenty of cinematic vigour to the proceedings. The chase sequence after Oliver's accusation of theft outside the bookshop is a case in point, with its speedy tracking shots, achieved by placing camera operator Oswald Morris in a pram and following the running boy. The sequence comes to a magnificent climax as the camera, now filming from

Oliver's point of view, crash zooms into the fist of a passer by, intent on stopping Oliver dead in his tracks. Lean later makes use of another striking tilt shot in Fagin's den, when Oliver, having been kidnapped in the streets while on an errand for Mr Brownlow, is quizzed by Sikes as to whether or not he has given away the location of the hideout. As Sikes grabs hold of the boy, the whole room tilts in dramatic fashion.

Even more than *Great Expectations*, *Oliver Twist* is a film of shadows, and its cleverest use of them comes in the scene in which Nancy meets Mr Brownlow on London Bridge to tell him about the kidnapping of Oliver and how she hopes to return him. The entire conversation takes place in silhouette. Nancy's disclosure to Brownlow leads to her murder. This being 1948, the brutal bludgeoning could only be implied, which Lean masterfully does by concentrating on the reaction of Sikes' dog as it claws and yelps at the door in a bid to get away. This leads to the chase of Sikes by the police and the mob, with Lean displaying his ability to control vast crowd scenes, all of which would prove useful later when tackling his epics.

When released in Britain in June 1948, *Oliver Twist* proved to be another box office success for Lean and Cineguild, backed by generally favourable reviews. Unfortunately, owing to the furore over Guinness's performance as Fagin, the film didn't receive a Stateside release until July 1951, by which time some 12 minutes of footage featuring the character had been edited out in a bid to make the film less offensive to Jewish sensibilities; the resulting reviews were mixed.

As with *Great Expectations*, Lean's version of *Oliver Twist* was by no means the first adaptation. There had been a 1922 silent starring Jackie Coogan as Oliver and master of disguise Lon Chaney as Fagin. There had also been a low-budget 1933 Hollywood version starring Dickie Moore and Irving Pichel as Oliver and Fagin, respectively. There have been numerous television adaptations too, as well as a Disney cartoon, *Oliver and Company*, in which the story is re-enacted by a kitten and some dogs. It is Lean's version that remains the definitive straight version of the story, although the Lionel Bart musical *Oliver!*, filmed in 1968 by Carol Reed, matches it for style and spirit. While *Oliver Twist* failed to earn a single Oscar nomination, *Oliver!* went on to win five, including best picture and best director.

Despite the consistently high quality of his work, the Oscar was curiously eluding Lean during his career. Nevertheless, he must have taken some consolation in his growing prestige both at home and abroad. Unfortunately, his next two productions didn't live up to his increasingly vaunted reputation. Lean was about to enter into the least memorable stretch of his career.

Eight

—》《—

ANN

The set up at Cineguild was a fairly flexible one, not entirely geared around David Lean as director. Having photographed and produced successfully, it was perhaps inevitable that at some stage Ronald Neame would make a stab at directing too, which he did in 1947 with *Take My Life*, a Hitchcockian thriller about a man accused of murdering an ex-girlfriend. Produced by Anthony Havelock-Allan, it had Guy Green behind the camera and Hugh Williams, Greta Gynt, Marius Goring and Francis L Sullivan in front of it. Generally well received, it was described by Dilys Powell in *The Sunday Times* as, 'An extremely confident and exciting British thriller,' and eventually led Neame to a healthy career directing *The Million Pound Note*, *Tunes of Glory*, *The Poseidon Adventure* and *The Odessa File*.

No doubt spurred on by his initial success with *Take My Life*, Neame began looking around for a second property to direct, finally landing on HG Wells' 1913 novel *The Passionate Friends* (which had already been filmed as a silent by Maurice Elvey). To script and produce the film, Neame turned to the acclaimed thriller writer Eric Ambler, author of such popular books as *Journey Into Fear* and *The Mask of Dimitrios*. Ambler had himself turned to screenwriting in the mid-Forties, and had already penned and produced *The October Man*, a superior character thriller starring John Mills, Kay Walsh and Joyce Carey, which had been directed by Roy Ward Baker in 1947 (Ambler would go on to write such classics as *The Card* [directed by Neame], *The Cruel Sea* and *A Night to Remember*).

The writing of the screenplay in safe hands, Neame began recruiting technicians, turning to such familiar Cineguild players as Guy Green to photograph, Oswald Morris to operate, John Bryan to design the sets, Jack Harris to edit and Richard Addinsell to provide the score. The cast Neame chose was no less impressive, top-billing Ann Todd, Marius Goring and Claude Rains. Unfortunately, before even a foot of film was shot, things began to go wrong. Lean and Stanley Haynes, who'd seen a copy of Ambler's script, found it to be far from perfect and suggested a complete re-write by themselves and Ambler, all of which pushed the film's start date back. When production finally did start almost a month later, the script was still far from complete, and after just four days filming, Ambler wearing his producer's hat, pulled the plug.

It was decided that Neame would step down as director and take over as producer, a role he'd comfortably filled for several years. Ambler simply took credit for the film's script (for which Lean and Haynes also received an adaptation credit), while the directing reins were handed over to Lean. It was also decided that Marius Goring should be replaced by Trevor Howard who, since working with Lean on *Brief Encounter*, had gone on to make such successes as *I See a Dark Stranger* and *Green for Danger*.

Like *Brief Encounter*, the story of *The Passionate Friends* is a straightforward one, but made to seem more complicated by its intricate use of flashbacks, and flashbacks within flashbacks. At the end of the day, the narrative revolves round a simple love triangle.

Mary (Ann Todd) has married wealthy banker Howard Justin (Claude Rains) for security rather than love, only to meet again her former true love Steven Stratton (Trevor Howard) while on holiday in Switzerland. Cue flashback to New Year's Eve some nine years earlier, when Mary and Steven, she already married to Howard, accidentally meet and re-kindle their romance from an even earlier time. Thus, within this flashback, we flashback further to the couple's first affair at college, when Mary refused to marry Steven, despite her genuine love for him. We then flash forward to the couple's rekindled romance after the New Year's Eve party, which ends with Howard's discovery of the re-ignited affair. We then flash forward again back to Mary's holiday in Switzerland, where she discovers that Stephen has the room next to hers (following this?). It seems that the romance is about to start up yet again (Mary briefly fantasises about this in a dream sequence), but Steven himself is also now married, and although happy to see Mary again, he has no intention of cheating on his wife. Unfortunately, Mary's husband Howard, who's been away on business, arrives in Switzerland to join his wife a day earlier than arranged, only to see Mary and Steven returning from a day in the mountains. He naturally misconstrues the scene, which isn't surprising given that Mary betrays her true feelings for Steven by waving to him wildly from her hotel bedroom as he leaves by boat for his train back home. Consequently, once back in London, Howard petitions Mary for a divorce, citing her supposed relationship with Steven as the reason. Not wishing to ruin Steven's happy marriage, Mary attempts to throw herself under a tube train, only to be rescued at the last moment by her concerned husband who, realising the error of his ways, takes Mary home. Phew!

All three roles are well cast. At the time, Ann Todd was arguably Britain's biggest female star. Born in 1909, she made her stage debut in 1928, which she closely followed by her first appearance in films with *Keepers of Youth* in 1931, the same year she also appeared in *These Charming People*, on which Lean had briefly worked. Much stage and film work followed in the Thirties (among her films being *Poison Pen* and *South Riding*), although it wasn't until 1945 that she became a truly international star with the success of *The Seventh Veil*, which resulted in a trip to America to work on Hitchcock's *The Paradine Case*. British-born Claude Rains, meanwhile, had by this time been long in Hollywood, having made a spectacular debut in *The Invisible Man*, which he'd followed with a string of classics, among them *The Adventures of Robin Hood* (as a memorable Prince John), *King's Row* and *Casablanca*. Like Todd, he'd also worked for Hitchcock, on *Notorious*, as well as for Gabriel Pascal on the notoriously expensive *Caesar and Cleopatra* (as Caesar).

Made at Pinewood rather than Denham, *The Passionate Friends* also took Lean and the company abroad on location to France (doubling for Switzerland) for the holiday sequences, with excellent use made of the lakes and mountains of the Chamonix and Haute-Savoie regions. Lean had made many trips abroad by this time, both on holiday and business, but this was the first time he'd filmed away from home, and it was during this sojourn that he began an affair with his leading lady. Kay

Walsh, not being involved in this production, was handily out of the way back home. Despite having worked with her husband again on *Oliver Twist*, Walsh and Lean's marriage was practically dead anyway, and Lean's affair with Todd proved to be the final nail in the coffin.

Work on the film proved slow, both on location and back at the studio, and while the end results are technically solid and well enough performed, they somehow lack that spark, perhaps because, despite all the tricks, the story is plain to begin with. Ann Todd is a little cold as Mary, while Trevor Howard offers a paler version of his role in *Brief Encounter*, leaving it to Claude Rains to steal the acting honours as the cuckolded Howard. This isn't to say *The Passionate Friends* is a bad film. It is competent and has an admirable professionalism to it. Certain scenes even stay in the mind, especially the confrontation between Howard, Steven and Ann, after Howard's discovery that the couple are seeing each other again (Rains' performance here is masterful in its understatement, so that when he yells at Steven to 'Get out!' it comes as a shock). Mary's attempted suicide is also effective in its use of Underground signs (Way Out) and angled shots of the tracks on which she is about to throw herself. As a variation on themes from *Brief Encounter*, however, it doesn't hit the mark.

When it was released in January 1949, *The Times* commented about the 'Sure handling of camera and soundtrack.' When released in America in June the same year, where it was re-titled *One Woman's Story*, *Variety* was also enthusiastic: 'Polished acting, masterly direction and an excellent script put *The Passionate Friends* in the top rank of class British productions.' Yet despite the press, the film, although it recouped its budget, was not a success of the size Lean was now used to. Artistically it was also a step back from *Great Expectations* and *Oliver Twist*. Despite being thrown in at the deep end, Lean mostly enjoyed making the film, no doubt because of his affair with Ann Todd, whom he subsequently decided to make his third wife.

This necessitated divorcing Kay Walsh who, although still very much in love with Lean, nevertheless agreed to dissolve the marriage, seeing little point in clinging on. Todd herself had to divorce too (also for the second time), losing custody of her daughter, Ann Francesca, in the process. The whole affair must have been distressing for all concerned, particularly Walsh who, like so many of Lean's wives and affairs, found herself left behind. They'd had some good years together and had made some notable screen collaborations. Lean and Todd were eventually married on Saturday 21 May 1949.

To get over the mess, Walsh threw herself into work, appearing in three films which were released the following year: *The Last Holiday*, which re-united her with Alec Guinness, *Stage Fright*, in which she was directed by Hitchcock, and *The Magnet*, a minor Ealing comedy. Lean and Todd also busied themselves looking for another project to make together. They eventually decided on the story of the notorious Madeleine Smith, a role which Todd had already tackled on the stage in a play by Harold Purcell titled *The Rest Is Silence* in 1944.

Man in the middle. This striking portrait of Trevor Howard, Claude Rains and Ann Todd (Mrs Lean number three) was taken by John Vickers during the making of The Passionate Friends.

Smith, the daughter of a wealthy Glaswegian architect, came to public attention in 1857. Having been accused of poisoning her French lover, one Pierre Emile L'Angelier, with arsenic, she was brought to trial. However, the evidence was inconclusive and the case was 'not proven,' although it was considered by most that Smith had literally got away with murder.

To turn the story into a script, Lean again turned to the reliable Stanley Haynes, who was also handed the producer's reigns, Anthony Havelock-Allan being busy producing *The Small Voice* for British Lion (starring James Donald and Valerie Hobson), while Ronald Neame no doubt felt it was perhaps time to take a break from producing for Lean, given what had happened with *The Passionate Friends*. In any event, Neame was setting up his next directorial effort, *The Golden Salamander* (for Pinewood Productions). This film, which Neame would also produce and co-write, was to star Cineguild favourite Trevor Howard, and was to be photographed by Oswald Morris, whom Neame promoted from camera operator.

Back at Cineguild, Nicholas Phipps was hired to help Haynes with the script. An assured light comedian in the upper class twit manner, Phipps had also successfully turned his hand to screenwriting, particularly for director Herbert Wilcox, for whom he penned *Piccadilly Incident*, *Spring in Park Lane* and *Maytime in Mayfair*, all of them starring Wilcox's wife Anna Neagle and her screen partner Michael Wilding. Despite his pedigree, Phipps nevertheless seemed a curious choice to help co-author *Madeleine*, given the film's serious subject matter and almost total lack of humour.

The result of Haynes' and Phipps' labours sticks pretty closely to the actual events. Against her father's wishes, the headstrong Madeleine falls in love with Frenchman Pierre Emile L'Angelier. Strong at first, this infatuation with L'Angelier eventually begins to subside when Madeleine comes to realise that it could well be her money the Frenchman is after, he after all being but a poorly paid clerk. Her love for L'Angelier now on the wane, Madeleine instead falls for the more suitable William Monnoch, much to L'Angelier's annoyance. L'Angelier now becomes something of a nuisance to Madeleine, his behaviour bordering on blackmail. Madeleine nevertheless continues to show him kindness by serving him hot cocoa whenever he visits her. However, when L'Angelier dies of arsenic poisoning, all fingers point to Madeleine, who has been purchasing arsenic allegedly to rid the house of rats.

To support Ann Todd in her role as Madeleine, Lean turned to continental star Ivan Desny (born in Peking, his father was Russian and his mother French). Well known in theatrical circles, Desny had only completed one film, *Le Bonheur en Location*, before securing the role of L'Angelier, which would lead to a lengthy career in both European and English-speaking films. As Madeleine's second lover, William Monnoch, Lean hired radio announcer turned Shakespearean actor, Norman Wooland, because of his impressive work as Horatio in Olivier's 1948 screen adaptation of *Hamlet*. Respected character star Leslie Banks (*The Most Dangerous Game*, *The Man Who Knew Too Much*, *Jamaica Inn*) was meanwhile taken on to play Madeleine's disapproving father, while Barbara Everest (*The Wandering Jew*, *Jane Eyre*) was hired to play her mother. The rest of the cast was decked out by Edward Chapman, Jean Cadell, Ivor Barnard, John Laurie, Amy Veness, Susan Stranks, Andre Morell and David Horne.

Susan Ridgefield (Ann Todd) introduces her fiancé Tony Garthwaite (Nigel Patrick, right) to her doomed brother Chris (Denholm Elliott) in The Sound Barrier, *the success of which put Lean's career back on track following the disappointments of* The Passionate Friends *and* Madeleine.

The filming of *Madeleine* was a lengthy process, extended further owing to an electricians' strike at the studio. Despite the best efforts of both the cast and crew, the results are a somewhat cold and artificial affair, especially as the film could side with neither Madeleine's innocence or guilt, given the not proven verdict. Consequently, much of the drama is dissipated. Despite the film being Lean's most atypical work, it is elegantly directed, Guy Green's photography is ravishing and John Bryan's period settings are perfect down to the last detail. Handsome visuals alone do not make a film though, especially when the story is inconclusive. The film was derided by both critics and audiences alike. Not a perfect film by any means, *Madeleine* has been unjustly neglected and perhaps should be re-evaluated.

There is one last interesting point. Lean depicts the boredom of L'Angelier's life as a clerk, checking numbers that have already been checked by others, doodling to pass the time away. This could have been Lean during his own brief tenure as an accounts clerk. Luckily, he got out in time, but the memories of all those mind-numbingly dull days obviously stayed with him.

Madeleine proved to be the last film made under the Cineguild banner. Neame, Havelock-Allan and Lean decided to disband the company and go their own separate ways. Lean and Neame would never work together again, although they remained on amicable terms with each other, despite the debacle over *The Passionate Friends*. Meanwhile, it would be almost 20 years before Lean and Havelock-Allan would collaborate again on *Ryan's Daughter*. The trio had a good run together but it was clear that as a team their best was now behind them. Lean moved from Rank to Alexander Korda's London Films for his next production, *The Sound Barrier*, a box office success which would restore his standing.

London Films had been formed by the Hungarian Korda (who'd been directing in Europe since 1914) in 1932, and the company made its mark on the world in 1933 with *The Private Life of Henry VIII*. Produced and directed by Korda, it won its leading actor, Charles Laughton, an Oscar, and was also nominated for best picture. Over the coming years, Korda, either as producer, director or executive producer, instigated a brilliant programme of films at Denham Studios, among his successes being *The Scarlet Pimpernel*, *Things to Come*, *Rembrandt*, *The Four Feathers*, *The Thief of Baghdad* and *The Third Man*. Among those directors who had worked for Korda were Rene Clair, Paul Czinner, Michael Powell and Carol Reed. That Lean should join this prestigious band was an inevitable step following his departure from Rank and the winding down of Cineguild.

The story for *The Sound Barrier* (or *Breaking the Sound Barrier* as it is known in America) came from a newspaper article about a squadron leader, one JSR Muller-Rowland, who had been killed when his plane, which had allegedly passed through the sound barrier, broke up. Taking this as the kernel for the film, Lean began to visit aircraft factories, looking for background material and a hook on which to hang the story. He eventually approached playwright Terence Rattigan (whose film version of *French Without Tears* he had edited) to flesh out the idea into a human drama, handing him the research notes he'd made during his field trips. After much deliberation with Lean, Rattigan centred the story around aircraft manufacturer Sir John Ridgeway, whose determination that his company be the first to produce a plane that will fly faster than sound loses him not only his son, but also his daughter's husband. The film's drama comes not only from the thrilling aerial sequences in which the pilots battle to prevent their planes from breaking up, but also from the devastating consequences Sir John's ruthless ambition has on his family.

Ann Todd was the natural choice to play Sir John's daughter Susan, while Ralph Richardson was persuaded play Sir John himself. Richardson was one on Britain's most respected stage actors, renowned for his work at The Old Vic. His film appearances were comparatively few however, most of them having been in Korda productions, in particular, *Q Planes*, *The Four Feathers* and *Fallen Idol*. His best supporting actor Oscar nomination for *The Heiress* in 1949 gave his screen career an

unexpected fillip. Although Lean initially had reservations about Richardson, Korda urged the director to use him, much to his eventual delight.

Playing Sir John's son Chris, who dies during his first solo flight, was an up-and-coming actor called Denholm Elliott, who would go on to have an astonishing film career, appearing in *Nothing But the Best*, *Trading Places* and *A Private Function*. Sir John's son-in-law Tony Garthwaite was played by Nigel Patrick, who excelled at playing jolly decent stiff upper lip types in *The League of Gentlemen* and *The Battle of Britain*. John Justin, memorable in Korda's *The Thief of Baghdad*, played another one of Sir John's test pilots, Philip Peel, who eventually breaks the sound barrier. They were supported by Dinah Sheridan (as John's wife Jess) and Joseph Tomelty (as Will Sparks, Sir John's chief engineer).

Given that this wasn't a Cineguild production, there was a new face behind the camera: cinematographer Jack Hildyard, for whom this would be the first of four films with Lean (Guy Green was at the same time photographing *The Beggar's Opera* for director Peter Brook). Hildyard began his career in 1932 as a clapper boy before graduating to camera operator, in which capacity he'd worked on *Pygmalion*. His first film as a cinematographer had been Peter Ustinov's 1946 film *School for Secrets* (starring Ralph Richardson), which in turn led to *Vice-Versa* (again for Ustinov), *The Chiltern Hundreds* and *Home at Seven* (the latter directed by and starring Ralph Richardson). Working with Lean proved to be the making of his career. The art department was now in the hands of Alexander Korda's brother Vincent, who was assisted by Joseph Bato and John Hawkesworth (John Bryan was producing *The Card* for Ronald Neame), while Norman Spencer, long Lean's production manager, was promoted to associate producer, with Lean taking on the role of producer (Alexander Korda oversaw as executive producer).

The Sound Barrier also marked the first time Lean used a second unit director, in this case Anthony Squire, who headed the aerial unit, capturing the breath-taking cloudscapes and test-plane footage needed for the film. Lean directed the actors in their close-ups in the cockpit sequences, which were mocked up back at the studio, with the aerial footage later matted in.

As with any pioneering story, *The Sound Barrier* proves to be an absorbing piece of entertainment, with its spectacular aerial sequences of heroism and derring-do balanced by well-judged domestic scenes, which help to establish the characters in reality, not merely as ciphers supporting the technology. Rattigan's script is very well structured, even if some of the 'jolly dee, old chap' dialogue seems stilted. The film also benefits from an excellent score by Malcolm Arnold, who would go on to score another two films for Lean. Arnold had only started composing for films a few years earlier in 1947, and *The Sound Barrier*, following on from work on such minor films as *The Ringer* and *Stolen Face*, proved to be a major stepping stone for him, going on to score *The Belles of St Trinian's*, *Suddenly Last Summer* and *Whistle Down the Wind*, not to mention even more acclaimed work for the concert platform. His work for *The Sound Barrier* more than lives up to Lean's faith in him, and is distinguished by its soaring strings and dancing piccolo work, which give the aerial sequences an almost balletic quality.

Lean presents an extremely slick and linear production, with the emphasis firmly on the thrust of the narrative. Superfluous directorial displays are kept to the minimum, although there is never any doubt that this is the work of a true craftsman. There are some inventive effects, however, such

David Lean offers some directorial advice to Charles Laughton during the making of Hobson's Choice. *Laughton no doubt politely listened, then did his own thing anyway, as was his wont.*

as Tony's tour of Sir John's aircraft factory, during which he and we hear, but do not see, the new jet engine being tested. As Tony later comments, 'I think it's the most exciting sound I've ever heard.' Other clever touches include Lean's introduction of Sir John, whom we at first only see partially as he enters the drawing room of his stately home. Lean has him pause in the doorway for a few moments as he argues with someone on the other side of it, so that all we see is his arm on the door handle, helping to build the impression of a formidable figure. Susan and Tony's trip to Cairo in a jet piloted by Tony is an expertly edited piece of montage, following the couple from their departure in England at 7.30am through to their arrival in Egypt some five hours later, during which we're treated to aerial shots of Paris and the Swiss Alps from 40 000 feet (or eight miles high, as Tony informs a surprised Susan).

   Lean also resorts to some tried and tested tricks. For example, Susan, now pregnant, finds out that Tony has been killed during a test while at the cinema. Family friend Philip turns up to take her home. No words are said, yet Susan obviously knows what's happened simply by Philip's presence. While the scene is playing, the jolly music of the film Susan has been watching is heard on the soundtrack, recalling the scene from *This Happy Breed* in which Frank and Ethel discover that their boy and his wife have been killed in a car crash (also remarkable is the fact that Susan is actually shown to be heavily pregnant, making it something of a first). Another familiar trick is Lean's use of the tilt shot during the test in which Philip finally breaks the sound barrier. Lean uses the device to show Sir John's anxiety during one particularly tense moment, the camera levelling off only once the danger has passed.

Perhaps the most subtle direction comes at the end of the film, when Susan and her baby son John Anthony visit her father in his observatory, where he is looking at the stars through his telescope. As she enters, Susan places the baby boy on a giant map of the moon. Husband John may have devoted his life to breaking the sound barrier. Who knows what his son might end up doing. Travelling to the moon, perhaps? Lean seems to intimate this as man's next big challenge, for he ends the film on a shot of Sir John's telescope and a model jet pointing skywards to the stars.

The success of *The Sound Barrier* both in Britain (where it was released in July 1952) and America (in November the same year) brought to an end Lean's brief dry period, earning excellent notices on both sides of the Atlantic. 'The most exciting film to be produced about the air anywhere,' enthused *The Daily Express*. *The Sunday Dispatch* was also full of praise, 'A peacetime film as exciting as any wartime one.' Added *Variety*, 'Technically, artistically and emotionally, this is a topflight British offering… Ann Todd's portrayal of the daughter correctly yields the emotional angle. David Lean's direction is bold and imaginative.'

The Academy Award committee was also impressed and nominated the film for Terence Rattigan's story and screenplay. Unfortunately, Rattigan lost out to fellow Englishman TEB Clarke who won for *The Lavender Hill Mob*, although the London Films sound department, headed by John Cox (who would go on to become another Lean regular), won the award for best sound.

The Sound Barrier also won three BAFTAs, for best film (any source), best British film and best actor, Ralph Richardson, who also won the New York Film Critics' Circle and DW Griffith award for best actor. Lean also took the best director gong home from the DW Griffith awards, which also recognised the picture as one of the year's best 'foreign' films, alongside *The Man in the White Suit* and *Beauty and the Devil*.

Laden with success and trophies, Lean was again back where he belonged, alongside Carol Reed and Alfred Hitchcock as one of Britain's top three film directors. He now had to build on this and secure his position. Again, he chose a completely atypical subject, but unlike *Madeleine*, this time he managed to pull the trick off.

The subject was the 1915 play *Hobson's Choice* by Harold Brighouse, a late Victorian comedy about a selfish Salford boot-shop owner, Henry Hobson, who since the death of his wife has relied on his three daughters to run his shop and make sure he has what he terms his 'rightful home comforts'. Unfortunately, Hobson's eldest daughter, the canny Maggie – whom Hobson deems past it at 30 – is determined to marry before it really is too late, and so chooses Hobson's talented but seemingly dim-witted boot-maker Will Mossop. Mossop, of course, is somewhat taken aback by Maggie's proposal but gradually comes to see things her way, and so not only agrees to marry her, but also to set up a rival boot shop, which they're able to do thanks to the financial help given to them by the well-to-do Mrs Hepworth, one of Hobson's customers who insists that Will – and only Will – makes her boots.

Once Maggie and Will have left her father and his shop, things go from bad to worse in the hands of Hobson's two remaining flighty daughters, who also want to flee the nest and get married. With the ball now in their court, Maggie and Will agree to go back and save Hobson and his shop, but only if he allows his other two daughters to leave and get married, and if the shop is re-named Mossop & Hobson. With no other options open to him, Hobson literally has to accept 'Hobson's choice' and go along with Maggie and Will's demands, resulting in a happy ending for all concerned – even the bullish Hobson.

The play of *Hobson's Choice* had been a long-standing favourite with audiences, and had already spawned two British screen versions: a 1920 silent starring Arthur Pitt as Hobson and a 1931 talkie starring Jimmy Harcourt. For his version, however, Lean had only one person in mind to play Hobson: Charles Laughton. So much so that Lean, working on the adaptation with his associate producer Norman Spencer (initially assisted by Wynyard Browne) tailored the script to Laughton's larger than life talents.

By the time he came to make *Hobson's Choice* in 1953, Charles Laughton was an international character star of some repute, having won a best actor Oscar for his performance in Alexander Korda's 1933 production of *The Private Life of Henry VIII*. Laughton, who'd had an interest in amateur dramatics as a teenager, graduated from RADA in 1926 following experience as a hotelier. He made his professional stage debut in *The Government Inspector* the same year, quickly establishing himself both on the boards and in front of the cameras. Hollywood beckoned and Laughton cemented his growing reputation in such films as *The Old Dark House*, *Island of Lost Souls* and *The Sign of the Cross*. Further success followed his Oscar in *The Barretts of Wimpole Street*, *Mutiny on the Bounty*, *Les Miserables*, *The Hunchback of Notre Dame*, *Jamaica Inn*, *The Canterville Ghost* and *The Paradine Case* (the latter with Ann Todd). Laughton had also made several more films for Alexander Korda, among them *Rembrandt* and the costly *I, Claudius* which, owing to various accidents and delays, was abandoned mid-way through production, since when Korda and Laughton had not worked together.

If Laughton wasn't entirely comfortable in a part, he would delay filming – no matter how much the cost – until he was. This had been the case on *I, Claudius* and several other pictures, so by the time he came to be cast as Henry Hobson, he had acquired a reputation for being awkward and difficult. He'd already turned down a film offer from Lean to appear in an adaptation of HE Bates' *The Cruise of the Breadwinner* which the director had toyed with making after completing *The Sound Barrier*. Nevertheless, despite having been spurned by the actor once, Lean was still keen on Laughton to play Hobson, as too was Korda, despite his previous problems with him. One can only assume that Korda thought enough water had passed under the bridge since then. In any case, Korda's involvement with the production would again be as a supervisory executive producer.

David Lean lines up a shot in Will Mossop's workshop in Hobson's basement during the making of Hobson's Choice. *He is assisted by camera operator Peter Newbrook (holding Lean).*

With Laughton in the title role, Lean began looking around for suitable actors to play Will Mossop and Hobson's daughter Maggie. His initial choice for Will was, somewhat surprisingly with hindsight, Robert Donat, remembered for such films as *The Thirty-Nine Steps* and *Goodbye, Mr Chips*, which won him an Oscar. Donat has also starred opposite Laughton in *The Private Lives of Henry VIII*, and Laughton was keen to work with him again. Unfortunately, Donat was prone to illness and had to pull out at the last moment owing to a severe bout of asthma. The door opened for John Mills to step in. Mills didn't seem an obvious choice either, his image at the time being that of the stiff upper-lipped officer, yet he surprised everyone and made the role his own. As did Brenda de Banzie with Maggie. Forty-two at the time of filming (she was supposed to be 30 in the story), de Banzie had had a long stage career previously. Even then she was only offered *The Long Dark Hall* (her debut in 1951) and *The Yellow Balloon*. *Hobson's Choice* turned her into a star, albeit briefly, and led to roles in *The Purple Plain*, *The Man Who Knew Too Much*, *The Entertainer* and *The Pink Panther*.

Maggie's sisters, Alice and Vicky were played by Daphne Anderson (*Trottie True*, *The Beggar's Opera*) and Prunella Scales (later to find fame in television's *Fawlty Towers*). The rest of the cast was filled out by Helen Haye (as the wealthy patron Mrs Hepworth), Richard Wattis and Derek Blomfield (as Alice and Vicky's intended husbands) and Jack Howarth (as Tubby Wadlow, Will's foreman at Hobson's [Howarth would later come to prominence as *Coronation Street*'s Albert Tatlock]).

Made at Shepperton, *Hobson's Choice* was photographed by Jack Hildyard on sets by Wilfred Shingleton, which included the Salford street on which Hobson's shop is situated, all of which were built on the back lot. Lean opens the film on this set on a windswept, wintry night, with the giant wooden boot hanging outside Hobson's shop creaking in the wind (echoes of *Oliver Twist*). We then cut to the smart but deserted interior of the shop, the camera tracking along a display of finely crafted shoes, among them boots, elegant ladies shoes and children's shoes, each pair accompanied by a brief burst of appropriate music by Malcolm Arnold (he titled this piece of music *The Shoe Ballet*). The camera carries on moving to the back of the shop, where we're shocked by the clock striking one and a branch rattling against the window in the gale outside. We then cut to the shop door, which bursts open to reveal a belching Hobson, drunk from his Mason's meeting across the road at the Moonrakers pub. Laughton couldn't have asked for a better entrance. Hobson's arrival alerts Maggie, who descends from upstairs to chide him and encourage him up to bed. However, he can only get up the stairs by taking a run at them, accompanied by a drum roll. Only just making it, he collapses into bed, to awake the following morning with a hangover.

A brilliant opening sequence, it quickly establishes the atmosphere and the characters of both Hobson and his eldest daughter. Straightaway we're into the action – and straightaway we know that this probably isn't the first time Hobson, all froth and bluster, has returned home from the pub in such a state, given Maggie's stern, no nonsense attitude. It's quickly established that Hobson is teetering on the edge of alcoholism, for the first thing he does after getting up late the next morning is to head, along with the other shopkeepers, over to the Moonrakers for a pint, all of them on the pre-text that they're popping out for 15 minutes on a bit of business.

Having introduced us to Hobson and Maggie, we then meet Alice and Vicky, as well as Mrs Hepworth, who arrives by carriage to enquire after who made her boots, and up pops Will (can that really be John Mills with the basin haircut?) from the cellar hatch. 'He's like a rabbit,' comments Mrs Hepworth, before telling Hobson that from now on Will, and Will alone, should make her boots.

These establishing scenes concluded, Lean is then able to lay down the main drive of the plot, with Maggie determined on finding a man to marry before it's too late. Scorning her at first, Hobson is soon boasting that he can do just as well without her and perhaps even her sisters: 'The domination of one woman is paradise to the domination of three,' he comments, without realising that without his daughters to run the shop and take care of him things would (and indeed do) quickly turn into a shambles.

Having set her cap at Will Mossop, Maggie sets out to convince him that she is the woman for him. The courting scenes are both moving and humorous, particularly the scene in which the awkward couple take the air one Sunday by the polluted River Irwell. 'I saw a river clean once,' says Will. 'Sunday school outing, up on the moors.' It's then that Maggie learns that Will is 'promised' to another, one Ada Figgins (Dorothy Gordon), daughter of his dragon-like landlady Mrs Figgins (Madge Brindley). Having none of this, Maggie heads over to Mrs Figgins' to sort the mess out and lay her claim on Will. As they head over to Will's lodgings, they pass a Salvation Army band, accompanied by the banner, 'Beware the wrath to come.'

The wrath comes pretty quickly. Will is told to wait outside in the street while Maggie lays down the law for the vile Mrs Figgins, a huge, greasy-looking woman wearing a flat cap. The front window is slightly open and Will hears Maggie standing up for him, telling the two women what a bright future he is going to have. Lean here closes on Will's face, and one can almost read the character's mind here, as he realises that things could be about to take a turn for the better. However, in a marvellous comic touch, Will is quickly brought out of his reverie by Mrs Figgins, who smacks him over the head with a dustpan. A ruckus ensues, but Maggie leaves with her man, telling him he never has to go back to Mrs Figgins' again. Clearly relieved by this, one can well imagine the dreadful life Will would no doubt have had had he remained in the clutches of the snivelling Ada and her domineering mother.

Maggie then asks Will to kiss her, against the backdrop of a dirty ginnel. Lean always had an eye for setting romantic scenes against unromantic backgrounds to heighten the moment further. Will, being a decent man, demurs at kissing Maggie in broad daylight, but we know that from this moment on, he admires her, will come to love her and that they will make a success of their lives together. One of the most moving scenes in the film, this can bring a lump to the throat and all without recourse to undue sentimentality.

Maggie and Will set their business up in a dingy basement, which also doubles as their home (before their marriage, Will stays at Tubby's), and it is from this unlikely venue that things really start to go their way. A superb piece of art direction from Wilfred Shingleton, the cellar contrasts sharply with Hobson's plush establishment. Set on two levels, the basement has a giant pipe running horizontally right through the middle of it, while overhead people clatter over the grating. Yet on his way home from their first day in the shop, Will looks up to the stars in the heavens – the skies really are the limit for him now.

From here the story moves steadily to its climax, with Maggie and Will returning in triumph to Hobson's shop. Yet on the way there is plenty of humour to keep the story bubbling along, most memorably Hobson's 'moonwalk' as he returns home, drunk from the Moonrakers again. As he walks across the cobbled street, he sees the full moon reflected in a number of dirty puddles, only for it to disappear as he approaches. Skilfully photographed by Jack Hildyard, this is the sequence most remember from the film. Hildyard and Lean also make use of double imagery to reflect Hobson's drunken state.

The other memorable sequence is Will and Maggie's wedding night. After the celebrations with Maggie's sisters and their intended in the basement shop, Maggie retires to bed. Will, obviously

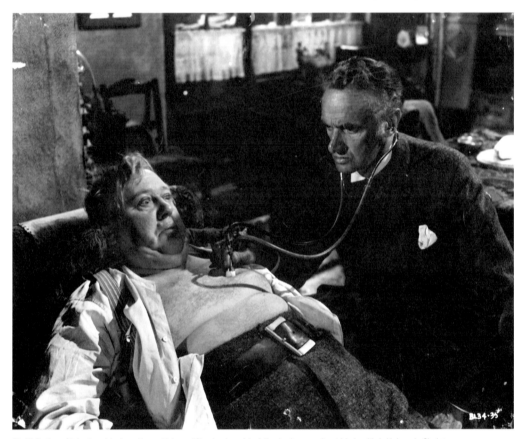

Dr McFarlane (John Laurie) gives Henry Hobson (Charles Laughton) the bad news about his health in Hobson's Choice.

nervous about following her, does everything in his power to delay the moment, taking off his collar and dickie and arranging them on the mantelpiece, after which he demurely changes into his night-gown. He also gives the fire a poke (innuendo anyone?). Maggie finally swings the bedroom door open and Will, accompanied by a bugle call care of Malcolm Arnold's score, heads off for bed. He obviously enjoys himself, for all he can say when he emerges the next morning is, 'By gum!'

It's Hobson's chronic alcoholism, diagnosed by his doctor (John Laurie) following a series of hallucinations (a giant daddy longlegs and a snickering mouse at the end of his bed), which brings Will and Maggie back to him. Although not before Hobson has been threatened with legal action for trespassing, having drunkenly fallen down the delivery chute and into the cellar of the corn merchant's Mr Beenstock (Raymond Huntley), only to be found there, snoring, the next morning. Unfortunately for Hobson, Beenstock is not only 'temperance,' but his son Freddy, who is training to be a solicitor, is courting Alice, thus making Hobson's literal downfall all the more painful.

Maggie (Brenda de Banzie), Henry Hobson (Charles Laughton) and Will (John Mills) go for a stroll down the street set art director Wilfred Shingleton built on the backlot for Hobson's Choice.

Earlier in the film, as Hobson makes his way over to the Moonrakers for his mid-morning refreshment, Beenstock beadily watches him from his shop window, commenting to his son, 'Freddy, you see where Hobson is going? There's a small spark of decency in that man that's telling him that at this very moment that my eye's on him.' Lean frames the shot from Beenstock's point of view, and just before Hobson enters the Moonrakers, he glances back over to Beenstock, ensuring one of the biggest laughs in the film.

The performances in *Hobson's Choice* are mostly bold and brassy, with none of the restraint found in *Brief Encounter*. Laughton has a field day playing the belligerent shopkeeper, although his Northern accent does occasionally slip, for he pronounces 'laughing,' 'nasty' and 'circumstances' in the Southern manner, despite being Yorkshire-born. Laughton's Hobson, sailing deliciously close to ham, easily ranks alongside his Captain Bligh and Quasimodo, as among his very best. Giving equal measure is Brenda de Banzie, whose no nonsense Maggie is full of spirit, while John Mills is a revelation as Will Mossop, timid as a mouse at first, but increasingly confident as the film progresses and he is brought to see his true worth. The supporting cast is excellent too, notably Madge Brindley as the awful Ma Figgins and Raymond Huntley in his brief but highly effective cameo as Beenstock (one almost wishes Beenstock and Hobson had a full-on verbal collision).

Technically, the film is masterful. Lean keeps a tight grip on the narrative and, although there is a slight lull in the third act, there is enough to take the eye and ear to keep one engrossed. Malcolm Arnold's rumbustious score adds immeasurably to the comic proceedings.

The film's rich performances and professional sheen were admired by both the critics and public, and the film went on to considerable commercial success when released in February 1954. *The Observer* praised the film's, 'High visual finish,' *Screencombers* added, 'Difficult to see how a better job could have been made of it.' Even though it didn't quite go down the same way in America (perhaps expectedly so) when released in June there, *Variety* also gave the film a positive review: 'There is a wealth of charm, humour and fine characterisation in David Lean's picture made under the Korda banner. The period comedy, with a Lancashire setting, is essentially British in its make-up… Although Laughton richly overplays every scene, his performance remains one of the film's highlights. Mills also makes a major contribution in his interpretation of the illiterate shoemaker's assistant who learns to assert himself. Brenda de Banzie captures top femme honours for her playing of the spirited daughter who triumphs over the ridicule of her father and sisters.'

Perhaps because of its very Britishness, *Hobson's Choice* failed to garner any Oscar nominations, although back home it received a BAFTA for best British film. During its making, Lean also received another very special award, a CBE (Commander of the British Empire), which was given to him by the Queen on Tuesday 21 July 1953.

Although things were going extremely well for Lean professionally, in his private life, his marriage to Ann Todd was over. There hadn't been a role for her in *Hobson's Choice* for obvious reasons, although even when she and David had worked together, things hadn't always been amicable. In 1954, Ann broke away to make the courtroom drama *The Green Scarf* for director George More O'Farrall, while Lean went on an extended vacation, taking in Egypt and India, supposedly to scout locations for a proposed film about the building of the Taj Mahal, to be financed by Alexander Korda. The film, of course, was never made, but by the time Lean returned from India, not only had he fallen in love with the country, but also with the woman who would become his fourth wife.

Nine

—⁓—

KATIE

Like Lean himself, Leila Matkar (nee Devi) was married when the two met in India. A local beauty prone to bouts of melancholy, she had nothing in common with the glacially cool Ann Todd, and it was this sharp contrast between the two that no doubt attracted Lean. As had happened before, Lean would now have to divorce one wife in order to secure himself another. Yet before all that could take place, there was the matter of making his first fully location-filmed feature *Summer Madness* (or *Summertime* as it is known in the USA).

Based on the 1952 play *The Time of the Cuckoo* by Arthur Laurents, it tells the story of Jane Hudson, a lonely, spinsterish American woman from Akron, Ohio who travels to Venice for a vacation, where she falls in love with both the city and a local man, whom she discovers is married. Shirley Booth had played Hudson on the Broadway stage, and the play, a single-set affair, centred around whether she would succumb to the Latin charms of her admirer and have a holiday fling, or retain her propriety. This being a David Lean film, there was obviously no way the action would be restricted to a single indoor set when the beauties of Venice called.

A noted playwright, Arthur Laurents (who would go on to provide the book for the musicals *West Side Story* and *Gypsy*) had already dabbled in screenwriting, having penned *Caught* for Max Ophuls and *Rope* for Hitchcock. He was hired to write the screenplay for *Summer Madness*. Unfortunately, he was too close to his own material and failed to 'open up' the play to Lean's satisfaction. The collaboration quickly ended (although Laurents received remuneration for the rights of his play) and Lean began to rework the play himself, assisted by novelist HE Bates, whose *The Cruise of the Breadwinner* he had previously toyed with turning into a film.

To write the script, Lean and Bates, accompanied by assistant producer Norman Spencer, travelled to Venice to soak up the atmosphere and local colour, all of which helped to bring the narrative to life – as did the fact that the film was made entirely on location, capturing the sights, sounds and almost the smells of the great city.

Given that the character of Jane Hudson carries the film, the casting of a strong actress in the part was paramount. Ann Todd, who was at the time playing Lady Macbeth at the Old Vic, was out of the picture, so Lean turned to Katharine Hepburn. One of the silver screen's greatest stars, Hepburn had made her first film, *Bill of Divorcement*, in 1932, before which she'd made her name on stage, most notably in the Broadway production of *The Warrior Husband*, which led to a long-term contract with RKO, where she made *Morning Glory* (which won her the first of her four best actress Oscars), *Alice Adams* and *Bringing Up Baby*. By the late Thirties, however, she was deemed 'box office poison' and returned to the stage with *The Philadelphia Story*, the film version of which revitalised

Jane Hudson (Katharine Hepburn) surrenders to the charms of Renato di Rossi (Rossano Brazzi) in Summer Madness, *the first Lean film to be made entirely on location abroad.*

her career. By the time she came to work with Lean, she'd made several notable films with Spencer Tracy – *Woman of the Year*, *Keeper of the Flame*, *Adam's Rib* – as well as *The African Queen* with Humphrey Bogart. If anyone could put a spark of life into Jane Hudson, there was no one better qualified than Katharine Hepburn. Hepburn and Lean hit it off together immediately and became life-long friends as a consequence of working together on *Summer Madness*.

The rest of the casting was done out of Rome, which is where the film's love interest, antiques dealer Renato Di Rossi, was found. This was romantic lead Rossano Brazzi, who had already made notable appearances in *Three Coins in the Fountain* and *The Barefoot Contessa* (although it is for his role in the musical *South Pacific* for which he is perhaps best remembered). These casting sessions also produced Isa Miranda (known in Europe for *Au-dela des Grilles*, *La Ronde*), who would play Signora Fiorina, the proprietor of Jane's pensione. However, child actor Gaetano Audiero, who almost steals the film as the streetwise Mauro, whom Jane befriends on her travels around the city, was found locally. The other American actors in the cast are Darren McGavin and Mari Aldon, who play the Jaeger's, an argumentative young couple, while Jane Rose and MacDonald Parke play the McIlhenny's, a retired couple doing Europe in typical American style (i.e. seeing everything, yet nothing).

The crew, meanwhile, was a blend of British (cinematographer Jack Hildyard, camera operator Peter Newbrook), Hungarian (art director Vincent Korda) and Italian (composer Alessandro Cicognini, assistant director Alberto Cardone). Again, Alexander Korda executive produced from the safety of his office in London's Piccadilly, while the on-set producer was the Italian, Ilya Lopert.

Hepburn and Brazzi aside, the real star of *Summer Madness* is the city of Venice itself, and from the opening shot it's clear that Lean had fallen in love with the place. As the film opens, Jane Hudson is arriving in the city on the Orient Express, photographing the event herself with her portable cine camera. Before she knows it, she's amid the bustle of the train station, the visual frenzy of which Lean and his sound recordists accompany with a montage of overlapping sounds (speaker announcements, train whistles, shouted conversations) to accentuate further the liveliness of the place. Then it's on to the pensione, taking in the breath-taking sights and architecture along the way, all of which is sumptuously photographed by Jack Hildyard. However, as the picture postcard views flick by to Alessandro Cicognini's swelling music, Lean cleverly turns cliché on its head by climaxing the sequence with a shot of a television aerial, accompanied by a comical riff from the score.

Jane learns quickly about Venice. When told she has to take the bus to her pensione, she automatically looks to the road outside the train station for the vehicle, only to be told that the bus is behind her, on the canal. On her way to the hotel, she's also surprised to see that the local fire engine, called out to action, is also a boat.

It's on the water bus that Jane meets the travel-weary McIlhennys, who it transpires are staying at her hotel. While the couple seem immune to the charms of Venice, Jane is busy recording everything with her camera (Lean himself, it must be noted, was an avid user of the cine camera whenever he was on holiday). Unlike the McIlhennys, it's clear that Jane is going to make the very most of her trip to the city (earlier, when asked by a passenger on the train if she thinks she'll like the place, she replies, 'Oh, I've got to. I've come such a long way').

As Jane is guided to the pensione, Lean treats us to the sights and sounds of Venice's labyrinthine alleyways, although again, Jane's romantic view of the place is interrupted when someone throws a pail of garbage into a canal from an upstairs window. Still, this doesn't prevent Jane from seeing Venice through rose-coloured glasses. Inside the pensione, Jane meets the proprietor, the worldly Signoria Fiorina, and quickly settles into the way of things, unlike the McIlhenny's ('This wop food has wrecked my digestion,' complains Mr McIlhenny on the terrace after dinner, much to the understandable offence of Signora Fiorina).

As Jane's holiday gets underway, despite her outer bravura, we quickly realise that she is desperately lonely, which is probably why she teams up with the streetwise Mauro, a miniature Chico Marx who shows her the sights, bums cigarettes off her and tries to sell her postcards (dirty

Rossano Brazzi and David Lean play with Gaetano Audiero during the filming of Summer Madness. *The young boy came close to stealing the film from under Katharine Hepburn's nose.*

ones, of course). It's while she's touring the city with the child that she spots a red goblet in the window of an antiques shop (its shiny red glass is the only colour of distinction in the shop), and she goes inside to get a closer look. Once inside, she realises that the proprietor, Di Rossi, is the same handsome man who'd been eyeing her in the Piazza San Marco the evening before when she was having a drink by herself.

Jane buys the goblet, allegedly 18th Century, and goes on her way. Again, that night Jane sees Di Rossi in the piazza, but again he fails to make a move (owing to the fact that she has ordered two drinks, to give the impression that she is not alone). However, the next day, Jane and Mauro just happen to pass by the antiques shop. Di Rossi isn't there, just a teenage boy (former British child star Jeremy Spenser, complete with fake tan and fake accent), so Jane contents herself by taking some cinefilm of the shop. Unfortunately, as she does so, she steps back into a canal, throwing the camera for Mauro to catch just as she's taking her unexpected dive. The comic highlight of the film, this is perhaps the biggest laugh to be found in any Lean film, and justifiably so, given its perfect execution.

That night Di Rossi turns up at Jane's pensione, the boy at the shop having told him that she'd called by. He thinks that she has been pursuing him and takes this as his cue to make his move. Given her background, Jane is at first reluctant to succumb to Di Rossi's charms, but finally she gives in, especially when he tells her the painful truth about herself which, thanks to Hepburn's brilliant performance, we've known practically all along: 'You make many jokes, but inside I think you cry.' Thus their brief encounter begins.

The following evening they go out together ('Two – that's the loveliest number in the world,' says Jane) and they finally kiss, and Lean isn't ashamed to cut to shots of exploding fireworks as they do so. However, as we've suspected, Di Rossi isn't everything he seems. It transpires that the McIlhennys have bought six goblets identical to Jane's '18th Century' goblet, revealing him as a con artist. It also turns out that the boy in Di Rossi's shop is his son and that he is married, albeit separated. Despite her earlier reservations about having an affair with Di Rossi, Jane accepts all this news comparatively calmly. The next day she announces that she is going home early ('You know, all my life I've stayed at parties too long because I didn't know when to go'), and off she heads for the station. Things end on a slightly more upbeat note, for as Jane's train is pulling out of the station, Di Rossi comes running down the platform. He tries to pass Jane a gardenia he has bought for her, but the train is going too fast. But Jane has seen the flower and noted the gesture, and as she waves frantically out of the window, we know that she is returning home comparatively happy.

Summer Madness is a wildly romantic film, both in the story and visually, yet its determined lack of sentimentality makes it all the more emotionally wringing; one truly feels for Hepburn's character, and it is this human centre that gives the film its heart. 'Few actresses in films could equal Hepburn's evocation of aching loneliness on her first night in Venice,' commented *Time* magazine. *Variety* agreed: 'Hepburn turns in a feverish acting chore of proud loneliness.' Back home, Dilys Powell wrote in *The Sunday Times* that, 'The eye is endlessly ravished,' to which the *Daily Worker*'s critic added, 'The acting and the travelogue, not the play, are the thing, and they turn a well-conceived piece of glossy romanticism into something sparkling and almost distinguished.'

The hard work of both Lean and Hepburn was rewarded with Oscar nominations for best director and actress, although both lost out: Lean to Delbert Mann for *Marty*, Hepburn to Anna Magnani for *The Rose Tattoo*. Jack Hildyard's rich Eastmancolor photography, which captured Venice from a variety of never-before-seen angles, surprisingly didn't rate a nomination. The film earnt itself a place in the DW Griffith Awards' annual 10 best, and Lean won the New York Film Critics' Circle Award for best director. Back home the film was nominated for a best British film BAFTA, but lost to Olivier's *Richard III*, which also took the best film (any source) award.

When Lean returned home after the completion of *Summer Madness*, his marriage to Ann Todd was truly at an end. He failed to return to their marital home and instead moved into rented accommodation, shutting Todd completely out of his life (it would be 30 years before they saw each other face to face again). The fact that Lean's third marriage was at an end and he was now having an affair with an Indian woman caused a few raised eyebrows both in his family and in the industry, all of which no doubt spurred him to find another film subject that would take him abroad.

The subject that first caught his eye was *The Wind Cannot Read*, Richard Mason's novel about an RAF pilot who falls in love with a Japanese language instructor in India in 1943. The setting obviously appealed to Lean on two counts. It would allow him to present India to the world David Lean-style; more importantly, location filming would mean he'd also be able to be with Leila.

Lean scouted locations for the film and even secured the acclaimed Japanese actress Kishi Keiko to play the role of the language instructor. The script, meanwhile, was co-authored by Mason and Lean. Sadly, Alexander Korda, who was to have financed the film, was unsatisfied with the screenplay and died before production began. The film with Lean was not to be and the property was sold on to Rank, where it was picked up by producer Betty E Box and director Ralph Thomas, who made it with Dirk Bogarde and Yoko Tani in the leading roles. Although the Lean–Mason script was used, Lean didn't receive a credit. Perhaps just as well, given *Variety*'s verdict of the script: 'The gradual falling in love of the two stars is written with trite dialogue but is directed charmingly.'

The Wind Cannot Read, although a success at the time, has not worn well, and seems like a romance very much in the Fifties' Rank manner today. Nevertheless, Lean was greatly disappointed that he didn't get to make it. Compensation was just around the corner, however, for the American producer Sam Spiegel had an offer Lean really couldn't refuse.

Ten

BRIDGE BUILDING

Sam Spiegel was not only one of the film industry's most enigmatic film producers, he was also one of its most successful, particularly from the early Fifties through to the early Seventies. Born in Austria in 1903, the multilingual Spiegel first broke into films in Hollywood in 1927, working as a story translator for Universal, although it would be in Europe that he would make his first forays into producing, beginning in Austria in 1933 with *Invisible Opponent*. The rise to power of Hitler in Germany saw Spiegel return to Hollywood in 1935 where, using the name SP Eagle, he gradually rose up the ladder, producing *Tales of Manhattan* and *The Stranger*. In 1951, he formed Horizon productions, through which he produced *The Prowler* and what would prove to be his breakthrough film, *The African Queen*, released in 1952. Directed by John Huston and starring Katharine Hepburn and Humphrey Bogart, it won Bogart an Oscar for his performance.

By 1954, Spiegel had won a best picture Oscar for *On the Waterfront* (which he produced under his real name), which also won a further seven Oscars, including best director for Elia Kazan and best actor for Marlon Brando. *The Strange One* followed in 1957, along with his most ambitious project yet, an adaptation of Pierre Boulle's 1952 novel *The Bridge on the River Kwai*. It tells the story of the building of the legendary bridge – in Burma in the book and film, in Thailand in real life – by British prisoners of war under the direction of the Japanese. Yet despite Spiegel's success and reputation, he was having difficulty in signing a director. Such notables as William Wyler, Howard Hawks, John Ford and Fred Zinnemann had already turned Spiegel down. It eventually fell to Katharine Hepburn, who'd worked for both Spiegel (*The African Queen*) and Lean (*Summer Madness*) to get the two together.

Spiegel had acquired the Boulle novel through writer Carl Foreman. Blacklisted as a communist at the time, Foreman had penned such notable films as *Champion*, *The Men* and *High Noon*, each of which had earned him Oscar nominations. Now working out of Britain, Foreman had optioned the book with the idea that Alexander Korda might produce it through London Films. Korda proved uninterested in the project, so Foreman teamed up with Spiegel. Unfortunately, when Lean came on board, he was far from impressed by Foreman's script, which he regarded as the antithesis of Boulle's book.

With Spiegel's permission, Lean set about writing a new script with Norman Spencer. This version was in turn worked on by Carl Foreman with variable results, the upshot being that Foreman finally left the project. Calder Willingham (author of *End as a Man*, produced by Spiegel from a script by Willingham) next joined Lean, although it wasn't long before he too went the way of Foreman. He was replaced by another blacklisted writer, Michael Wilson, who'd won an Oscar

David Lean discusses a scene with Alec Guinness during the making of The Bridge on the River Kwai.
The film would win both men an Oscar.

(with Harry Brown) for his screenplay for *A Place in the Sun*. This time things worked out much better, with Wilson remaining to finish the shooting script with Lean (Wilson would later go on to adapt another of Boulle's books, *Monkey Planet*, for the screen, as *Planet of the Apes*). However, given that Wilson was a blacklisted writer, he didn't receive a screen credit. Similarly, neither did

3-PUB90

Foreman, nor Lean, nor Calder Willingham, nor Norman Spencer. Amazingly, Spiegel gave the writing credit to Pierre Boulle, who hadn't written a single word of the screenplay. This later caused all kinds of problems when the film went on to win the best adapted screenplay Oscar. It wasn't until 1985, over a quarter of a century later, that the oversight was partially rectified, when Foreman (who'd died in 1983) and Wilson (who'd died in 1978) were awarded posthumous Oscars for their work, although Lean and Spencer's unaccredited work still went unacknowledged. It wasn't until 1992 that a widescreen video release of the film restored Foreman and Wilson's credits to the film.

While the script was slowly taking shape, locations were being scouted and the decision was made to film in Ceylon, where the building of the bridge (engineered by Husband and Co. of Sheffield, built by The Equipment and Construction Co. of Ceylon) began a full year before the cameras began rolling. Thoughts were also seriously turning to the casting.

The story's central character is that of Colonel Nicholson, who takes a stand against Colonel Saito, the Japanese commander of a prisoner of war camp. The other main roles are that of an American marine, Shears, who has escaped the camp is recruited by Major Warden, the leader of a crack group of British commandos. Among those considered for the role of Nicholson were, surprisingly, Charles Laughton (too portly for a POW) and Noel Coward (too 'drawing room'). Also considered were Ralph Richardson, Anthony Quayle, Ronald Colman, Laurence Olivier, James Mason and even Spencer Tracy. The role went to Alec Guinness, who was persuaded to take it on after having already turned it down. Considerations for the role of the American, Shears, included Montgomery Clift and Cary Grant, with the role finally going to William Holden, one of Hollywood's hottest properties following his success in *Sunset Boulevard*, *Stalag 17* (another POW story which had won him a best actor Oscar), *The Bridges of Toko-Ri* and *Love Is a Many-Splendored Thing*. It appears that Jack Hawkins (*Mandy*, *The Cruel Sea*) was always the choice to play Major Warden. The role of Colonel Saito meanwhile went to Sessue Hayakawa, a Japanese actor who had made his name in American silents, such as Cecil B de Mille's sensational 1914 production of *The Cheat*, in which he had memorably branded Fanny Ward. Shears' momentary love interest with a nurse (insisted on by Columbia, which was financing the film) came in the guise of newcomer Ann Sears, sister of British film star Heather Sears, while the British medico, Dr Clipton, was played by James Donald, who'd also been the MO in *In Which We Serve*.

Filming on location for eight months was a tough and sometimes unpleasant experience for all concerned, given the searing heat and soul-destroying humidity. Tempers were short and Lean often found himself up against the actors and the crew, who failed to see the director's wider view of things. Lean and Guinness are also on record for disagreeing over how Nicholson should be played. Lean and producer Spiegel were often at loggerheads too, notably over the film's budget

David Lean goes over the day's shooting script with actor William Holden. Lean admired Holden greatly and thought he brought a touch of Hollywood glamour to the film.

Poster artwork for The Bridge on the River Kwai.

and Spiegel's unwarranted interference. Yet, despite the arguments and personality clashes, the results were spectacular.

The film opens with a tracking shot through the jungle (over which the credits are played) and comes to rest on a railway line, graves by its side. A train then trundles along, escorting prisoners, under armed guard, to the end of the line where they are to work on the continuation of the railway. The sequence immediately sets the scene: heat, harsh conditions, death.

We then cut to the arrival of a new group of troops at Saito's prisoner of war camp, camp 16. Defiant to the last, the prisoners whistle Colonel Bogey as they march in, the vulgar lyrics to which British audiences would have been familiar with at the time. Covered in grime and sweat, their clothes and shoes falling apart, they look like they've come to the end of their tether. However, as Saito warns them in his greeting, they're not in for an easy time. Escape, he tells them, is also an impossible consideration. 'There is no barbed wire, no stockade, no watchtower. We are an island in the jungle,' he says, to the ceaseless accompaniment of insects on the soundtrack. The men are then informed that they are to work on the continuation of the Bangkok–Rangoon railway and should be, 'happy in your work.'

Very subtly, Colonel Nicholson (Alec Guinness) turns the tables on Colonel Saito (Sessue Hayakawa).

Nicholson's confrontation with Saito follows, along with Nicholson's stay in 'the oven' and Shears' escape. The pace, direction and photography are almost indifferent during these establishing sequences, and it is the performances of Guinness and Hayakawa, especially in their head-to-head confrontations in Saito's quarters, that carry the film. Directorial displays are pretty thin on the ground, until Dr Clipton (James Donald) makes his famous comment about Nicholson and Saito: 'Are they both mad, or am I going mad? Or is it the sun?' after which he looks up to the sun. Lean then cuts to a shot of the sun, into which the escaping Shears stumbles, some 100 miles downstream. The river has by now dried up, and as he shambles along, vultures circle overhead. It's only when Shears mistakes a child's kite for a vulture – another clever piece of cutting – that he realises he's made it back to humanity.

Back at the camp, the bridge is way behind schedule, and Saito berates his chief engineer, pointing to missed dates on a Western pin-up calendar in his quarters. It's not long after this that Saito

Lieutenant Joyce (Geoffrey Horne) and Shears (William Holden) show the injured Major Warden (Jack Hawkins) the object of their arduous journey in The Bridge on the River Kwai *as two Siamese bearers look on.*

capitulates to Nicholson, who literally turns the tables over Saito's dinner table. 'He's done it!' cry Nicholson's men when they realise Saito has caved in, losing a great deal of face. Saito cries, defeated.

Nicholson and his officers take over the building of the bridge, meeting with Saito and providing him with detailed engineering plans (although where they got all this paper and technical drawing equipment from isn't explained). Realising that Nicholson is going to make a better job of the bridge than he ever could have done, Saito agrees to all of Nicholson's suggestions ('I have already given the order,' says Saito). It's at this point that we come to realise that Nicholson has become obsessed by the project, particularly when one of his men informs him that they are building the bridge with elm, which should last 60 years. 'That would be quite something,' replies Nicholson. Clipton, the objective observer of the increasing madness simply inquires, 'Must we build a better bridge than they could have built themselves?'

Mad dogs and Englishmen. Colonel Nicholson (Alec Guinness) and his men bake in the sun having arrived at the prisoner of war camp.

Meanwhile, Shears has been recruited by Major Warden to return and blow up the bridge (when Shears arrives at Warden's commando HQ, he sees a car pull out which we are led to believe is occupied by 'Lord Louis'). Joining them on the mission will be a group of crack commandos, among them one Lieutenant Joyce, (Geoffrey Horne, whom the film 'introduced'), who it is revealed was an accountant in civilian life. 'I just checked columns and columns of figures which three or four people checked before me. And there were other people who checked them after I had checked them!' Lean, it would seem, was having another dig at his past.

The trek through the jungle is an arduous one, yet the group makes it to the bridge on the eve of its opening. Nicholson is taking a walk over his creation and is joined by Saito, who comments, 'Beautiful,' about the setting of the sun. Nicholson misconstrues, thinking Saito is congratulating him on the completion of the bridge ('Yes, first rate job'), which prompts a reverie about his past. This is Nicholson's most human moment in the entire film, and it is superbly played by Guinness, whom Lean cleverly has perform the scene with his back to the camera. Saito also seems to have softened during this scene.

Then, while Nicholson and his men enjoy a celebratory stage show to mark the completion of the bridge, Shears and the commandos lay the charges for its destruction, any noise they make being drowned out by the music from the show (violin and drums can be heard, yet they're never shown – nor is a gramophone player – making one wonder where the music is actually coming from). Unfortunately, the water level in the river drops during the night, exposing the cables leading to the charges. The train is already on the way (we can hear it approaching for several minutes) when Nicholson spots the wires and alerts Saito ('He's leading them right to it – our own man,' exclaims Warden). In the ensuing chaos Shears, Saito and Nicholson are all killed, with Nicholson falling dead onto the plunger and destroying the bridge ('What have I done?' he gasps in realisation), leaving Clipton to make the final comment, 'Madness! Madness!' as the film ends with a helicopter shot of the destroyed bridge (the bridge remains intact in the novel).

Performance-wise, Guinness's blinkered Nicholson is undoubtedly the focus of the film (despite the fact that the actor is third billed in the credits behind Holden and Hawkins). His judgment throughout the film is masterful, for really, Nicholson is something of a bore – the ultimate jobsworth – yet behind the sheer bloody-mindedness of the man, Guinness is able to reveal the character's inner depths. These moments are necessarily few, yet their impact earns our sympathy, even though Nicholson's determination to follow the letter of the law almost leads him to an act of treason.

Hawkins and Holden are equally fine in their roles, despite the fact that their characters are little more than ciphers to carry forward the plot. Also impressive is Hayakawa's Saito, particularly in his scenes of capitulation and humiliation, which generate sympathy, despite the fact that he is clearly the villain of the piece.

Less impressive is Jack Hildyard's photography, which for the most part curiously lacks the vigour and invention of his work on *The Sound Barrier*, *Hobson's Choice* and *Summer Madness*. Perhaps he felt encumbered by the unwieldy widescreen CinemaScope process. His work is undeniably solid, yet it does lack flair. Meanwhile, Peter Taylor's editing seems somewhat leisurely, despite the fact that he had Lean over his shoulder in the cutting rooms, plus an astonishing eight assistants, among them Eric Boyd-Perkins and Teddy Darvas, who would go on to become respected editors in their own right. Malcolm Arnold's music can also be irritating, being little more than thunderous orchestral noise at times, while Lean's direction, particularly in the early scenes, lacks inspiration and the kind of intimate detail found in his previous films. The script is intelligent though and full of the kind of irony lacking in most wartime spectaculars. A film of broad, bold strokes, it is a completely different kettle of fish compared with the detailed miniatures Lean had previously made.

The Bridge on the River Kwai was a worldwide smash hit and was praised to the skies by the critics on both sides of the Atlantic when it was released in December 1957. 'If ever there was a nearly perfect motion picture in every way, this is it,' enthused *The Hollywood Reporter*, while back at home the *Evening News* commented, 'As thrilling an adventure film as was ever made.' *Variety* was also highly complimentary: '*The Bridge on the River Kwai* is a gripping drama, expertly put together and handled with skill in all departments. From a technical standpoint, it reflects the care and competence that went into the $3 million-plus venture, filmed against the exotic background of the steaming jungles and mountains of Ceylon... [Guinness] etches an unforgettable portrait of the typical British army officer, strict, didactic and serene in his adherence to the book.' Dylis Powell in *The Sunday Times* added, 'Splendidly professional, finely directed and excitingly photographed. I have rarely seen, in a film of action, a better cast.'

The result was queues round the block wherever the film played, while Kenneth J Alford's Colonel Bogey March found itself in the hit parade, thanks to a cover version by Mitch Miller. The film also swept the board at the Oscars, winning best actor (Alec Guinness), best adapted screenplay (Pierre Boulle), best cinematography (Jack Hildyard), best music (Malcolm Arnold), best editing (Peter Taylor) and best picture (Sam Spiegel, beating *Peyton Place*, *Sayonara*, *Twelve Angry Men* and *Witness for the Prosecution*). After three times nominations, Lean finally got his statue, picking up the best director Oscar. The only person who failed to turn a nomination into a win was Sessue Hayakawa, who lost out on the best supporting actor award to Red Buttons, who won for his frankly far from special performance in *Sayonara*.

The film also won four BAFTAs (best film any source, best British film, best actor, best screenplay), four DW Griffith awards (one of the year's 10 best, best director, best actor, best supporting actor), three New York Film Critics' Circle Awards (best film, best director, best actor) and three Golden Globes (best motion picture drama, best director, best dramatic actor).

After this success, Lean was at the peak of his profession. Even his private life seemed to be bucking up, his divorce from Ann Todd having been granted in July 1957, while he was still away in Ceylon filming, leaving the path clear for him to marry Leila, although there remained the obstacle of family disapproval. Rich, lauded and secure, the world was Lean's oyster. Yet it would be almost four years before his next film would see the light of a projector. It would be worth the wait, for while *The Bridge on the River Kwai* had made Lean a prince in his profession, *Lawrence of Arabia* would make him King.

Eleven

—◊—

IT IS WRITTEN

Lean was inundated with offers. Kirk Douglas was keen for him to direct *Spartacus*. MGM wanted him for their expensive remake of *Mutiny on the Bounty*. Lean turned both down, although the Bounty story intrigued him and he would return to it 20 years later. There was another offer from MGM, this time to direct the chariot race in *Ben-Hur*, while Sam Spiegel suggested adapting another Pierre Boulle novel, *The Other Side of the Coin*. None of these projects came to pass for Lean.

Nor did Lean's long-cherished hope to direct a film about Gandhi. The subject had fascinated him for years. It would also mean he'd be able to shoot in his beloved India and be close to Leila. Lean hired Emeric Pressburger to write a script for him, got Sam Spiegel interested in financing the project, and persuaded Alec Guinness to take on the role of Gandhi. This would of course have involved Guinness 'blacking up' for the role. This might have been acceptable in the less politically correct late Fifties and early Sixties, when white actors frequently made themselves up to play Othello, yet it would have dated the film for later audiences. Lean obviously failed to see this, for although Gandhi eventually fell through for him, it didn't prevent Lean from hiring Guinness to play a Brahmin some 25 years later in *A Passage to India*, a move that resulted in almost universal condemnation.

Gandhi would eventually be released to cinemas in 1982, and neither Lean, Alec Guinness, Emeric Pressburger nor Sam Spiegel were involved. Produced and directed by Richard Attenborough, with the Anglo-Indian actor Ben Kingsley in the title role, the film was an international blockbuster and went on to win eight Oscars, including best picture, best director and best actor. Apparently, Lean never saw the film, despite the fact that it co-starred John Mills and Trevor Howard, with both of whom he had frequently worked.

The collapse of *Gandhi* was a great disappointment to Lean. But there were other things to occupy his mind. He married Leila in July 1960, by which time he and Spiegel had committed themselves to telling the story of another 20th-Century historical figure, Thomas Edward Lawrence, the British soldier who, during World War One, united the Arabs and joined them in their fight against the Ottoman Turks, during which they liberated Damascus and set up the United Arab Council.

There had been attempts before to capture on film Lawrence's exploits in the desert, most notably by Rex Ingram in the late Twenties, Alexander Korda in the Thirties and Anthony Asquith

David Lean and producer Sam Spiegel square up to each other during the filming of Lawrence of Arabia *in Jordan. Although both men won an Oscar for the film, it proved to be the last time they collaborated together.*

in the Fifties (from a script by Terence Rattigan, which was later turned into the stage play *Ross*, with Alec Guinness playing Lawrence). These proposed films had been variously scuppered by Lawrence himself, his surviving brother AW Lawrence (who had become Lawrence's literary executor after his death in 1935), government opposition and even revolution.

When Lean and Spiegel became interested in the project, their first hurdle was to convince AW Lawrence to relinquish them the rights to *Seven Pillars of Wisdom*, his brother's account of his time in the desert. They did this by hiring Michael Wilson to write a treatment of the story. They also screened *The Bridge on the River Kwai* for Lawrence, who was extremely impressed with the picture. The result: Spiegel acquired the rights for the bargain price of £22,500. The film was announced to the world on Wednesday 17 February 1960, with Marlon Brando, who had won an Oscar for Spiegel's *On the Waterfront*, in the title role.

Location scouting in Jordan followed, with King Hussein offering both his blessing for the film as well as any help Lean and Spiegel might need. Meanwhile, Michael Wilson continued working on the script. Fortunately for the film, Brando in the end decided to decline the role of Lawrence, instead opting to play Fletcher Christian in MGM's remake of *Mutiny on the Bounty*. The film was a troubled one, with the original director, Carol Reed, being replaced during production by Lewis Milestone. In no way comparable with the 1935 version starring Charles Laughton as Bligh and Clark Gable as Christian, the remake does have some spectacular sequences, while Trevor Howard makes an excellent Bligh. Unfortunately, so ludicrous is Brando's English accent it scuppers the whole enterprise. One can only hope that Lean later saw the film and realised how close he had been sailing to disaster in casting Brando as Lawrence.

When he returned to London, Lean began looking for a replacement for Brando, and turned to up-and-coming actor Albert Finney, testing him at length. Finney too eventually turned down the role, despite the fact that Spiegel had lavished an incredible $100,000 on the tests. Luckily, a visit to the cinema soon after Finney's decline introduced Lean to another up-and-coming actor called Peter O'Toole. The film was *The Day They Robbed the Bank of England*, a period caper yarn directed by John Guillermin and co-starring Aldo Ray, Elizabeth Sellars, Joseph Tomelty and Miles Malleson. It was only O'Toole's third film, following *Kidnapped* and *The Savage Innocents*, yet straightaway Lean saw the actor's potential.

Although born in Connemara in Ireland in 1932, O'Toole spent his developing years in Leeds where, after leaving school early, he trained as a reporter with *The Yorkshire Evening Post*, during which time he also developed a taste for amateur dramatics. After his national service (in the Navy), O'Toole decided to take up acting professionally, studying at RADA in London. He eventually made his stage debut in 1955 at the Bristol Old Vic. He made the jump to films four years later, although it would be Lean's faith in him that would turn O'Toole into an international star.

With things gradually taking shape, Lean turned to the casting of the other key roles in the film. An early choice was to re-unite with Alec Guinness, who'd take the role of Prince Feisal to make up for his disappointment over Gandhi. Another member of the Lean alumni, Jack Hawkins, returned, this time as General Allenby. Claude Rains would be on board as Mr Dryden, as would

Lawrence (Peter O'Toole) gets the order from General Murray (Donald Wolfit) to go and find Prince Feisal in the desert. Mr Dryden (Claude Rains) manages to secure Lawrence more time for his task.

Anthony Quayle as Colonel Brighton. Quayle had, of course, made a brief appearance in *Pygmalion* back in 1938, since when he'd had a distinguished career in the theatre (he'd been the Director of the Shakespeare Memorial Theatre in Stratford from 1948–1956), as well as in films, most notably in *Ice Cold in Alex*, another desert-set adventure.

New to the group was Arthur Kennedy (a five-time Oscar nominee for *Champion*, *Bright Victory*, *Trial*, *Peyton Place* and *Some Came Running*) who'd take the role of the American journalist Jackson Bentley, whose newspaper reports do much to bring Lawrence to the attention of the Western world. Edmond O'Brien was the original choice to play Bentley. Unfortunately, after filming just a handful of scenes he suffered a heart attack, and so was replaced by Kennedy. Another acclaimed American star, Jose Ferrer (a best actor Oscar winner for *Cyrano de Bergerac*), was meanwhile cast as the Turkish Bey with whom Lawrence has a clash, for which he is flogged (and possibly raped). The role of the Arab leader Auda Abu Tayi was given to the powerful Mexican-born Hollywood star Anthony Quinn (himself a two-time best supporting actor Oscar winner for *Viva, Zapata* and *Lust for Life*).

El Aurens (Peter O'Toole) admires his newly acquired togs in the reflection of his dagger having successfully proved that the Nefud can be crossed. The dagger will later reflect a much-changed Lawrence.

O'Toole wasn't the only comparative newcomer featured in *Lawrence of Arabia*. For the role of Sherif Ali Ibn el Karish, Lawrence's friend and ally, Lean originally had his eye on German star Horst Buchholz (*Tiger Bay*, *The Magnificent Seven*). Unfortunately, Buchholz had signed to do the Billy Wilder comedy *One, Two, Three* with James Cagney. Frenchmen Alain Delon (*Plein Soleil*) and Maurice Ronet (*Lift to the Scaffold*, *Carve Her Name with Pride*) were considered as alternatives. Spiegel even went as far as signing Ronet for the role. Lean unfortunately found Ronet entirely unsuitable, and so he was let go, leaving the door open for Egyptian star Omar Sharif to step into the role. Lean had spotted Sharif's photograph while looking for actors to play minor Arab roles. Sharif (real name Michel Shalhoub), a former soccer international for Egypt, had been a major star in his homeland since the mid-Fifties, appearing in such films as *The Blazing Sun* (his debut), *Land of Peace* and *Goha*, using the names Omar el Cherif and Omar Cherif. After the inescapable screen tests, he secured the role of Sherif Ali and became a world-wide star as a consequence.

Behind the cameras, there were also a few new faces. Gone was cinematographer Jack Hildyard after four films, to be replaced by Freddie Young. Something of a legend, Young, born in 1902, had entered the industry in 1917 as a lab technician for Gaumont. In the late Twenties he became a second cameraman on *The Flag Lieutenant* (directed by none other than Maurice Elvey) and *The Somme*, before graduating to director of photography in 1928 with *Victory*. Over the next 30 years he would become Britain's most distinguished cameraman, working with directors such as Herbert Wilcox (on 20 films, including *Bitter Sweet*, *Victoria the Great* and *Nurse Edith Cavell*), Tom Walls (on eight films, including *Rookery Nook* and *Plunder*), Jack Raymond (on 12 films, including *Mischief* and *A Royal Divorce*) and Michael Powell (twice, on *Contraband* and *The 49th Parallel*). He also worked with Sam Wood (*Goodbye, Mr Chips*), Gabriel Pascal (*Caesar and Cleopatra*) and Carol Reed (*The Young*

Lawrence (Peter O'Toole) attempts to persuade Auda Abu Tayi to join his campaign against the Turks. Sherif Ali Ibn el Karish (Omar Sharif) and Majid (Gamil Ratib) look on sceptically.

Mr Pitt), while for MGM his work took in *Mogambo* (for John Ford), *Invitation to the Dance* (Gene Kelly), *Lust for Life* (Vincente Minnelli) and *Bhowani Junction* (George Cukor). His path had already crossed Lean's a couple of times, on *The 49th Parallel* (which Lean had edited) and *Major Barbara* (on which Young had worked briefly).

The film's production design was meanwhile in the very capable hands of John Box (*The Inn of the Sixth Happiness*, *Our Man in Havana*), who's success with Lean on *Lawrence of Arabia* and other films helped to secure him such prestigious jobs as *A Man for All Seasons*, *Oliver!* and *Nicholas and Alexandra*. John Bryan, Lean's designer in the Forties, had originally intended to return to design the film after years as a successful producer (*The Card*, *The Spanish Gardner*). Unfortunately, illness prevented him, and Box, assisted by art director John Stoll, found himself facing his biggest challenge. Also working on her biggest production to date was editor Anne V Coates (*The Pickwick Papers*, *Tunes of Glory*), who landed herself the job after impressing Lean by editing the Albert Finney screen test (Lean had also wanted the test's cinematographer, Geoffrey Unsworth, but he was committed to working on the Danny Kaye 'comedy' *On the Double*). Phyllis Dalton, the film's costume designer made the jump from screen test to movie too.

With the cast and crew in place, an almost insurmountable problem presented itself: Lean didn't like Michael Wilson's script; Wilson left the project. The fact that Wilson was still a blacklisted writer resulted, as it had with *The Bridge on the River Kwai*, in a lack of screen credit for his work. (Making one wonder to whom Spiegel would have given the credit had Wilson remained on the project. Pierre Boulle? TE Lawrence, perhaps, who'd been dead since 1935?) Despite having laid the groundwork, Wilson again found his efforts overlooked on screen.

Enter stage left playwright Robert Bolt. Born in Manchester in 1924, Bolt, a former English teacher, was then enjoying his second big success at the time, *A Man for All Seasons* (the first had been *Flowering Cherry*), and this impressed Spiegel enough to hire him to take over from Wilson. The original assignment was for a seven-week re-write job for which Bolt received the impressive sum of £10,000 (a fortune in the early Sixties). Of course, these seven weeks stretched into many, many more. In the meantime, to keep things going while Bolt beavered away, another screenwriter and playwright, Beverley Cross (*Half a Sixpence*, *Jason and the Argonauts*), was also assigned, to work on some of the second unit action sequences, the plotting of which he helped Lean to devise.

Filming finally began in mid-May 1961. For this, not only did the cast and crew have to assemble in the desert, but a catering corps to feed them, accompanied by sleeping tents, equipment trucks, horse and camel wranglers, plus the vast amounts of food and water to keep the livestock fed and watered. The making of *Lawrence of Arabia* was practically a military operation, with Lean the commander-in-chief.

Bolt was still working on the script when Lean called action for the first time, so the director concentrated on filming Lawrence's first trek across the desert to find Prince Feisal, in which he is led by the guide Tafas (Zia Mohyeddin, making his film debut). This lengthy sequence involves Lawrence's first meeting with Sherif Ali (Sharif), who emerges from a mirage and shoots Tafas, who has been using his well. One of the most famous sequences in film history, it required the use of an extremely long lens to capture the shimmering mirage. At first, Ali is little more than a distorted black blob on the horizon, seemingly floating in the haze. It is only when he gets closer that we realise that this is a man on a camel. Sharif couldn't have asked for a better entrance.

It took 20 months to film *Lawrence of Arabia*, during which cast and crew had to endure the scorching heat of the desert during the day and the freezing cold at night, not to mention sand storms, plagues of insects and being cut off from civilisation for weeks at a time. Inevitably, romances blossomed under these often adverse conditions. Lean succumbed, despite been married to Leila for only a short time, he began an affair with his continuity girl Barbara Cole.

After several months of filming in the deserts of Jordan, the unit broke for a few weeks, allowing Lean to return to London to view the footage so far shot. The unit then re-convened in Spain, where parts of Seville doubled for Cairo, Damascus and Jerusalem. This is where the majority of the film's interiors were shot, including Lawrence's encounters with General Allenby, Mr Dryden and General Murray (Donald Wolfit). The Arab council sequences and the scenes in the officers' club were also shot here. The charge into Aqaba was meanwhile filmed at Carboneros in Almería, where John Box built the entire city in a dried-up river bed leading down to the sea. A brilliant illusion, the Aqaba set could only be filmed from one angle, being little more than a series of cleverly constructed facades, complete with a giant gun. Filming this sequence was an enormous undertaking, and Lean was aided in staging parts of the attack on Aqaba by a second unit director, Andre de Toth. A director in his own right (*Dark Waters*, *House of Wax*), de Toth worked unaccredited on the scene with up-and-coming cinematographer Nicolas Roeg (who'd go on to photograph such Sixties classics as *A Funny Thing Happened on the Way to the Forum* and *Far from the Madding Crowd*, before turning to direction with *Performance*, *Walkabout* and *Don't Look Now*).

Lean gives Omar Sharif a few last second instructions during the filming of the sequence at Auda's well in Lawrence of Arabia. *The film's success would catapult Sharif to international stardom.*

Finally, the unit moved on to Morocco, where the massacre of the Turks took place, with Lawrence shouting the immortal command, 'No prisoners! No prisoners!' Then it was back to Britain to film the opening, Lawrence's fatal motorbike crash and the subsequent memorial service at St Paul's Cathedral.

Despite the vast amount of footage, Lean and his editor, Anne V Coates, had only four months to cut the picture, for Spiegel had managed to get *Lawrence of Arabia* selected as the Royal Film Performance of 1962, to be held in the presence of the Queen on Monday 10 December. Consequently, Lean, Coates and her various assistants worked round the clock, seven days a week, until the film was ready. Meanwhile, Spiegel had the idea of having three composers work on the film: Benjamin Britten (to write the military marches), Aram Khatchaturian (the Arabian sequences) and Maurice Jarre (the 'dramatic' scenes). Britten and Khatchaturian quickly fell by the wayside, as did Broadway composer Richard Rodgers (*South Pacific*, *The Sound of Music*), whom

Spiegel also had working on the music at one stage. Other considerations included William Walton and Malcolm Arnold, the latter an obvious choice after his Oscar win for *The Bridge on the River Kwai*. Ultimately, the job of scoring the entire film fell to Jarre.

Born in 1924, Jarre had studied at the Paris Conservatoire de Musique (under Arthur Honegger, who'd written the score for *Pygmalion*), after which he had worked primarily for the Jean Louis Barrault Theatre Company, after which he became the music director for the Theatre National Populaire. Jarre scored his first film, the short *Hotel des Invalides*, in 1952, which he followed with *Toute la Memoire du Monde* (another short), *Les Yeux sans Visage* and *Crack in the Mirror*. However, it was his 1962 score for *Cybele ou les Dimanches de Ville d'Avray* (*Sundays and Cybele*) that brought Jarre to the attention of Spiegel. Learning that the assignment was finally totally his, Jarre was also informed that he had just six weeks to both score and record the music for the film, which Lean and Coates were still working on, fine tuning the cut.

Jarre's score, played by the London Philharmonic Orchestra, was to have been conducted by Sir Adrian Boult, who receives a credit for doing so. Conducting to screen action was not something Boult was familiar with, however, and he almost immediately handed the job back to Jarre, who re-recorded the cues Boult had tried to lay down. Jarre had to fight to make sure that Boult didn't receive a credit on the subsequent soundtrack LP, for which he would have received a share of Jarre's royalties for doing absolutely nothing.

Work on *Lawrence of Arabia* came to an end just two days before the royal premiere. The ultimate cost was a then-staggering $13m. At the end of the day, even the money-pinching Spiegel couldn't argue that the film wasn't worth every penny.

From its very opening – that incredible Maurice Jarre overture with its thunderous kettledrum intro – *Lawrence of Arabia* is a film rich with style, each shot being beautifully composed for maximum visual impact. The credits (which carry the line, 'Introducing Peter O'Toole') play over a high-angled shot of Lawrence as he works on his motorcycle – the same bike on which he will shortly meet his death. Lean films the scenes of Lawrence speeding through the English countryside in a series of lengthy shots which capture the breathtaking velocity of Lawrence's hair-raising journey. We know from the outset that he is going to die, and the journey seems fraught with unexpected dangers, including road works and a sign warning of danger. Yet it is a couple of delivery boys cycling on the wrong side of the road that prove to be Lawrence's downfall. He brakes to avoid them, skids and flies over a hedgerow. The sequence ends with his goggles dangling from a bush.

Scenes inside and outside St Paul's Cathedral follow, in which Allenby, Brighton and Bentley confess that although they were acquainted with Lawrence, they 'didn't know him well' (after the premiere, this sequence was cut from the film, and wasn't reinstated until the film was restored in 1988). So who was Lawrence? We're introduced to him in the next scene, which shows him in his days as a mapmaker in Cairo working for General Murray. Obviously bored by his duties, Lawrence entertains his workmates with a trick that involves extinguishing a match with his fingers without flinching. A colleague asks what the trick is. Lawrence replies, 'The trick, William Potter, is not minding that it hurts.' Here lies the key to Lawrence. During the rest of the film we see him endure the heat of the

The Arabs, united by Lawrence, charge on Aqaba.

desert, go without water, murder a man in cold blood and order a massacre, during all of which he keeps his emotions concealed. He doesn't mind the hurt — at times he seems positively to revel in it.

Summoned to see General Murray, Lawrence is told that he is to be sent into the desert to find Prince Feisal and assess the Arab situation. A briskly written scene in which Lawrence's casual way with authority figures ruffles the General's feathers ('It's my manner,' he says by way of explanation), it concludes with a close-up of Lawrence, having lit a cigarette for Mr Dryden, the general's advisor, blowing out the match. We then jump-cut to the desert where, after a few seconds, the sun gradually begins to rise over the horizon. A masterful touch, it is a visually startling introduction to the desert. Several lovingly composed tracking shots follow, as Lawrence and his guide Tafas make their way across the dunes. Ravishing to look at, one can only imagine what Sixties audiences, fed on a diet of black and white kitchen sink dramas, thought of the rich colour and fantastic widescreen image. Even today, some 40 years on, these shots are staggeringly beautiful to behold. Lean and Freddie Young really were operating at the height of their artistic powers.

As Lawrence and Tafas make their way through the desert they become friends, Lawrence giving Tafas his gun as a present. Next comes the introduction of Sherif Ali through a mirage as Lawrence and Tafas fill their waterbags at a well ('Turks?' Lawrence nervously enquires of the approaching figure. 'Bedu,' comes the disdainful reply). Tafas draws his newly acquired gun on the approaching Ali, only to be shot dead in turn. To be befriended by Lawrence, it seems, is to be cursed by him. The well, it transpires, belongs to Ali. Tafas, it seems, is from a rival tribe and is not welcome to use it. 'He is nothing, the well is everything,' explains Ali.

Now guideless, Lawrence continues his journey to find Feisal, aided only by his army compass. Seemingly alone, he takes advantage of the situation by singing *The Man Who Stole the Bank at Monte Carlo* at the top of his voice as he rides through an echoing gorge, only to be brought up short by Colonel Brighton who, knowing that someone has been sent from Cairo, has been watching Lawrence progress through the canyon. Telling Brighton that he has been sent to 'appreciate the situation,' Lawrence is taken by Brighton to meet Feisal, whose enormous camp is being attacked from the air by the Turks. The casualties are many and Brighton warns Feisal that he must travel further into the desert if he wants to avoid the might of the Ottoman Turks.

During a meeting later on in Feisal's tent (in which he again meets Sherif Ali), Lawrence gradually persuades the Arabs that destiny can be of their own making, that they are more than capable of taking the port of Aqaba from the Turks if the disparate tribes can only be persuaded to join forces. 'Aqaba is over there – it's only a matter of going,' Lawrence tells Sherif Ali.

Not quite, it involves a 20-day trek across the Nefud Desert – the sun's anvil – the searing, dust-dry heat of which Young and Lean brilliantly capture. By this time Lawrence has acquired two servant boys, Farraj (Michel Ray) and Daud (John Dimech), who already hero worship the Englishman. Soon he gives them – and the other Arabs – real reason to do so. Having successfully crossed the furnace-like Nefud, it is noticed that one of the group's number, Gassim (IS Johar), has fallen off his camel and has become separated from them. Without any hesitation, Lawrence turns back into the Nefud to rescue Gassim, only to be told by his companions to leave the man to die. 'It is written,' one of them shouts. But Lawrence has made up his mind. Another jump cut follows to Gassim as he shambles across the desert. As the sun slowly rises, Gassim's shadow stretches across the baked sand, getting shorter and shorter as the sun gets higher and higher. Finally, Gassim can take the incredible heat no longer and collapses. Lawrence reaches him just in time and returns to the group in triumph ('Nothing is written,' he tells them). As a consequence, the Arabs call him El Aurence and, having finally reached a water hole, garb him in robes and give him a ceremonial dagger. Now, he is truly Lawrence of Arabia.

Exhilarated, Lawrence rides off into the desert to celebrate his new-found identity, which he does by parading about in his newly acquired robes, only to meet Auda Abu Tayi. Auda, whose well Sherif Ali and his men have been watering at, is angered that a rival tribe is using it without his permission. However, Lawrence manages to persuade the rival Arabs to join forces, fight the Turks and take Aqaba, promising the still dubious Auda riches beyond his wildest comprehension as an extra incentive (gold in a great box). The night before the proposed taking of the port, there is an

Lawrence (Peter O'Toole) returns to the desert in triumph, this time accompanied by a band of thuggish bodyguards.

altercation, and one of Auda's men is killed by one of Sherif Ali's men. The culprit turns out to be Gassim. In order to keep the peace and retain the honour of the opposing tribes, Lawrence offers to execute the man himself, which he does by firing six shots into Gassim. Says Auda: 'It *was* written then. Better to have left him.'

Their internal squabbling laid to rest, the Arabs go on to capture Aqaba with ease, the port's giant gun impotently and immovably pointing in the wrong direction – out to sea (there's even washing hanging on a line from it). This is arguably Lawrence's finest moment, and Lean shoots the ride into the port in long, sweeping takes, showing the ease with which the Arabs are able to achieve their objective.

During all of the aforementioned sequences, Lean makes as much use of startling sound effects as he does imagery to impose on his audience the other world of the desert. As Sherif Ali approaches Lawrence and Tafas from the mirage, all we hear is the gentle pad, pad, pad of the feet of Ali's camel

Sherif Ali (Omar Sharif) cautions restraint before the charge on the Turks.

as it makes its way towards the well, all of which adds to the building tension. Later, when Lawrence is alone in Feisal's tent, persuading the Prince to commit men to the taking of Aqaba, the tent's wooden poles creak as they gently sway in the evening breeze, adding to the atmosphere of the scene. Meanwhile, in the desert, as the Arabs revive themselves from a rest period in the Nefud, their camels sound like so many motorbikes revving up ready for action. Finally, after the taking of Aqaba, we're refreshed by the sound of waves crashing thunderously on to the beach as Lawrence rides along the coast in triumph. Indeed, this is the first time we see a body of water in the film, and after the heat and dust of the Nefud, one can almost feel the coolness of the foamy waves.

Aqaba now conquered, Lawrence decides to trek across the Sinai to inform Allenby what's happened. He is accompanied on the journey by Farraj and Daud. Unfortunately, on the journey, Lawrence not only loses his compass in a sandstorm (more incredible sound effects), but Farraj is swept away to his death in quicksand. Bereft, Daud and Lawrence continue the journey by themselves, first to the Suez Canal (where they're treated to the curious sight of a ship seemingly sailing behind a sand dune) and on to Cairo, where Lawrence, still garbed in his desert clothes, takes Farraj into the officers' bar only to be greeted by hostility ('What do you think you look like?' 'Get that wog out of here'). It's only after Lawrence tells Brighton and Allenby that they – the Arabs – have taken Aqaba that Lawrence is hailed a hero (Robert Bolt, visiting the set in Seville, can be seen during this sequence smoking a pipe as Lawrence chats with Allenby in the club's courtyard).

Allenby urges Lawrence, whom he promotes to Major, to return to the desert. 'I want you to go back and carry on the good work,' he says. But Lawrence has reservations, citing the death of Daud and Gassim. There's something that bothers him about their deaths, particularly his cold-blooded execution of Gassim. The reason finally comes. 'I enjoyed it,' he confesses. Promised money, guns, armoured cars and field artillery by Allenby, Lawrence is nevertheless persuaded to return to the desert to continue the campaign against the Turks, urging Allenby to aim for Jerusalem in the meantime. However, as Lawrence heads back to the dunes, Mr Dryden urges caution with Lawrence. 'He's riding a whirlwind,' he comments. 'Let's hope we're not,' comes Brighton's retort. All this and we're only halfway through!

The second part of the film opens with the arrival in Aqaba of the American reporter Jackson Bentley (for whom read Lowell Thomas), where he meets the newly installed Prince Feisal. Bentley desperately wants to tell Lawrence's story. Armed with an introductory letter from Feisal, he journeys into the desert, where he chronicles Lawrence's exploits, which include the spectacular devastation of a Turkish train (the actual explosion of which was filmed by second unit director Andre de Toth). Lawrence parades in victory on the train, which the Arabs proceed to loot. However, a surviving Turk shoots Lawrence in the arm, only to be dispatched by Auda's sword. 'Jimminy! Never seen a man killed with a sword before!' exclaims Bentley. 'Why don't you take a picture?' asks Lawrence. 'Wish I had,' comes the cynical reply. However, while Lawrence is happy to bask in Bentley's attention, posing for photographs at every opportunity, Auda is suspicious of Bentley's cameras, destroying one of them for taking away his virtue. Lawrence, it seems, has no such problem.

As the campaign moves on, Lawrence's army dwindles at every turn, the Arabs happy to loot and then return to their home camps. Auda too yearns for his home camp, along with something honourable to take back to his people. Jump-cut to an open-topped train of horses, including a white stallion. Auda has found his honourable prize, and so he too now returns home, leaving Lawrence with an ever-diminishing band of followers. Things go from bad to worse; while attempting to mine a stretch of railway, Farraj is badly wounded by a detonator. Not wanting to leave him for the Turks to pick up and torture, Lawrence kills him with his pistol.

With only a straggle of men now left, Ali accuses Lawrence of wanting the men to walk on water for him. Later, when Lawrence and Ali travel to assess the situation in the town of Deraa, where there is a Turkish garrison, Lawrence purposely walks through a large puddle instead of around it. Perhaps he can walk on water? He is quickly brought down to earth when he is arrested in the street and taken before the Turkish Bey in charge of the garrison. The Bey, bored with his post ('I couldn't feel more lonely if they'd sent me to the dark side of the moon'), seems drawn by Lawrence's blue eyes, blond hair and white skin, which he touches ('Your skin is very fair'). From the close-up of Lawrence startled eyes and the Bey's moist lips, we can guess the Turk's designs. So too can Lawrence, who punches the Bey in the stomach. As a consequence Lawrence is beaten, but like his trick with the match, he hides the pain. When thrown out on to the street where Ali is waiting for him, it seems that Lawrence has endured something more than a beating. Despite the hints – perhaps too subtle in a bid to avoid vulgarity – most audiences failed to realise that Lawrence has been sodomised by the Bey.

Recovering at Kerak, Lawrence realises that, for now, things have come to some kind of conclusion. 'I've come to the end of myself,' he tells an incredulous Ali, and so heads to see Allenby in Jerusalem. The desert is in Lawrence's blood by now, and it's clear that he doesn't fit in with the other army officers, particularly when feigning enthusiasm for their new squash court in the club. 'Lays it on a bit thick,' comments one officer. (Immediately after this exchange, Bentley approaches

Lawrence: in the long shot it's Edmond O'Brien, although the close-up is of Arthur Kennedy, the actor who replaced him). Given his inability to fit in, it isn't long before Allenby is able to encourage Lawrence to return to the desert to carry on with the campaign. 'I believe your name will be a household word, where you'd have to go to the war museum to find who Allenby is,' the General flatters Lawrence.

Lawrence succumbs to Allenby's pandering and returns, his aim being to give Damascus to the Arabs before the British get there. It is clear that Lawrence has somehow changed since his return, for when the newly formed Arab army comes across a village that has been ransacked by the Turks, Lawrence orders the massacre of the soldiers responsible. 'No prisoners! No prisoners!' he cries in revenge, providing one of the film's most enduring moments. A blood bath follows, the only survivors being two lambs ('Oh, you rotten man. Here, let me take your bloody picture for the rotten bloody newspapers,' condemns Bentley).

Yet Lawrence successfully delivers Damascus to the Arabs. The various tribes, despite forming a supposedly united Arab council, fail to put their past differences aside and prove unable to govern together. Gradually, they leave for their home camps, and this proves to be the last time Lawrence sees Auda and Sherif Ali. Indeed, the diminished council is even unable to look after the 2000 Turkish wounded in the hospital, which Lawrence, dressed in his Arab robes, visits, only to be slapped in the face by a disgusted British medical officer ('Outrageous! Outrageous! the MO repeatedly exclaims).

By now it's clear that Lawrence is finished in Arabia, his hope for the council in ruins. It's down to Allenby, Brighton, Prince Feisal and Mr Dreyden to sort out the political mess now that the fighting is over. Allenby promotes Lawrence to Colonel (so that he can have his own cabin on the ship home) and sends him packing. 'What I owe you is beyond evaluation,' says Feisal as Lawrence departs through a pair of diaphanous curtains. Ironically, Lawrence meets the MO who slapped him on the way out. 'May I shake your hand? Just want to be able to say I've done it,' he says proudly, not realising that Lawrence was the 'wog' he slapped at the hospital.

So was it all the fighting worth it? 'On the whole I'd wish I'd stayed in Tunbridge Wells,' dryly comments Mr Dreyden to Prince Feisal, leaving Lawrence to journey back to England, with the film coming full circle as his car, travelling to the docks on a dusty desert road, is overtaken by a speeding motor bike.

Unlike most epics made in the Fifties and Sixties, *Lawrence of Arabia* benefits enormously from its script by Robert Bolt, which adds intellect, wit and irony to a story of dubious heroism (Lawrence's personal acts of endurance are heroic, the self-serving manner of his motivations less so). While *Ben-Hur* and *Quo Vadis?* entertain by their spectacle, *Lawrence of Arabia* commands our attention and concentration. Audiences could be forgiven for not clearly being able to follow the events and politics at times, as Bolt and Lean take it almost as written that people will be familiar with them (there are no subtitles or voiceovers to clue in the stragglers). Momentary confusion in the narrative aside, however, this is a spectacular piece of cinema. Lean's direction throughout is masterful, making the most of the stunning desert vistas, yet at the same time providing subtlety and nuance in the dialogue sequences. Freddie Young's photography is the best colour photography you'll see anywhere, while Maurice Jarre's deliriously romantic music makes a perfect

COLUMBIA PICTURES presents THE SAM SPIEGEL · DAVID LEAN Production of

LAWRENCE
OF ARABIA

WINNER OF
17 ACADEMY
AWARDS

ALEC GUINNESS · ANTHONY QUINN · JACK HAWKINS · JOSE FERRER
ANTHONY QUAYLE · CLAUDE RAINS · ARTHUR KENNEDY
OMAR SHARIF as 'ALI' and introducing **PETER O'TOOLE** as 'LAWRENCE'

ROBERT BOLT
SAM SPIEGEL
DAVID LEAN

A HORIZON BRITISH PRODUCTION IN TECHNICOLOR

Poster artwork for Lawrence of Arabia.

accompaniment to the stunning scenery (his use of such electronic instruments as the Onde Martinote and cithare add to the desert's more curious sights).

Performance-wise, Peter O'Toole is Lawrence, capturing and conveying the outer bravura and inner doubt of the man, while Omar Sharif provides Sherif Ali with a genuine air of dignity, particularly in the scenes where he acts as Lawrence's conscience. Anthony Quinn's Auda is loud, proud and imposing, teetering on the edge of ham, and all the better for it, while Alec Guinness's Prince Feisal is suitably clipped, reflecting his character's formal education. As the British contingent, Jack Hawkins artfully conveys General Allenby's easy authority, while Claude Rains' Mr Dryden provides some welcome wit, wryly put over. Anthony Quayle conveys Brighton's initial doubt and later admiration of Lawrence (his tears when he realises he will never see him again add a touch of humanity to what otherwise could be misconstrued as a straightforward performance), while Arthur Kennedy makes Jackson Bentley's cynicism, both humorous and despairing, a joy to behold.

Despite the last minute rush to complete the editing and mixing, the royal premiere of *Lawrence of Arabia* was a triumph for all concerned, resulting in some of the best reviews Lean ever had. 'The direction of David Lean is masterly,' wrote the critic of *The Sunday Express*. The paper's daily edition was also bowled over: 'Made me proud of the cinema as a medium of entertainment.' *The Financial Times* agreed, commenting, 'A landmark in the history of cinema.' *The Evening Standard* could barely contain itself: 'Here is an epic with intellect behind it, an unforgettable display of action staged with artistry. A momentous story told with moral force.' The Americans were also suitably impressed. *Variety*: 'Authentic desert locations, a stellar cast and an intriguing subject combine to put this in the blockbuster league.' Only Pauline Kael seemed to waver, commenting, 'Fails to give an acceptable interpretation of Lawrence, or to keep its action intelligible, but it is one of the most literate and tasteful and exciting of expensive spectacles.'

Nevertheless, cuts were made to the original 222-minute print, reducing the running time by 20 minutes to make the film more acceptable to audiences. It also enabled cinemas to screen an extra showing of the film each day. Among the scenes to go was the shot of Lawrence's goggles on the bush, the memorial service at St Paul's, the spectacular entry into Auda's camp, a dialogue scene between Allenby and Brighton in Alleby's quarters, and parts of Lawrence's return to the desert, accompanied by his newly acquired bodyguards. These sequences wouldn't be seen again for over 25 years, re-emerging in 1988 when the film was fully restored in a director's cut supervised by Lean. In the meantime, controversy grew over who ordered the cuts. Lean often accused Spiegel of being responsible, although it has since been revealed that Lean not only knew of the cuts, but suggested and sanctioned them. In any form, the film is a truly spectacular experience – for completeness and clarity, however, one must side with the original/restored widescreen cut.

Critics and filmgoers weren't the only people enamoured of *Lawrence of Arabia*. The Academy of Motion Picture Arts and Sciences nominated the film for 10 Oscars, including best picture and best director. It went on to win in seven categories: best picture (Spiegel, beating off *The Longest Day*, *The Music Man*, *Mutiny on the Bounty* and *To Kill a Mockingbird*), best director (Lean), best photography (Young), best music (Jarre), best editing (Anne V Coates), colour art direction and set decoration (John Box, John Stoll, Dario Simoni) and best sound (John Cox). The three losers were Peter O'Toole, who lost out on the best actor award to Gregory Peck for *To Kill a Mockingbird*; Omar Sharif, who lost best supporting actor to Ed Begley for *Sweet Bird of Youth*; and Robert Bolt, who lost the best adapted screenplay award to Horton Foote for *To Kill a Mockingbird*. Bolt would eventually go on to win two Oscars for other films. Sharif would never be nominated again, and while Peter O'Toole would go on to be nominated a further six times, he'd never win. *Lawrence of Arabia* made O'Toole an international star, yet he'd never again work with Lean.

Internationally, the film also did extremely well on the awards circuit, going on to pick up four BAFTAs (including best actor and screenplay), two DW Griffiths awards, the Italian Silver Ribbon, two Italian 'Davids,' four Golden Globes and the Japanese Kinema Jumpo award for best foreign film. Lean, it seems, would need many cabinets to house all his trophies. Unquestionably, he was now at the pinnacle of his career. What was next for the celebrated director? How about a little second unit work – unaccredited, of course.

Twelve

RUSSIA, SPANISH STYLE

ean did much travelling after completing *Lawrence of Arabia*, visiting Italy, France and Egypt among other places. However, his companion on these trips was not his wife Leila, from whom he was becoming increasingly remote, but Barbara Cole. During these travels, Lean considered various projects. However, the one that he agreed to do surprised many: to direct some second unit scenes – unaccredited.

A mammoth portrayal of the story of Christ, *The Greatest Story Ever Told* was being produced and directed by George Stevens, whom Lean admired greatly. Known for *A Place in the Sun* and *Giant*, both of which won him best director Oscars, Stevens was also responsible for such hits as *Woman of the Year*, *I Remember Mamma* and *Shane*. However, as critic Andrew Sarris later succinctly pointed out, 'He [Stevens] was a minor director with major virtues before *A Place in the Sun*, and a major director with minor virtues after.'

Bankrolled by United Artists to the tune of $15m, the film was a lavish, star-studded affair, featuring top drawer names: Charlton Heston, Sidney Poitier, Dorothy McGuire, Shelley Winters, Sal Mineo and John Wayne, although like *Lawrence of Arabia*, the leading character was played by a comparative newcomer, Max Von Sydow, known to art-house audiences for his work in the films of Swedish director Ingmar Bergman (among them *The Seventh Seal* and *The Face*). Also like Lean's last film, *The Greatest Story Ever Told* was intended as the pinnacle of George Stevens' achievements.

Unfortunately, the film, which was being shot in Utah and the Nevada desert, was overschedule and overbudget, so Stevens approached Lean through fellow director Fred Zinnemann to take on some of the sequences. Surprisingly, Lean accepted the offer, agreeing to direct the scenes involving King Herod and Herod Antipas. That these roles were played by Claude Rains and Jose Ferrer, respectively, must have been an added incentive for Lean to take the work on, for which he was paid scale, handing his fee over to charity (the Screen Directors' Guild Benevolent Fund). The film would mark the only time Lean would film in a Hollywood studio – or in America.

Working with cinematographer Charles Lang (an Oscar winner for his work on the 1933 version of *A Farewell to Arms*), Lean completed his chores on *The Greatest Story Ever Told* in just under two weeks. He was not the only director approached to take on extra scenes. Jean Negulesco (*Humoresque*, *Three Coins in the Fountain*) handled the film's nativity sequences. Oddly enough, these two scenes are the best in the film. However, although sumptuously photographed in UltraPanavision by William C Mellor and Loyal Griggs (who were Oscar nominated for their efforts), with eye-catching art direction care of Richard Day and William Creber, the end product is a stately affair. The original running time of the completed film was a backside-numbing four

The entertainment event of the year. Poster artwork for Doctor Zhivago.

hours and 20 minutes. Like *Lawrence of Arabia*, this was reduced after the premiere, with subsequent versions running from three hours and 58 minutes down to two hours and seven minutes. Whatever the running time, the critics savaged it. Far from being George Stevens' *Lawrence of Arabia*, it turned out to be his *Madeleine*.

'Who but an audience of diplomats could sit through this thing,' dismissed *Life*, to which the *New Yorker* added, 'We can only sit and sullenly marvel at the energy for which, for more than four hours, the note of serene vulgarity is triumphantly sustained.' Critic John Simon turned the knife with, 'God is unlucky in *The Greatest Story Ever Told*. His only begotten son turns out to be a bore… As the Hallelujah Chorus explodes around us stereophonically and stereotypically it becomes clear that Lazarus was not so much raised from the tomb as blasted out of it. As for pacing, the picture does not let you forget a single second of its four hours.'

Sadly, the film remains a monument to Steven's overindulgence, remembered solely, if at all, for John Wayne's guest appearance as a centurion during the crucifixion. His only line, drawled in his usual style, is, 'Truly, this man was the Son of God.' Perhaps it is just as well that Lean chose not to be credited for his work.

Afterwards, Lean headed off on a cruise with his wife Leila, and it was during this trip that he finally decided what his official follow-up project to *Lawrence of Arabia* would be — an adaptation of Boris Pasternak's *Doctor Zhivago*, which he'd been given by his agent to read on the voyage. Pasternak had written *Doctor Zhivago*, the story of a doctor and his love for two women during the Russian Revolution, in 1954. However, the Soviet authorities banned the book's publication and it wasn't until 1957 that it saw the light of day, when an Italian publishing house in Milan managed to produce an edition based on a manuscript smuggled out of the Motherland. A worldwide hit thanks to the publicity created by Pasternak's nomination for the Nobel Prize for Literature, which he at first accepted and then later refused (for fear of exile), the book was subsequently bought by the Italian producer Carlo Ponti, who wanted to cast his wife, Sophia Loren, in the role of Lara.

Carlo Ponti was born in 1913 (some sources say 1910), and following success with home-grown product such as *Piccolo Mondo Antico* and *La Strada*, he began to turn increasingly towards star-studded international productions like *War and Peace*, *Boccaccio '70* and *Operation Crossbow*. Having acquired the rights to *Doctor Zhivago*, Ponti approached MGM to finance the film, which its president, Robert O'Brien, was happy to do, as long as Lean was in the director's chair, hence Lean's agent sending him the book to read on his ocean voyage.

Lean was eager to go to MGM to make the film for several reasons: he would be free of Sam Spiegel, who he'd never been able to trust entirely as far as financial matters were concerned, Robert Bolt would be writing the script, he'd receive an enormous up-front salary plus a percentage of the profits and producer Carlo Ponti would leave him to his own devices during filming.

Given the length of Pasternak's book, with its many characters and plot twists, work on the script was slow moving. There was also the problem of making Zhivago's extramarital affair acceptable. Bolt concentrated on the bare bones of the narrative.

Following the death of his mother, the young Zhivago goes to live in Moscow with his mother's friends the Gromekos, Alexander and Anna. As a student, Zhivago turns to medicine and becomes a doctor, by which time he has fallen in love with the Gromeko's daughter, Tonya, whom he later marries. Meanwhile, across town, Lara, the daughter of a high-class dressmaker, is trying to prevent her fiancé, Pasha Antipov, from being arrested for handing out revolutionary leaflets. She also finds herself the object of sexual advances from her mother's financial advisor, Monsieur Komarovsky, with whom she subsequently has an affair. When her mother finds out — she has also been involved with Komarovsky — she tries to commit suicide. Komarovsky manages to persuade his friend Professor Kurt to tend to Lara's mother. The Professor agrees, taking his protégé Zhivago along with him. This is the first time Zhivago sees Lara and, although they do not meet, he seems to have been greatly affected by her.

But Zhivago and Lara are not destined to be together just yet, for the Revolution and the First World War are about to explode. By now, Lara has married Pasha and had a daughter, but Pasha soon after disappears, transmogrifying into the militant leader Strelnikov. Lara meanwhile becomes a nurse, finally meeting and working with Zhivago in a military hospital. After the war, Zhivago returns to his wife and family, taking them to the remote town of Varykino for safety, only to learn that Lara is living in the next village. However, before Zhivago can take up his affair with Lara, he is kidnapped by a band of revolutionaries and made to serve as their medical officer. After two years, Zhivago finally deserts, returning to Lara. By this time, his wife Tonya (with whom he has had two children) has escaped to Paris with her father, leaving Zhivago, Lara and her daughter to live in peace in Varykino, where Zhivago writes his love poems about Lara – until, that is, the arrival of Monsieur Komarovsky, by now Minister of Justice, who warns them to leave before being arrested. Lara, her daughter and Komarovsky escape, but Zhivago stays behind, never to see his beloved again. To enhance the story further, Bolt topped and tailed the whole narrative with scenes involving Zhivago's half-brother Yevgraf, who is searching for the daughter Zhivago never knew he had, whom Lara was carrying when she left Zhivago for the last time.

MGM and Carlo Ponti had some curious casting ideas for the film, hinting that either Burt Lancaster, Peter O'Toole or Paul Newman should play the title role (O'Toole turned down the opportunity). Jeanne Moreau, Yvette Mimieux, Jane Fonda and Sophia Loren were meanwhile mooted as Lara, while James Mason and Marlon Brando were considered as Monsieur Komarovsky. Omar Sharif was also ear-marked for the young revolutionary Pasha Antipov. Of all these considerations, only Omar Sharif made it to the film, winning the title role. Since his success in *Lawrence of Arabia*, Sharif had gone on to enjoy a high-profile career, appearing in such epics as *The Fall of the Roman Empire*, *Behold a Pale Horse* and *Genghis Khan*, so there was no worry that he wasn't a big enough name to carry the picture (although Lean's name, like de Mille's and Hitchcock's, was big enough in itself).

Yet Lean still had no Lara. He eventually found her, along with his Pasha Antipov, while watching *Billy Liar*. Her name was Julie Christie and she was playing Liz, one of Billy's many girlfriends.

An up-and-coming actress, Christie, who'd been born in India and educated in France, had trained at London's Central School for Music and Drama, making her official debut in 1957 at the age of 16. Work in television later followed, notably in *A for Andromeda*, which she followed with a couple of minor appearances in two comedies for director Ken Annakin: *Crooks Anonymous* and *The Fast Lady*. These brought her to the attention of director John Schlesinger, who cast her as Liz in *Billy Liar*. When Christie received the news that she would be playing Lara for Lean, she was by then in Ireland working with another great director, John Ford, on his Sean O'Casey biopic *Young Cassidy*. Christie may have been up-and-coming at that point but *Doctor Zhivago* would turn her overnight into a star.

Christie's co-star in *Billy Liar*, Tom Courtnay, also found himself jumping from relatively small – albeit successful – British films (*The Loneliness of the Long Distance Runner*, *Private Potter*) to the international blockbuster thanks to his casting as Antipov/Strelnikov.

Also joining the *Doctor Zhivago* cast was heavyweight character star Rod Steiger (*On the Waterfront*, *Al Capone*, *The Pawnbroker*) who would be playing Monsieur Komarovsky. Lean also brought back a few familiar faces from the past, among them Alec Guinness, who'd be playing Zhivago's half-brother Yevgraf, and Ralph Richardson, as Alexander Gromeko, Zhivago's adopted father. The role of Tonya, Zhivago's wife, was given to Charlie Chaplin's daughter Geraldine, who'd be making her film debut,

'Do you know this man?' Yevgraf Zhivago (Alec Guinness) questions Tonya (Rita Tushingham) about her parents.

earning the film plenty of additional publicity. The rest of the cast was filled with Rita Tushingham (as Zhivago and Lara's grown-up daughter, also named Tonya), Geoffrey Keen (as Professor Kurt), Klaus Kinski (as Kostoyed, the cynical prisoner Zhivago and his family encounter on the train to Varykinow), while the role of the young, orphaned Zhivago was played by Omar Sharif's son Tarek.

As always, Lean brought back plenty of talent familiar to him to work behind the scenes, most notably production designer John Box, who found himself not only having to build an entire Russian street, complete with trolley cars, but also the ice palace at Varykinow where Zhivago and Tonya, and later Zhivago and Lara, retreat from the outside world. The former was built on the CEA studio back lot in Madrid, where much of the film was shot, the latter on the Spanish plains at Soria (Carlo Ponti had hoped to make the film in Russia, but this proved impractical, as did Yugoslavia and Finland, so Spain it was).

After their successful collaboration on *Lawrence of Arabia*, Lean was keen for Freddie Young to photograph *Doctor Zhivago*. Unfortunately, Young was lined up to photograph *Khartoum* for director

Basil Dearden, so Lean instead offered the job to Nicolas Roeg, who'd photographed some of the second unit sequences. In the time since, Roeg had photographed *The System* and *Nothing But the Best*, both of which had been regarded as pictorially innovative in the swinging Sixties style. Landing *Doctor Zhivago* was a coup for Roeg, even if Lean's approach was at variance with Roeg's more 'with it' outlook. This clash of styles revealed itself very soon, so despite having photographed remarkable scenes such as the burial of Zhivago's mother, Lean and Roeg parted company. As a stop gap, Manuel Berenguer, the film's second unit cinematographer, took over Roeg's job while negotiations went on to buy Freddie Young out of his *Khartoum* contract. This achieved, Young took over for the film's remaining 15-month shooting schedule.

Also back on continuity was Barbara Cole, with whom Lean was still having an affair, costume designer Phyllis Dalton and art director Terence Marsh. Another essential member of the *Doctor Zhivago* team was props man Eddie Fowlie, who'd first worked for Lean on *The Bridge on the River Kwai*, since when he and Lean had become good friends. On *Lawrence of Arabia*, Fowlie had built the well for Sherif Ali's first appearance, and had also been responsible for the arduous task of keeping the desert sand smooth, clean and free from footprints between takes. *Doctor Zhivago* proved to be a greater challenge. In the heat of the Spanish summer, Fowlie had to convert a meadow into a frozen lake for one of the film's battle sequences (which he did by covering it with compacted marble dust) and create the effect of ice inside the house at Varyikinow (achieved by covering the set with dripping hot wax).

Not only did *Doctor Zhivago* film in Spain, Lean and the crew also travelled to Finland to shoot some of the train sequences. Second units were also dispatched to Finland and Canada to capture snow vistas unobtainable in Spain, where an unusually mild winter meant that the thin snowfall had to be continually augmented by marble dust, white tarpaulin and whitewash to create the desired effect.

All the effort was worth it for the film is visually stunning from beginning to end. Lean sets up the premise for the film's flashback swiftly, with Yevgraf Zhivago's meeting with the young Tonya at the dam where she works. Is she really the daughter of Yuri Zhivago and *the* Lara of the Lara poems? The first scene in the flashback shows the burial of Yuri's beloved mother, and is one of the film's most memorable. Seen from the child's point of view, it has echoes of the opening of *Great Expectations*. The wind is howling, the trees are bending, and the burial itself seems almost brutal, with clods of earth unceremoniously shovelled in on top of the coffin with a loud thud. The pièce de résistance, however, comes when Lean cuts to a shot inside the coffin, showing Yuri's mother lying serenely in state. It is an unforgettable image.

The film is full of memorable images and details, such as the insistent tap of a branch against Yuri's bedroom window as he tries to sleep after the funeral (echoes of the opening scene in *Hobson's Choice*); the distant sound of music coming from his mother's balalaika as it stands in the corner; the shocking cut back to her grave as it is assaulted by the relentless wind, the wreathes blown away, almost wiping her from the face of the earth.

When Zhivago is a teenager studying medicine, there is the moment when, unbeknownst to each other, he and Lara back into each other on a tram. As they do so, Lean cuts to a spark on the

The charge of the dragoons down the Moscow street in Doctor Zhivago*, as seen from Zhivago's viewpoint on the balcony of his home.*

overhead power line. Then, as Komarovsky takes Lara to dinner, there's the remarkable whip pan that takes us from Lara and Komarovsky on the dance floor back to their table, just as they are sitting down. The slaughter of the demonstrators is also inventively handled, for instead of concentrating on the bloodshed, as had been the case with the massacre of the Turks in *Lawrence of Arabia*, we instead watch Zhivago's face as he witnesses the horror from a balcony.

Elsewhere, the fact that Lara loses her virginity to Komarovsky is relayed by her wearing a scarlet dress when next dining with him, this time in a private room. One of the most remarkable camera moves comes when Lara's mother tries to commit suicide. Having discovered her, Komarovsky races through the house to get a servant to go for help. However, Lean observes the action from outside the house, the camera dollying past the various windows. Having helped Professor Kurt save the woman's life, Zhivago then wanders through the machine room where, through a glass partition, he sees Lara sitting alone in a dark room, and until Komarovsky bursts in to tell her that her mother will live, all we see of her is her hand, resting on the arm of a chair. Perhaps the moment that survives least well is when Komarovsky forces himself on Lara and, after a moment of struggle, she gives in and seems to enjoy it ('Don't delude yourself this was rape,' says Komarovsky afterwards. 'That would flatter us both'). Not exactly politically correct.

There are many more visual touches to compensate: the candle in the window which melts the frost to reveal Lara telling Pasha that she's been sleeping with Komarovsky; the parade of the conscripts (recalling the return of the soldiers from war in *This Happy Breed*); the frozen hand sticking out from the snow during the winter assault; the petals falling from the sunflower as Lara and Zhivago depart after serving as doctor and nurse together; the drabness of the Gromeko house after the communists take it over as a commune; the sound of Tonya ironing, which reminds Zhivago of Lara doing the same thing; Zhivago's cap as it lies in the road after his kidnapping by the revolutionaries; the charge over the frozen 'lake', complete with moored boat; the massacre of the boys from St Michael's Military School, mistaken for soldiers; the sled ride to the ice palace, the sled almost taking off when it hits a bump in the road; Zhivago's last sighting of Lara as he travels on a Moscow tram, only to suffer a fatal heart attack when he tries to pursue her; the final shot of Lara as she walks down as street dominated by a giant poster of Stalin. Then comes Yevgraf's conclusion to Lara's story, bringing things full circle: 'She died or vanished in one of the labour camps, a nameless number on a list that was afterwards mislaid. That was quite common in those days.'

Filming on *Doctor Zhivago* was completed early in October 1965, and as had been the case with *Lawrence of Arabia*, Lean had to rush the editing to meet the American release date of 22 December, which would also qualify the film for the all-important Academy Awards (UK cinema audiences had to wait until April 1966 to see the film). Moving to Hollywood for the editing process, Lean worked round the clock with his chief cutter, who this time was Norman Savage. This meant that Maurice Jarre, who Lean brought back to score the picture, again had a very short period to score a movie that was over three hours long.

In the three-year period since the completion of *Lawrence of Arabia*, Jarre had not been idle, having scored 14 films, among them *The Longest Day*, *The Train* and *The Collector*. Good as some of these are, Jarre's music for them is not particularly notable, presumably because he was restricted from flying his musical colours owing to the nature of the films. There would be no such restrictions with *Doctor Zhivago*. A visual tour de force, it called for lush, sweepingly romantic music. Jarre more than delivered here, penning *Lara's Theme*, one of the cinema's most immediately recognisable pieces of music.

To play it, Jarre was keen to use balalaikas. Not just a single instrument, but a whole orchestra of them. But there weren't too many balalaika players in Los Angeles, where the score was recorded. Jarre solved the problem by visiting a Russian Orthodox church one Sunday morning, where one of the congregation managed to put him in contact with a number of players. However, none of them could read music, so they had to learn their parts by ear, which were then added to the rest of the orchestra (if one listens carefully to the balalaika segments of the score, it's always the same 16 bars of the theme that are played).

Pasha Antipov (Tom Courtnay) hands out leaflets inciting revolution, much to the consternation of his future wife Lara (Julie Christie).

Lara's Theme proved an instant hit across the world for Jarre, and the subsequent soundtrack LP for the film stayed at the number one spot in America's Billboard Hit Parade for six weeks, closely followed by The Beatles' fourth album, *Revolver* (the theme also charted in Britain, reaching the number 16 spot in a song version titled *What Now, My Love?* as sung by The Mike Sammes Singers, and the number 42 spot in an instrumental conducted by Geoff Love). Yet the theme didn't come easily to Jarre, who took four attempts at it before Lean was finally happy with the results. Time was ticking while Jarre toiled. However, once he latched on to the tune, the rest of the scoring went smoothly, with the composer again making use of unorthodox instruments to pepper his music, among them a Moog synthesiser, a zither, a koto (Japanese harp), two Shamisens (Japanese banjos), a harpsichord, a novachord, a sonovox and an electric piano.

Jarre finished recording his score on 14 December, eight days before the premier. The music of course consisted of many more themes, motifs and narrative passages than *Lara's Theme*, even

The peasants attempt to keep warm during the gruelling train journey to Varykinow. Sasha (Jeffrey Rockland), Tonya (Geraldine Chaplin) and Yuri (Omar Sharif) look suitably dishevelled.

if it is this piece that everyone remembers. The most descriptive passage comes towards the end of the film as Yuri sits writing poetry in the ice palace. As he writes down the title of his first poem, Lara, Jarre cleverly accompanies the pen strokes of the name's four letters with the opening four notes from *Lara's Theme*. As Yuri then starts to work on the poem, Jarre describes in musical terms what the character is thinking as he writes. Hesitant at first as Yuri searches for the opening line of the poem, the music becomes increasingly confident and faster-paced as Yuri's ideas coalesce.

Another effective piece of music plays over the burial of Yuri's mother. After a rendition of *Kontakion*, Jarre accompanies the shovelling of the earth into the grave with four thunderous claps of music (kettle drums, tubular bells, zither) as the earth hits the coffin, adding aural shock to what is already a stunning visual. The effect is startling in both its starkness and finality.

Despite the visual beauty of *Doctor Zhivago*, the reviews were somewhat mixed. 'It is all too bad to be true; that so much has come to so little, that tears must be prompted by dashed hopes instead of enduring drama,' condemned *Newsweek*. John Simon was more humorous, writing, 'David Lean's *Doctor Zhivago* does for snow what his *Lawrence of Arabia* did for sand.' The London *Evening Standard*'s critic, Alexander Walker, jibed, 'When a director dies he becomes a photographer.' Pauline Kael was also dismissive, commenting, 'It isn't shoddy (except for the music); it isn't soap opera; it's stately, respectable and dead. Neither the contemplative Zhivago nor the flow of events is intelligible, and what is worse, they seem unrelated to each other.'

There's perhaps something to be said for Kael's last comment about the flow of events being unintelligible. At times, the plot does jump about somewhat. Still, those critics who were in favour of the film were more concerned with its beauty. The *Hollywood Reporter* said, 'A majestic, magnificent picture of war and peace, on a national scale and scaled down to the personal. It has every element to make a smash, long-run box office hit.'

That is exactly what happened. Thanks to positive word of mouth, *Doctor Zhivago* went on to make a fortune for MGM, ultimately ranking only second behind *Gone with the Wind* as the studio's most profitable film, beating even the mighty *Ben-Hur*. The film's popularity was also reflected at the Oscars, where it went on to win five awards from a healthy 10 nominations: best adapted screenplay (Robert Bolt), best colour cinematography (Freddie Young), best art direction and set decoration (John Box, Terry Marsh, Dario Simoni), best costume (Phyllis Dalton) and best music (Maurice Jarre). The film failed to win the coveted best picture award, which went to the equally popular *The Sound of Music*. Lean also lost out on a third best director Oscar, which went to Robert Wise, for *The Sound of Music*. The other losers were Tom Courtnay (best supporting actor), Norman Savage (best editing) and Franklin Milton and AW Watkins (best sound). Julie Christie won the best actress award. However, this wasn't for *Doctor Zhivago*, but for *Darling*, a film she managed to make after *Doctor Zhivago*. It also managed to pick up four Golden Globes (best motion picture drama, best director [Lean], best screenplay, best music and best actor [Omar Sharif]), yet surprisingly no BAFTAs.

To this day, *Doctor Zhivago* has a special niche in many people's hearts – and not just because of the music, scenery, photography and story. It's the performances of Omar Sharif and, moreover, Julie Christie as Lara that stay in the mind. With *Lawrence of Arabia*, it was obvious that Lean had fallen in love with the desert. With *Doctor Zhivago*, the object of his cinematic love was Julie Christie and the film is all the more remarkable for it.

Thirteen

—ɯ—

A TOUCH OF BLARNEY

Lean and Leila had endured a long separation while he concentrated on *Doctor Zhivago*, and this put a strain on their already fragile marriage. Lean's relationship with Barbara Cole was as strong as ever and they even set up a home together in Spain. It was only a matter of time before the break with Leila would come. However, so delicate was her state of mind by this time, Lean had to tread extremely carefully when handling the situation. Then came the added complication of a further love interest for Lean, one Sandy Hotz, who helped to run one of the hotels he frequented when visiting India. The upshot of all this personal drama was that Lean left Barbara Cole and took up with Hotz, although it would be over a decade before he finally divorced Leila.

During the meantime, there was the matter of finding a film with which to follow *Doctor Zhivago*. For a while Lean and Bolt toyed with the idea of resurrecting the *Gandhi* project, but again things came to nought. Other books and plays were also read, considered and discarded, until Robert Bolt came up with the idea of doing a variation on the themes found in Gustave Flaubert's *Madame Bovary*. The script went through various versions and re-writes, emerging as *Ryan's Daughter*. Set in the small village of Kirrary in western Ireland during the 1916 Troubles, it tells the story of Rosy Ryan, the daughter of a publican who falls in love with and marries her former school teacher, only to realise she's made a mistake when a handsome but shell-shocked British officer arrives at the nearby garrison.

By the time Lean and Bolt had finished with it, the story was far more complicated than this simple pastoral romance. The British officer, a Victoria Cross winner for bravery in the trenches of the Western Front, latches on to a plot by the IRA to gun run German arms. When he foils this plot, the locals, who know about Rosy's affair, assume that she has colluded with him, and so shear her hair as punishment. There is a tragic end for the officer, who commits suicide by blowing himself up. Yet despite being cuckolded, Rosy's husband stays with her in the end, and they head off for a new life together in Dublin. Add to this further subplots involving the local priest, the village idiot and Rosy's publican father, who is the true informant to the British, and you have enough material for a rich and complex film. The original intention was to produce a tightly knitted, fast-moving narrative. The end result lasted almost four hours.

Bolt had written the script for his second wife, actress Sarah Miles, whom he had in mind as Rosy. At first Lean wasn't keen on the idea, even though he'd briefly considered Miles for the part of Lara in *Doctor Zhivago*. Born in 1941, Miles had trained at RADA. She first came to public attention in the 1962 film *Term of Trial*, playing a flirty student who seduces her schoolmaster

(Laurence Olivier, who became her real life lover for a time). This she followed with *The Servant*, *Those Magnificent Men in Their Flying Machines* and *Blow Up*. She married Bolt in 1967, by which time she was considered one of Britain's leading actresses.

As Lean and Bolt worked on the script, Lean managed to persuade Anthony Havelock-Allan to produce. Although they'd remained friends, the two hadn't worked together since the dissolution of Cineguild, since when Havelock-Allan had gone on to produce *The Young Lovers*, *Othello*, *Up the Junction* and *Romeo and Juliet*. Almost two decades had passed, yet Lean and Havelock-Allan quickly settled into the old routine — as did John Mills, whom Lean cast as the village idiot Michael. It had been 15 years since he'd last been directed by Lean on *Hobson's Choice*, but the passage of time quickly evaporated, and Lean and Mills enjoyed their most fruitful collaboration on *Ryan's Daughter*.

Given Lean's commercial success with *Doctor Zhivago*, MGM was the natural studio home for *Ryan's Daughter*, although there were certain stipulations attached to the $9m investment, primarily the involvement of at least one major star name to give the film some value. Lean selected Robert Mitchum to play Rosy's ineffectual schoolteacher husband Charles Shaughnessy, which surprised many given Mitchum's tough guy persona, seen to best advantage in such films as *Out of the Past*, *The Big Steal*, *Night of the Hunter* and *Cape Fear*. Yet casting against type appealed to Lean, so Mitchum adopted an Irish accent and took the role of Charles. Little did he know that he'd be on the picture for a year when he signed on the dotted line.

Lean and Mitchum didn't get on at all, which caused much disruption to the shooting schedule, and Lean must have wished that he'd cast one of his other considerations in the role, among them Gregory Peck, George C Scott and Paul Scofield. Lean also had trouble with Christopher Jones, the actor hired to play the shell-shocked British officer, Major Randolph Doryan, to whom he turned after his preferred choice, Marlon Brando, proved unavailable owing to a conflict of schedules. Lean had spotted Jones in the thriller *The Looking Glass War*, which had been produced by his former production designer John Box. Lean hadn't realised that Jones was American and had been dubbed by another actor in the film (he was subsequently also dubbed in *Ryan's Daughter* by Julian Holloway, son of Stanley Holloway). Jones also proved somewhat somnambulistic on set, often refusing to perform. It was only afterwards that it was discovered that Jones was in deep grief over Sharon Tate, the film star wife of director Roman Polanski, with whom he had been having an affair before her murder by the Manson gang.

Mitchum and Jones may not have been easy to work with, but Lean got on fine with the rest of the cast, among them Trevor Howard, who again entered Lean's life after an almost 20-year gap, this time to play the gruff Father Hugh Collins, a role about as far as one could get from his romantic doctors in *Brief Encounter* and *The Passionate Friends*. Instead of indulging in a little extramarital activity, this time he would provide the voice of conscience as Rosy has her own brief encounter with Major Doryan.

Elsewhere the cast includes such respected names as Leo McKern (the stage and film versions of Bolt's *A Man for All Seasons*) as Tom Ryan, Rosy's publican father, Barry Foster (*The Family Way*, *Twisted Nerve*) as the IRA hero Tim O'Leary, Evin Crowley as the vindictive Moureen Cassiday and

Gerald Sim (*The Pumpkin Eater*, *King Rat*) as the cowardly Captain who signs over the garrison to Major Doryan before heading for the front.

Having won Oscars for both *Lawrence of Arabia* and *Doctor Zhivago*, it was inevitable that Freddie Young would return to photograph *Ryan's Daughter*, which he did in 70mm. Also back on board were camera operator Ernie Day (who'd operated for Young on *Lawrence of Arabia* and *Doctor Zhivago*), editor Norman Savage and composer Maurice Jarre. Given that John Box was – at least at the time – now producing his own films, Lean turned to production designer Stephen Grimes (*Reflections in a Golden Eye*) to build the village of Kirrary, which he did, complete with church, from scratch on the Dingle Peninsula in western Ireland.

The location may have been breathtaking, but the area suffered some of the wettest weather in the country, all of which caused delay after delay to the shooting of the picture. So much so that not only did the unit have to go to Cape Town in South Africa to capture some of the beach scenes, but a bluebell wood also had to be created in a small studio for close-ups of Rosy and Doryan's main love scene, so bad had the weather become.

The only time Lean and the crew welcomed the poor weather was during the filming of the storm sequence, during which a German boat drops off palettes of arms for the IRA, which the villagers run to help Tim O'Leary and his comrade O'Keefe (Niall Tiobin) rescue before they smash up on the rocks. Lean had intended the scene to be the storm sequence to end all storm sequences, and in this ambition he certainly succeeded, aided by the contributions of second unit directors Roy Stevens and Charles Frend (the latter having worked with Lean as an editor on *Major Barbara* before becoming a respected director in his own right with *The Cruel Sea* and *The Long Arm*). Shooting was a treacherous affair for all concerned, while the driving rain caused problems with the cameras. Freddie Young solved these by using a revolving glass screen directly in front of the lens – akin to the Clear Screens used on ships – which immediately dispersed any water, including a direct hit from a wave.

By the time Lean returned from South Africa, filming was all but finished. Now lay ahead the Herculean task of editing down a year's footage and adding the score. The result is one of Lean's most visually romantic films.

The opening credit sequence is played over some spectacular shots of forming clouds, after which we're straight into the action, as we see Rosy walking along the cliffs, a solitary figure dwarfed by the enormity of the landscape. Her parasol is caught by a gust of wind and goes flying into the atmosphere, only to be caught in the waves below by Father Collins, who's been out fishing for lobster with Michael.

Rosy runs down to the beach to retrieve her parasol from Father Collins. It turns out she's been waiting for the school teacher, Charles Shaughnessy, to return from his trip to Dublin where he's been for a conference, only she tells Father Collins she's simply idling her time away. 'Doin' nothin's a dangerous occupation,' scolds Father Collins, on which Lean cuts to the nearby village, where indeed the youngsters are doing nothing, which seems to be the main occupation in Kirrary. Until, that is, Michael comes along with one of the lobsters he and Father Collins have caught, only to find his catch used as a football in an impromptu game.

David Lean and ace cinematographer Freddie Young line up a shot during the making of Ryan's Daughter. *Young would win his third Oscar for the film.*

Rosy finally gets to greet Mr Shaughnessy on the beach – all the main character introductions are done on the beach in a sequence of scenes lasting almost 20 minutes – and from the outset it's obvious that Rosy has a crush on her former school teacher, although Shaughnessy doesn't seem to see this. Or perhaps he chooses not to, for he leaves Rosy on the beach to go and pay respects to his wife in the cemetery on the dunes. Left alone on the beach, Rosy wanders along, placing her feet in the footprints left by Charles. Rosy is determined to get her man, and so hot foots it to the schoolhouse, where she waits for Shaughnessy to return. He does, and in a clever touch, we hear – but do not see – him enter the rooms next to the classroom, for Lean focuses the camera on the partitioning wall, and we follow the action via sound through the wall. Charles eventually enters the classroom, where he's surprised to find Rosy, whom he presumes has come to help lay out the class for the next day. But Rosy finally has the courage to tell Charles that she loves him. It transpires that her attention has not been wasted at all, and the couple kiss.

Next, we're introduced to the film's subplot with the arrival of IRA hero Tim O'Leary and his comrade O'Keefe, who are gun-running. As they drive their horse and cart across the countryside, they're spotted by a local copper, who they subsequently shoot dead for fear of being reported, hiding his body, along with the cart, down a disused mineshaft. Again, sound effects are cleverly used as we hear the cart fall down the mineshaft, seemingly taking forever to reach the bottom, which it does with a great noise, followed by a cloud of dust shooting out at the top.

Rosy and Charles are now set to wed, and it falls to Father Collins to tell Rosy a little about the facts of life. It seems that Rosy is under the impression that sexual congress with her husband-to-be will be a life-altering experience. 'What are you expecting?' asks Father Collins. A shot of hovering gulls follows. 'Wings, is it?!'

O'Leary and O'Keefe, who are posing as tinkers, arrive in Kirrary ('If they're two tinkers, I'm the Bishop of Cork,' comments Father Collins). It's Rosy's wedding day, as O'Leary discovers when he and O'Keefe call in at Ryan's pub for a drink, where they spot a photograph of Ryan with O'Leary taken in Dublin some years earlier. Ryan being a boastful sort of chap shows off the photo to the two men without realising that he's speaking to O'Leary, who's more than a little disgusted at hearing Ryan blab so easily ('Talk – this whole cursed country will capsize with talk!').

Rosy and Charles' wedding reception follows, and Lean almost presents Rosy as the Virgin Mary as she sits at the top table with her new husband, the locals meanwhile jigging away to the music, making the most of the celebrations. Finally, it comes time for Rosy and Charles to make their way upstairs, although not after all the men have tried to kiss the bride goodnight – including the unfortunate Michael, who Rosy inevitably rejects in horror. Upstairs in the bedroom, we're treated to a scene not dissimilar to the wedding night scene in *Hobson's Choice*, although here the fumbling and uncertainty is played straight. The villagers downstairs seem to think it's a laughing matter, for when Charles turns out the light, they throw grain up at the window and shout, 'Charles, how you gettin' on?'

Charles makes love to Rosy, and in one of his most unsubtle pieces, Lean cuts to the fiddle player downstairs, his bow going up and down in a somewhat suggestive manner. The act of lovemaking proves a disappointment to Rosy and she and Charles fall asleep back to back. An ill omen for the marriage indeed. Consequently, Rosy concentrates her energies in married life to turning Charles' rooms at the schoolhouse into a home, and soon the couple have settled into a routine of unexciting domesticity, she sewing and he pressing flowers (for which read his stifling of her). Rosy expresses her doubt about the marriage to Father Collins, who gives her a slap for being so ungrateful for what she has. He also warns her, 'Don't nurse your wishes, or sure to God, you'll get what you're wishing for.' At which Lean cuts to the arrival of Major Doryan.

Like Michael, Doryan has a bad leg, which he received through injuries at the front. Unlike Michael, however, Doryan is extremely handsome, and as he is driven from the bus stop to the garrison, it seems inevitable that he and Rosy will at some point meet (as the truck drives past the schoolhouse, he notices her red bloomers hanging on the washing line). However, Doryan isn't entirely welcome at the garrison. Comments one of the soldiers, 'That's all we're short of here – a crippled bloody hero.' The departing Captain fills in Doryan on the local scene, telling him that

The cuckolded Charles Shaughnessy (Robert Mitchum) follows the footprints of his wife and Major Doryan along the beach in Ryan's Daughter.

the local publican, Ryan, is an informer, while if it's crumpet he's after he'd better think again: 'It's married or virgin here.' We also discover that Doryan suffers from shell shock. Bad enough in itself, this is compounded by the fact that the garrison's generator sounds like gunfire as it powers up.

Realising that the audience is probably already one step ahead regarding Doryan's affair with Rosy, Lean quickly cuts to the chase. Doryan makes his way to the pub for a drink ('Peg leg,' taunts Moureen Cassiday as he walks down the street). Rosy is minding the bar, and it's clear that, as she serves him, she finds him attractive. Michael is the only other customer in the place, and as he sits in the corner, he begins to bash his boot again the settle (accompanied by a burst of military-style music from Maurice Jarre's score), the noise of which sets off Doryan's shakes. Rosy quickly ushers Michael out of the place and locks the door. Lean cuts to a shell exploding, followed by Doryan diving for cover in a trench. He cuts to a close-up of Doryan, surrounded by darkness. Rosy's hand enters the shot, gently calming him. Doryan looks up, and they kiss. The background fades up and we're back in the bar, and the romance has started. A brilliantly economic sequence told purely in visual terms, it displays Lean's cinematic talent at its best.

Ryan returns, having bought Rosy a blood mare at the fair, providing her with an excuse to go off riding and secretly meet Doryan behind her husband's back. That night, Rosy's horse calls out to Doryan's horse at the garrison, after which we hear the generator gear up. Lean cuts to close-ups of Rosy and Doryan, and it's obvious that they are thinking about each other. Again, a word isn't said in this sequence, yet the message is clearly and cleverly conveyed.

Next day, Rosy and Doryan meet by the crumbling tower on top of the cliffs, and Doryan takes her into the woods to make love to her. It's obvious from Lean's use of close-ups, including the use of wind blowing through the leaves of the trees, that Rosy has finally got her wings. Later, back at home, Rosy lies to Charles about her meeting with Doryan, telling him that she took a fall on the horse and that Doryan helped her. 'The mare's not properly broke,' she tells him. Charles cottons on that something is not right, and he asks her, 'Rose, you'd never be unfaithful to me?' Her lie comes easily, for the deed has already been done.

Charles' suspicions are confirmed when, taking his class down to the beach to search for cuttlefish shells, he sees two sets of footprints on the beach. One set is obviously a woman's, while the other leaves a drag in the sand. Charles puts two and two together and follows the prints, imagining Rosy and Doryan together. Later, back at home, Charles not only discovers particles of sand in the brim of Rosy's riding hat (despite her claims that she's been riding on the moors), he also finds a shell Doryan gave on the beach hidden in her underwear drawer. It seems that Charles is the last to know of Rosy's infidelities. The whole village is buzzing with the affair, as Rosy also discovers when she gets short shrift at the local store. 'The way I see it,' says Mrs McCardle, the owner, 'there's loose women, there's whores and there's British soldiers' whores!'

But distraction is soon after at hand. Tim O'Leary and his men turn up at Ryan's pub. A German boat is expected to drop off a shipment of arms that night and they've come to pick up the rafts from the beach as the tide brings them ashore. To make sure their operation goes unnoticed, the local constable is bound and gagged and Ryan is told to cut the telephone wires, which he does, although not before calling the garrison to inform on O'Leary and his men. We then cut to the film's most spectacular sequence, the storm. A superb montage of howling wind, driving rain and gigantic waves crashing into sand and rock, it displays the violent force of nature in breathtaking style.

Realising what's happening, Father Collins and all the villagers turn out on the beach to help O'Leary and his men retrieve the arms. One of the schoolchildren meanwhile rushes to tell Charles and Rosy what's going on, and they too head for the beach to watch the spectacle. However, as O'Leary and his men are about to leave in their truck, Doryan and his men turn up to arrest them. O'Leary makes a run for it, but Doryan is too quick for him. Jumping up on to the roof of an army truck, he shoots the escaping O'Leary in the leg, bringing him down. Unfortunately, the sound of the gunshot brings on his shakes. Without realising what she's doing,

Fag break. David Lean and John Mills, in full character make-up, take a break outside Mrs McCardle's grocery store during the filming of Ryan's Daughter.

Rosy rushes to comfort him, much to the surprise of the crowd (Moureen Cassiday laughs with almost orgasmic glee – this will provide her with gossip for years!).

O'Leary has been stretchered back to the army truck, where he delivers the film's most telling line to Doryan: 'Get out of my country!' Many of Lean's films have contained hints of anti-Britishness (*Bridge Over the River Kwai*, *Lawrence of Arabia*, *A Passage to India*), although this is its most vehement. 'What'll they do to them?' an old woman asks Father Collins of the fate of O'Leary and his men. Comes the simple reply, 'They'll hang 'em!'

That night, Rosy leaves the marital bed to be with Doryan. As they meet and kiss on the hill at the back of the schoolhouse, Maurice Jarre's music swells, only to stop abruptly as Lean cuts back to Charles, who is watching the couple from a back window. Unable to stand the humiliation any longer, he disappears on to the beach in his nightgown, leaving Rosy to take class the next morning. But many of the children leave ('My father says I'm not to speak to you'). However, when Charles returns, Rosy tells him that the affair is finally over, despite the fact that nothing has been said between herself and Doryan ('As close as that, are you?' Charles asks incredulously).

The villagers want revenge for the arrest of Tim O'Leary and his men, believing it was Rosy who betrayed them to the British. Rosy is dragged into the schoolyard, stripped and shorn, her father unable and unwilling to tell the truth in order to save her the humiliation. Meanwhile, down on the beach, Doryan comes across Michael, who has found some explosives washed up on the shore. Deciding to end it all, Doryan uses the explosives to blow himself up, killing himself just as the sun is setting on the horizon (this is one of the sequences for which the unit went to South Africa). However, Lean doesn't show the explosion, he cuts back to Charles, who is striking a match in his quarters so as to light an oil lamp. As in *Lawrence of Arabia*, the match is shown in giant close-up, although instead of marking the beginning of a new day in the desert, here it marks the end of a day – and a life – on the beach.

There's little point in Rosy and Charles remaining in Kirrary now, and so they decide to move away to Dublin, and despite – or perhaps because of – their troubles, it looks likely that they will stay together. As they wait with Michael and Father Collins for their bus to arrive, Rosy's hat blows off in the wind, revealing her shorn and cut head, much to Michael's astonishment. It seems that Rosy, whom Michael has idolised, isn't so perfect after all. When the bus finally arrives, Father Collins offers Charles a parting word, that despite indications to the contrary, he doesn't believe Charles and Rosy will separate. 'That's my parting gift to you – that doubt.' The bus drives off over the hill, taking Rosy and Charles to a new beginning.

With a running time of 196 minutes, *Ryan's Daughter* is an epic production, despite the basic simplicity of its story line. Perhaps more than any other of Lean's films, it's the detail that matters here, and the director wallows in technique, to the point that the story almost becomes irrelevant. Lean takes his time over every sequence in the film, although this isn't to imply that the film is slow moving or dull. There's simply too much for the eye and ear to take in for that to be the case, even though Lean could effectively have told the story in half the running time. Had that been the case, however, we would have lost the myriad of intimate touches, the accumulation of which make *Ryan's Daughter* the joy it is to experience. The critics of the day, however, didn't see it that way. The cinema of the late Sixties and early Seventies, it seemed, had moved on from the kind of well-crafted epics Lean made, and had instead adopted the more youthful, guerrilla-style of filmmaking found in *Easy Rider*.

When it was released worldwide in December 1970, *Ryan's Daughter* was attacked from all sides. 'Instead of looking like the money it cost to make, the film feels like the time it took to shoot,' sniped Alexander Walker in the London *Evening Standard*, to which *The Sun* added, 'It's an all-star six million quid bore.' *The Times* was also dismissive, commenting that the film was, 'Too bad even to be funny.' *Variety* was slightly more upbeat, describing the film as being, 'A brilliant enigma. Brilliant because director David Lean achieves to a marked degree the daring and obvious goal of intimate romantic tragedy along the rugged geographical and political landscape of Ireland in 1916. An enigma because its overlength of perhaps 30 minutes serves to magnify some weakness of Robert Bolt's original screenplay, and to overwhelm [the] outstanding photography and production.'

Worse was to come. *New Yorker* critic Pauline Kael described *Ryan's Daughter* as being little more than, 'Gush made respectable by millions of dollars tastefully wasted.' She also went on to attack Lean's, 'gentleman-technician's tastefully colossal style,' criticising his films for having, 'a gleaming pictorial look, a prepared look,' and that, 'everything is posing for a photograph.' True, perhaps, but what photographs!

If this wasn't bad enough, Lean was invited to attend a meeting of the National Society of Film Critics in New York, attended by Kael and Richard Schickel, at which he found himself the subject of a brutal verbal attack. Lean was mortified, so much so that he lost all faith in himself as a director, mostly thanks to Pauline Kael's abusive attitude. Thus began a period of self-exile for the director, Lean didn't direct a feature again for almost 14 years, despite the fact that *Ryan's Daughter* played in one London cinema for over a year and went on to earn four Oscar nominations: best actress (Sarah Miles), best supporting actor (John Mills), best photography (Freddie Young) and best sound (Gordon K McCallum and John Bramall), of which it won two: best cinematography (richly deserved) and best supporting actor.

Fourteen

THE LONG RETURN TO TRIUMPH

In his 14-year absence from the screen, David Lean didn't exactly fritter away his time, nor is it true that he didn't at least try to set up a film, despite the blow the dismissive reviews for *Ryan's Daughter* gave his confidence. At first, he turned his attention to travel, taking in America, Europe, India, New Zealand, the Middle East, Tahiti and Africa, travelling by plane, boat and, more often than not, car (his beloved Rolls Royce went practically everywhere with him, despite the cost of transporting it). He also bought a house in Rome, which he shared with his lover Sandy Hotz, using it as a base from which to travel.

It was during this period that Lean also became re-acquainted with his family, in particular his brother Edward, of whom he had seen little owing to the long periods of time he had been away on location making films. Sadly, not only was Edward to die (in 1974), so too did Lean's father (in 1973, at the ripe old age of 95).

Yet despite being away from the cameras, film-making can't have been too far from Lean's mind, for there was yet another attempt to set up the *Gandhi* project the year after *Ryan's Daughter* opened. Again, it came to nothing.

During this time, many of Lean's associates continued to work. Robert Bolt turned to directing in 1972 with *Lady Caroline Lamb*, which he again penned for his wife, Sarah Miles. A solid historical drama co-starring John Mills and Ralph Richardson, it is very much in the Lean style (the film was photographed by Lean's former camera operator Oswald Morris and edited by Norman Savage, who died not long after completing it). Meanwhile, Freddie Young worked on the Sam Spiegel-produced *Nicholas and Alexandra*, which was designed by John Box, who won another Oscar for his efforts. Young also photographed a television remake of *Great Expectations*, which had originally been intended as a musical. As it was, it was scored by Maurice Jarre. Carlo Ponti was also involved in a television remake of one of Lean's old classics, *Brief Encounter*, starring his wife Sophia Loren and Richard Burton in the Celia Johnson and Trevor Howard roles (Loren may have missed out on playing Lara in *Doctor Zhivago*, but at least she had now made a David Lean film of sorts).

In addition to the failed *Gandhi* project, Lean had also considered making a biopic about Captain Cook and his discovery of Australia. Instead, he eventually channelled his energies into another Pacific-set story, a re-telling of *The Mutiny on the Bounty*, based on Richard Hough's 1972 revisionist version of events, *Captain Bligh and Mr Christian*. By now the year was 1977, and the kind of films Lean was known for were no longer vogue, the latest trend being for science fiction thanks to the success of *Star Wars*. Still, Lean and Robert Bolt made for Bora-Bora in the South Pacific to work on the script, which they managed to interest Warner Bros in producing.

Like *Ryan's Daughter*, however, what started out as a comparatively modest production quickly blossomed into a full-blown Lean epic, involving the building of a Bounty replica, to be designed by John Box. Unfortunately, Lean and Bolt scuppered their chances of getting the film off the ground when they insisted on doing the story as a two-parter. With the budget already spiralling for the original single film, Warners balked and Lean refused to compromise. Subsequently, in 1977, Italian producer Dino de Laurentiis, a former partner of Carlo Ponti and now successful producer on the international scene in his own right, agreed to take on the two-part project, tentatively titled *The Lawbreakers* and *The Long Arm*. De Laurentiis was certainly no stranger to big-budget epics, having produced *Barabbas*, *The Bible* and *Waterloo*, so finding upwards of $40m to finance the two proposed films didn't phase him in the slightest. After all, the year before he'd blown $20m on a dismal remake of *King Kong*, and would do the same again with a misguided remake of *Hurricane*, also being shot in Bora-Bora at the same time Lean and Bolt were working on their script.

While Lean and Bolt continued to work, the go ahead was finally given to build the Bounty replica. It would seem there was now no turning back. Yet despite the pressures to finish the scripts, Lean nevertheless found time to devote energy to a parallel project. A television documentary entitled *Lost and Found*, it chronicled the discovery of one of Captain Cook's anchors, lost in 1773, but miraculously found by Lean's propman Eddie Fowlie, who was also out in the Pacific with Lean and Bolt, prepping the Bounty films. Given Lean's fascination with the subject, he agreed to bankroll the raising of the anchor out of his own pocket, to the tune of $10,000. He also agreed to narrate the accompanying film, to be financed by South Pacific TV. Produced by George Andrews and directed by Wayne Tourell (with more than a little assistance from Lean), the 40-minute film has been little seen outside New Zealand and Australia, although *Variety*, who managed to review it, dismissed the effort as lacking, 'signs that it is the work of a major cinematic talent.' Such a put-down can only have undermined Lean's confidence at the time, given that he hadn't directed a feature for almost a decade and was about to embark on what was proving to be his most expensive project.

Sadly, the vast budgetary over-runs accrued by *Hurricane* (whose original director, Roman Polanski, had been replaced by Jan Troell) were to have a knock-on effect on Lean's project. Complex behind-the-scenes financial and contractual wrangling followed, the upshot being that Lean had to find a new backer for the film, while at the same time taking over the cost of the pre-production to date from de Laurentiis, which came to almost $2m. If Lean failed in this quest, Bolt's scripts would become the property of de Laurentiis, who was still paying the writer for his (and Lean's unofficial) continuing work on them. For a while, American producer Joseph E Levine, a man in the de Laurentiis mould who had produced such costly blockbusters as *The Carpetbaggers* and *A Bridge Too Far*, expressed an interest in taking over the two scripts. Despite great contractual compromises by Lean, the association came to nothing. Lean managed to interest United Artists in the scripts. Unfortunately, just as *Hurricane* was causing de Laurentiis financial problems, so too was

Michael Cimino's epic western *Heaven's Gate* causing headaches for United Artists. Seeing financial problems ahead, United Artists also jumped ship.

It was at this point that Lean, by now desperate, turned to his old sparring partner Sam Spiegel. Robert Bolt then suffered a heart attack followed by a stroke. Unable to work, Lean now had to find a new writer to take over the scripts. This he did, taking on author and television producer Melvyn Bragg (known in Britain for LWT's *The South Bank Show*). Lean also had to face the fact that two films were untenable. Work proceeded to tell the story in one epic film.

Lean didn't feel this new script to be what he was after and so proceeded by himself, finishing work in late 1979. Spiegel was dithering about the project, while Dino de Laurentiis, thanks to a new deal brokered with Paramount, was interested again. After all the effort, legal wrangling and emotional hardship, Lean had come full circle. With Spiegel now out of the frame and Lean unwilling to team up with de Laurentiis again, he instead turned to producer Arnon Milchan, then on the cusp of making *Once Upon a Time in America*, *Brazil* and *Legend*. Milchan managed to get United Artists interested again, but *Heaven's Gate* quickly destroyed any hope. So out of control did *Heaven's Gate* become that it bankrupted the studio.

Exhausted by the whole experience, Lean jumped ship. Dino de Laurentiis did go on to produce a single film version of *The Bounty* based on Bolt's script, which the author worked on having recovered from his stroke. The film, directed by New Zealander Roger Donaldson (then known chiefly for such local films as *Sleeping Dogs* and *Smash Palace*), didn't see the light of day until 1984. Although it looks good thanks to Arthur Ibbetson's photography, and has an intriguing cast (Anthony Hopkins as Bligh, Mel Gibson as Christian, not to mention such supporting players as Laurence Olivier, Daniel Day Lewis, Liam Neeson and Edward Fox), it was not a major success. 'This misshapen movie doesn't work as an epic,' commented Pauline Kael, hitting the nail on the head, to which the *Monthly Film Bulletin* added, 'A long voyage to nowhere.' The great David Lean film that never was, one can only imagine what his version would have been like.

Lean turned his attention to a production of Karen Blixen's *Out of Africa*, but again stumbled at the starting post. The film would go on to be made by the respected American director Sydney Pollack (*The Way We Were*, *Tootsie*), who would win an Oscar for his efforts (the film won a total of seven Oscars). Instead, at the suggestion of producer John Brabourne, Lean turned his attention to the works of EM Forster, being captured by one book in particular, *A Passage to India*. Lean had always had a passion for India. Ironically, Lean and the increasingly unstable Leila had finally been divorced in 1978, leaving the door open for the director to marry Sandy Hotz, which he finally did on Wednesday 28 October 1981. It was Sandy not Leila with whom he would return to India to make, what he didn't know at the time, would be his last film.

Forster's novel, published in 1924, had already been the subject of a stage adaptation by Santha Rama Rau, featuring Zia Mohyeddin. Lean had seen this production in London some time in 1960

Back in the director's chair. David Lean observes the action in the Marabar Hills during the filming of A Passage to India.

and subsequently cast Mohyeddin as Tafas in *Lawrence of Arabia*. This stage production was in turn was adapted for television in 1965. Directed for the BBC by Waris Hussein, it again featured Zia Mohyeddin, along with Cyril Cussack, Sybil Thorndike and Virginia McKenna. As produced by Peter Luke for the channel's *Play of the Month*, it earned some respectable reviews ('I feel half-inclined to rave about it,' commented Maurice Richardson in *The Observer*).

Inspired by Forster's own experiences in India in the early Twenties, the novel follows a visit to the country by an impressionable Englishwoman, Adela Quested, who has travelled there to visit her husband-to-be, Ronny, who is a magistrate. Accompanied on the trip by Ronny's mother, Mrs Moore, Adela is determined on seeing something of the real India, as opposed to the gentrification of it by the English.

After a meeting with a teacher, Mr Fielding, at a bridge party, Adela gets her wish, and is introduced to a local doctor, Aziz, who subsequently invites Adela and Mrs Moore on a trip to the mysterious Marabar Caves. However, it is following a trek to one of the more remote caves with Aziz that Adela is discovered running down the mountainside in great distress. From what her friends can discern, Adela has been raped by Aziz, who is subsequently arrested. Fielding suspects something is amiss about Adela's accusation, and so gives his support to Aziz, much to the consternation of the English. Events come to a head in a court case, the outcome of which takes all concerned by surprise.

Despite pleas from many top directors, Forster wouldn't release the film rights to *A Passage to India* during his lifetime. It wasn't until 11 years after his death in 1970 that John Brabourne was able to secure the rights for himself and his partner Richard Goodwin, with whom he'd had success with such films as Franco Zeffirelli's *Romeo and Juliet* (produced with Anthony Havelock-Allan), *Tales of Beatrix Potter*, *Murder on the Orient Express* and *Death on the Nile*. A script, by Santha Rama Rau was commissioned, and Brabourne and Goodwin set about securing a director, hence Brabourne's suggestion that Lean read the novel.

Although enthused by Rau's initial work, Lean proceeded to work on a new version of the script alone. The arduous experience of writing the *Mutiny on the Bounty* scripts with Robert Bolt had no doubt taken its toll, and Lean felt compelled to crack the novel himself. There was certainly no approach to Bolt to help him with the screenplay. In any case, Bolt was at work adapting the *Mutiny on the Bounty* scripts (again) for the Dino de Laurentiis film, which he would follow with an original script about two 18th Century Jesuit priests in the jungles of South America entitled *The Mission*. Lean ploughed ahead by himself, streamlining the book and solidifying some of its more ambiguous moments, making the events cinematic rather than literary or theatrical. He even added several scenes not in the Forster novel, most notably Adela's discovery, while cycling alone in the Indian countryside, of an ancient temple covered with erotic statues, the sight of which, we subsequently discover, has aroused her seemingly dormant sexuality.

Given the length of time Lean had been away from the screen, coupled with his reputation for being a perfectionist, John Brabourne and Richard Goodwin found *A Passage to India* a difficult project to finance. However, after much wheeling and dealing, they secured the film's budget through a number of companies, among them HBO, EMI and Columbia. With the script completed and the scene now set for Lean's comeback, pre-production began in earnest, the first step being to scout locations and start designing sets, the latter job being placed in the capable hands of John Box, whose biggest challenge was to build a large section of the city of Chandrapore, which he did in the grounds of an obliging maharaja in Bangalore.

Also returning to the Lean fold after the long absence was composer Maurice Jarre, prop and effects man Eddie Fowlie, sound editor Winston Ryder and camera operator Ernest Day, who was now promoted to lighting cameraman, presumably because Lean felt Freddie Young, then in his early 80s, was too old for the job (despite the fact that Lean himself would hit 75 during filming). Only one of Lean's old friends found himself in the cast. This was Alec Guinness, who was brought in to play the Brahmin, Professor Godbole. The rest of the cast was filled with actors new to Lean, among them Peggy Ashcroft as Mrs Moore, James Fox as Fielding, Nigel Havers as Ronny, Judy Davis as Adela Quested and Victor Banerjee as Dr Aziz.

Of these actors, Lean was most keen to work with Peggy Ashcroft (a fellow Croydonian), although at first the actress, whose screen appearances were rare (*The Wandering Jew* for Maurice Elvey, *The Thirty-Nine Steps* for Hitchcock, *The Nun's Story* for Zinnemann), demurred, having already spent a considerable period of time in India making the epic television drama *The Jewel in the Crown*. Lean was very persuasive and the actress relented. As did James Fox who, since making *Performance* back in 1970, had only made one film, *Runners*, which was released in 1983, making his absence from the screen almost as long as Lean's. Australian-born Judy Davis had meanwhile made a name for herself in such films as *My Brilliant Career* (which won her a BAFTA for best actress) and *Winter of Our Dreams*, while Victor Banerjee was a newcomer to British films. As too was one Sandy Hotz, who Lean coaxed into playing Stella, Mrs Moore's daughter whom Fielding ends up marrying.

The shoot for *A Passage to India* was not a troubled one technically, but personally it had its ups and downs. Despite his lengthy absence from the screen and the occasional self-doubt that accompanied this, Lean was in his element, and pictorially the film ranks among his very best. The performances are uniformly good too, although it's common knowledge that on this film in particular, Lean had run-ins with several members of the cast, most notably Judy Davis, who felt that his vision of her role, from which he wouldn't waver, restricted her own interpretation of the part.

Following the titles, played over a series of murals, Lean opens the picture with an overhead shot of a sea of black umbrellas in a wet London street. We then cut to a shot of Adela Quested as she looks through the window of a travel agent. It is here that her adventure begins, for she books a passage to India for herself and Mrs Moore. It is also here that she gets the first glimpse of what the future might hold for her, for while the clerk is writing out the tickets, she looks at a number of pictures on the wall depicting the Marabar Caves. The scene is brief, but masterfully written, directed and edited, for in it Lean sets up the whole film, lays down Adela's reasons for travelling to India and gives us a foretaste of what she is to find there.

The scene concludes with a comment from the clerk. 'You should have an interesting voyage. The Viceroy's on board. Tends to liven things up.' One of Lean's famous cuts follows, for next we see Adela and Mrs Moore arriving in India on board their steamer. It's a grand affair with cheering crowds, streamers and confetti, and marching bands, all out to receive the returning Viceroy and his wife, who glide through the tumult with impeccable poise. The shots of them walking up through the Gateway of India and then sitting motionless and emotionless in their carriage would be the visual highlights of many another film. Here, they are segments of a stunningly framed montage in a film barely five minutes into its running time.

Lean then contrasts the calm and collected arrival of the Viceroy with that of the other passengers, who have to battle through the crowds of baggage handlers, street hawkers and beggars. This is Adela and Mrs Moore's introduction to the real India, and already Mrs Moore seems overwhelmed by the heat and the bustle. But in the scene, Lean has deftly made his point, contrasting the life of everyday Indians with that of the British, who seem to notice little of their surroundings, preferring to cocoon themselves in their own world, a careful recreation of life back home. Lean makes this point again and again throughout the film, building irony upon irony in his use of this always effective device. In fact the crowds of Indians aside, Adela and Mrs Moore could be arriving at an English port, so complete has the colonisation by the British been. So much so that it seems quite natural for Mrs Moore to say to the driver of their carriage, 'Now, Victoria Station,' from which we cut to interior shots of the station, which could well be the London terminus of its namesake.

We follow Adela and Mrs Moore on their train journey to Chandrapore, on which they are joined by Mr Turton, The Collector/Chief Administrator (Richard Wilson) and his wife (Antonia Pemberton), both of whom seem unable to hide their distaste for both India and the Indians. Yet despite their barely disguised racism, which manifests itself in their superior attitude, they are amusing characters, sublimely unaware of the offence they are causing. When Mrs Moore professes to wanting to meet some Indians during her trip, the Turtons' response is total disdain, which they voice in the old cliché, 'East is east.' This certainly seems to be the case as Lean then contrasts the luxurious sleeping quarters of Adela and Mrs Moore with those of a group of poor Indians sleeping rough on the platform of a remote station. To make sure the point is clear, there is even a close-up of a huddled Indian, coughing in the night cold. Lean also shows the vastness of the continent through which Mrs Moore and Adela are travelling with several wide-angle shots of the train passing over vast plains. Adela and Mrs Moore, it seems, are merely specks in the wider picture.

Next day the train pulls in at Chandrapore where there is a crowd and band out to greet the Turtons. It's here that Adela meets her fiancé Ronny (Nigel Havers), whom we learn is a rather straight-laced magistrate. The car journey to Ronny's home follows via the local bazaar, in which we're introduced to Dr Aziz, when Turton's car knocks him and his friend Ali (Art Malik) off their bicycles. The Turton's driver doesn't stop to see if the two men are alright. Meanwhile, as Ronny's car makes its way through the bazaar, Adela and Mrs Moore get another taste of the real India, as Lean tracks his cameras past stalls of brightly coloured spices, as well as a funeral procession ('Is that a body?' Adela enquires). The sound recording during this brief sequence is absolutely superb, perfectly capturing the atmosphere of the bazaar, even down to a curious echo as the cars pass through a stone archway (a hint of the echoes to come in the caves?).

Dr Aziz (Victor Banerjee) does his Douglas Fairbanks impersonation in A Passage to India. *Banerjee performed the stunt for real over a 100ft gorge.*

Ronny's home could very well be in the home counties, so perfectly English is the decor and furniture, and Mrs Moore's subsequent tour of the local community – the church, the hospital, the war memorial, the barracks – also seems to indicate that the British seem to think they're living somewhere near Tunbridge Wells. The tour is capped by a visit to the club, where Adela and Mrs Moore are treated (or rather subjected) to a show. A delightful scene, it shows the Brits at their ghastly worst, much to Adela's disappointment, for she still harbours hopes of meeting some real Indians. Says Mrs Moore, 'My dear, life rarely gives us what we want at the moment we consider appropriate. Adventures do occur, but not punctually.'

However, a small adventure for Mrs Moore does occur punctually, for she steps out from the club for some fresh air, and wanders over to a nearby temple, where Dr Aziz is praying. At first he thinks Mrs Moore is a ghost – Lean certainly suggests she has an ethereal quality throughout the film – only to then reprimand her for entering the temple. But she has rightly removed her shoes. Aziz apologises, telling her that most Englishwomen wouldn't bother if they didn't think anyone was watching. 'God is watching,' replies Mrs Moore, at which she and Aziz become more friendly.

Together in the moonlight they look out over the Ganges. 'Sometimes I have seen a body float past,' says Aziz, adding to the mystical quality of the scene.

There is certainly nothing mystical about the bridge party that follows. Arranged by the Turtons to 'bridge' the gap between the Indians and the British, it is their attempt to introduce Adela and Mrs Moore to the locals. Unfortunately, the result is like a garden party at Buckingham Palace, with a band playing *Tea for Two* as everyone, immaculately dressed, sips tea and pretends to have an interest in each other. 'They hate it as much as we do,' says Mrs Turton in perhaps her most prescient statement. Disgusted by the spectacle, Mrs Moore tells Ronny, 'My only consolation is that Mrs Turton will soon be retiring to a villa in Tunbridge Wells' – possibly with Mr Dryden as a neighbour!

Adela and Mrs Moore finally get to meet some 'real' Indians soon after, when Mr Fielding invites them to a party of his own, attended by Dr Aziz and Professor Godbole. It is here that Aziz invites the Englishwomen to a trip to see the Marabar Caves. This shocks not only Ronny, but also the friends of Aziz, who know this is an extravagance he can ill afford. It is Ronny's superior attitude about Aziz and the trip that finally compels Adela to tell him she doesn't want to marry him anymore. She does this at a polo match, and Lean times the news to coincide with one of the players taking a fall from his horse, which helps to convey the impact.

Next comes a little adventure for Adela, for as she's riding by herself through the local countryside, she comes across a narrow pathway, which she decides to explore. Down it she discovers a derelict temple, covered in erotic statues. Through her reaction to the statues – and a brilliant piece of descriptive music by Maurice Jarre – we realise that something has been awakened in her. The scene comes to startling conclusion when Adela is chased from the shrine by a pack of monkeys. What she has seen has clearly had an effect of her, for it is soon after this experience that she tells Ronny she will marry him after all. This short sequence relays in visual terms Adela's feelings, without having to resort to prose or dialogue. In a bid to drive home the effect of the experience at the temple has had on her, Lean later shows Adela lying in bed – the net curtains billowing in the night breeze and the smell of frangipani heavy in the air – with her thinking of the statues, shots of which he cuts to as she lies dozing. A quietly erotic scene, it is Lean the director and editor working at his best.

The story soon after switches into high gear with the visit to the Marabar Caves, for which everyone has to rise early. Unfortunately, owing to Godbole's extended prayers, Fielding and the Brahmin miss the train (Godbole sees the barrier coming down across the road as an ill omen), although Fielding vows to catch up with the party later. The train journey up the mountains affords Lean the opportunity to show us some spectacular scenery, and when the train passes over a particularly vertiginous precipice, he has Aziz making his way along the side of the train, Douglas Fairbanks-style, to the carriage where Adela and Mrs Moore are having their breakfast, which is being prepared by the toilet by a servant ('Rather a strange place to do the cooking,' comments Mrs Moore, producing perhaps the biggest laugh in the film).

Once the expedition has reached base camp, Aziz unveils his surprise – a painted elephant, on which he, Adela and Mrs Moore, followed by the rest of the party, make the journey to the caves

Mrs Moore (Peggy Ashcroft) arrives in Chandrapore. The role won Ashcroft a richly deserved Oscar.

themselves. This parade begins in grand style in a small village, with the locals cheering the spectacle, although it's not long before the party is in the quiet of the mountains, the only sound to be heard being the bells on the elephant's feet. A memorable image, this shot of the elephant and the party making their way up a rocky slope became the poster for the movie (it's also during this sequence that Lean cuts to an eagle hovering overhead, making one wonder whether this is a tribute of sorts to his old sparring partner Sam Spiegel).

Then we're into the first of the caves, with the guide showing off the strange echo. Unfortunately, Mrs Moore gets caught in the crowd at the back and, feeling claustrophobic, rushes out. Collapsing into a chair, she looks skyward, only to be confronted by a giant image of the moon. Clearly, Mrs Moore doesn't have long left in this world, and Lean's way of conveying this visually (again) is both startling and arresting. Not up to the climb to the higher caves, Mrs Moore suggests that Adela and Dr Aziz go on ahead, accompanied only by the guide. 'Enjoy yourselves,' she says, at which Lean cuts to a long shot of Adela and Aziz climbing up the rocks. During the climb, Aziz stretches out his hand to help Adela, and an intimacy, it seems, is formed between them.

When they get to the top of the ridge, Aziz pardons himself from Adela and the guide to have a quick smoke, during which Adela ventures into one of the caves, alone. Inside, she lights a match and the cave begins to echo. Hot and confused, Adela seems on the verge of fainting, especially when Aziz presents himself at the mouth of the cave, although Adela stays in the shadows, not responding to his calls. What happens to Adela during these moments has puzzled many readers of the novel, for Forster presents things somewhat ambiguously. For those who care to pick it up, Lean is rather more definite about what has happened. Sexually confused, Adela has had her first orgasm, a point which Lean succinctly makes by cutting from her contorted face to a shot of the elephant taking its bath. As the elephant slips into a small pool, Lean cuts to a close-up of water pouring over the edge. At one and the same time, this image is both extremely subtle (many fail to pick up its meaning) and extremely vulgar. Yet it offers an excellent explanation for Adela's subsequent actions and accusations.

We next see her running down the mountainside in confusion, stumbling through a cactus patch along the way. Rescued by a passer-by (one Mrs Callendar [Ann Firbank]), she is driven back to Chandrapore, and while she is being cared for she accuses Aziz of rape. Fielding is incredulous, and decides to side with Aziz, who is subsequently arrested. The British are naturally outraged that Fielding could do such a thing. Says Godboli, 'My philosophy is, you can do what you like, but the outcome will be the same,' a comment which recalls the Arabs' philosophy in *Lawrence of Arabia*: it is written.

A trial is inevitable, but before it can take place, Mrs Moore leaves India for home. As her train pulls out of the platform at Chandrapore, she is compelled to look out of her window, only to see Godbole, his hands raised in salute to her, the assumption being that she and the Brahmin are kindred souls (it's Godbole's assertion that Mrs Moore is an old spirit, which ties in with Lean's frequent hints that she is an other-worldly character). Sadly, Mrs Moore dies on the voyage back home (she has a heart attack while looking at the night sky), but by this time the trial has started. Owing to his personal interest in the case, Ronny has to hand the proceedings over to his Indian deputy Das (Rashid Karapiet), much to the consternation of the British.

Aziz is represented by India's top lawyer, Amritrao (Roshan Seth), but his services are almost redundant, for while being questioned by her own QC, McBryde (Michael Culver), Adela withdraws her accusation and the trial collapses, much to the outrage of the British. Says Godboli, 'Who could have foretold that Aziz would be saved by his enemy!'

In the chaos following the trial, the dazed Adela is left wandering the streets in the rain, only to be rescued by Fielding. Aziz sees this as the ultimate betrayal, and vows never to have anything more to do with Fielding. In fact, the trial has left such a mark on Aziz that he leaves Chandrapore for Srinagar, a town in Kashmir, where he is joined by Godboli, who has been offered the post of Minister for Education. It is only years later that Fielding and Aziz meet again amid the splendour of the Himalayas (another fine excuse for Lean to treat us to some spectacular shots). In the meantime, Aziz has refused to answer Fielding's letters, believing him to have married Adela. This proves not to be the case, however, for Fielding has in fact married Mrs Moore's daughter Stella (Sandy Hotz), tying up all the ends.

Fielding and Aziz are now able to part as friends (in the book they ride off on horseback in different directions, agreeing to disagree), only leaving it for Aziz to write to Adela, telling her of

Lean on set

Fielding's visit, and that from this distance in time he can now forgive her, even finding in himself the ability to praise her bravery in recanting her accusation when the wheels of the law were so fully in motion. At home in England, Adela reads the letter in her room. Having done so, she looks out of the window. It is raining outside, and the film ends, full circle, with her mournfully looking through the rain-speckled glass.

A Passage to India was a triumph for David Lean, for not only does he manage to tell a complex and often ambiguous tale calmly and clearly, he had also invests it with his legendary visual flair. In many ways the film is his most visual, and not merely in terms of scenic splendour. Through clever cutting, choice of shots and framing, one can at times see the characters thinking. The most notable examples involve Adela, particularly at the derelict temple, and later when she fantasises about the statues in bed. Also, in the courtroom, Lean often shows her looking about the room, taking in the various details for us.

But the film doesn't live or die by Lean's touch. The performances are uniformly of a high calibre (including Sandy Hotz's silent but eye-catching turn as Stella), with only Guinness's Godbole striking a wrong note. The actor had played a variety of foreigners in his long and distinguished career (one only has to think of his Prince Feisal in *Lawrence of Arabia*). Yet by 1984, it seemed inappropriate and politically incorrect for him to be donning the darker shades of make-up when there were many Indian actors more than capable of taking on the role. Still, Guinness plays Godbole with dignity throughout and mercifully avoids slipping into a Peter Sellers routine. Despite his best efforts, it is an uncomfortable piece of casting (Lean insisted that Guinness, and only Guinness, was right for the part).

Where the film also triumphs is in its frequent contrast of British and Indian life. Lean could quite easily have fallen into the trap of patronising the Indians, as so many western filmmakers have done in the past. It is the snobbery and superior outlook of the British that instead comes in for a bashing. The Brits may have given India a good railway system, but at what cost? Even Fielding thinks the British should be kicked out.

A commercial hit on both sides of the Atlantic when released in December 1984 (USA) and February 1985 (UK), *A Passage to India* earned Lean some of his best reviews since *Lawrence of Arabia*. 'Impeccably faithful, beautifully played,' enthused *Variety*, to which Roger Ebert added, 'One of the greatest screen adaptations I have ever seen. Lean places these characters in one of the most beautiful canvases he has ever drawn.' Pauline Kael, of all people, also found much to admire in the film, commenting, 'Lean knows how to give the smallest inflections an overpowering psychological weight,' to which fellow *Ryan's Daughter* detractor Richard Schickel added, 'Like Forster, Lean uses India not just as a colourful and exotic setting, but as a decisive force in shaping the story he is telling, almost as a character.'

Acclaimed by practically all around him, Lean was again at the top of the cinema ladder, a fact reflected by *A Passage to India*'s 11 Academy Award nominations, which took in best picture (John Brabourne and Richard Goodwin), best director (Lean), best screenplay (Lean), best photography (Ernie Day), best music (Maurice Jarre), best art direction and set decoration (John Box, Hugh Scaife), best costume (Phyllis Dalton), best sound (Graham Hartstone, Nicholas Le Messurier, Michael A Carter, John Mitchell), best actress (Judy Davis) and best supporting actress (Peggy Ashcroft). The film was worthy of winning in every one of these categories. But it was the year of *Amadeus*, which took the lion's share of the major prizes (best film, best actor, best director, best screenplay, best art direction, best costume, best sound, best make-up), leaving Lean's film with only two: best supporting actress and best music, both of them richly deserved. Despite his three nominations, Lean came away empty handed, losing the best director award to Milos Foreman (*Amadeus*), the screenplay award to Peter Shaffer (*Amadeus*) and the editing award to Jim Clark (*The Killing Fields*).

Lean was completely overlooked at the BAFTAs, with best film going to Woody Allen's *The Purple Rose of Cairo*, while the best director trophy wasn't even awarded that year! Peggy Ashcroft did win best actress, while Lean was more than compensated with a knighthood, which he received from the Queen at Buckingham Palace on Tuesday 30 October 1984.

Commercially viable again, feted as a great artist and filmmaker, and now knighted, Sir David Lean had truly scaled the heights of his profession. The question now was, where from here?

ENDGAME

For a while after *A Passage to India*, it seemed likely that Lean's next film might be an adaptation of JG Ballard's 1984 novel *Empire of the Sun*, which revolves round an 11-year-old English boy's adventures in a Chinese internment camp during the Second World War. Lean couldn't get an angle on the story and the rights eventually ended up in the hands of Steven Spielberg, himself a great admirer of Lean's films (he has often cited *Lawrence of Arabia* as one of his greatest influences). Spielberg's version of *Empire of the Sun*, based on a script by playwright Tom Stoppard, was eventually released in 1987 to general acclaim. However, more than one critic pointed out that in style, the film was very much in the Lean manner. Earning Oscar nominations in six categories (but not for best director), the film did much for Spielberg's standing as a serious film-maker following *ET* and the first two *Indiana Jones* films.

After years of living out of a suitcase, albeit in some of the world's best hotels, Lean decided to put some firm roots down in Britain. He and Sandy bought some derelict warehouses on the Thames, which they had converted, at considerable cost, into a luxurious home. Despite their plans, they would never live in the place together, for Lean had met another woman at a dinner party, an art dealer named Sandra Cooke. Lean's marriage to Sandra Hotz was winding down and after he and Sandy mutually agreed on a divorce, they decided to go their separate ways. This became official on Tuesday 12 November 1985, making way for Cooke to become the sixth, and last, Mrs David Lean, although this didn't happen until five years later.

During this period, Lean kept himself busy, for in addition to trying to get *Empire of the Sun* together, he was also asked to supervise the restoration of *Lawrence of Arabia*. Although the film was just over 25 years old, no print of the original 222-minute premiere version existed. The project was spearheaded by Robert A Harris and Jim Painten (with assistance from Steven Spielberg and Martin Scorsese, whose names helped give the proceedings weight). They were determined on restoring some 30 minutes to the running time, which had been cut over the years to make the film more acceptable for general release and, later, television showings. Much of the missing material was discovered in the Columbia vaults, although in some instances without sound. Consequently, over a quarter of a century after completing the film, Peter O'Toole, Omar Sharif, Alec Guinness, Anthony Quayle, Arthur Kennedy and Charles Gray (doubling for the late Jack Hawkins, as he had done during Hawkins' later years when the actor lost his voice to throat cancer) gathered in various recording studios around the world to re-dub their dialogue for the restored sequences.

Following a premier in 1988 in Los Angeles, the film (the restoration of which had been the subject of a BBC documentary, *A Tickling of Talents*) was given a showing at the Cannes Film Festival in 1989, an event that was attended by Lean, Peter O'Toole, Omar Sharif and Anthony Quinn. It was a grand occasion, with the red-carpeted steps up to the cinema lined with boys dressed as Arabs. Audience reaction was astonishing, as it was throughout the rest of the world when the film went on general release. Acclaimed by many as not only Lean's masterpiece, but one of the true masterpieces of the cinema, the film earned plaudits wherever it played.

By the time *Lawrence of Arabia* was playing in the cinemas again, Lean was already well into preparing his next film. After a suggestion from members of The Cambridge Film Society, to whom he had given a talk, Lean had opted for an adaptation of Joseph Conrad's *Nostromo*, the story of a heroic but corrupt sailor who agrees to help smuggle silver out of a South American country (the fictitious Costaguana), only to end up keeping the treasure for himself, with the inevitable consequences.

To work with him on the screenplay, Lean first turned to celebrated playwright Christopher Hampton, known for *The Philanthropist* and *Les Liaisons Dangereuses*. *Nostromo* would by no means be Hampton's first screenplay. He'd already adapted Ibsen's *A Doll's House* for director Patrick Garland and Graham Greene's *The Honorary Consul* for John MacKenzie, while in 1988 he would win an Oscar for his adaptation of *Les Liaisons Dangereuses* (known to cinema audiences as *Dangerous Liaisons*). He'd even worked on an adaptation of *Nostromo* before for BBC television. The project, which was to have been directed by Stuart Burge, was shelved when it became prohibitively expensive.

The Hampton–Lean collaboration seemed to work well, and the script progressed steadily, to the point that casting choices started to be made, among Lean's wish-list being Marlon Brando, Paul Scofield and Isabella Rossellini, with French–Greek stage actor George Corraface (known primarily for appearing in Peter Brook's marathon presentation of Jean-Claude Carrière's adaptation of *The Mahabharata*) being chosen to play Nostromo. And just as Albert Finney had been the subject of a lavish and expensive screen test for *Lawrence of Arabia*, so too was Corraface for *Nostromo*.

With the script completed, Lean had a meeting with Steven Spielberg, who was to produce the film through his own company, Amblin, and Warners (Spielberg had a strong relationship with Warners, having directed *The Color Purple* and *Empire of the Sun*, and produced *Gremlins* for them). Spielberg and Lean failed to see eye to eye on the project and it began to collapse. By this time, Hampton and Lean's collaboration had run its course, leaving the door open for Robert Bolt to enter. Despite the fact that Bolt was still recovering from his stroke, he and Lean quickly slipped into their long-established working pattern, which was observed by Melvyn Bragg for an episode of *The South Bank Show*.

This was by no means the first *South Bank Show* programme to be dedicated to Lean. In 1985, he had been the subject of a two-hour documentary chronicling not only his career in general, but the making of *A Passage to India*, in particular. Broadcast on 17 February, the programme shows Lean at work on set in India, filming such scenes as the introduction of Aziz in the bazaar, Aziz's visit to Fielding's apartment and the departure of Mrs Moore before the trial. Fascinating stuff it is, being able to see the master at work both on set and in his editing suite. The second programme, aired in 1989, concentrated on Lean's working relationship with Bolt, and included interviews with both men (Bolt occasionally having to be subtitled, owing to his speech impediment after his stroke). Bolt and Lean were also shown working on the script together at Lean's warehouse home on the Thames.

This work went well, and the film, now to be produced by Polish-born Serge Silberman (*The Diary of a Chambermaid*, *The Discreet Charm of the Bourgoisie*, *The Phantom of Liberty*, *That Obscure Object of Desire*, *Ran*), looked set to go ahead, with Columbia (for whom Lean had made *Bridge Over the River Kwai* and *Lawrence of Arabia*) coming in as distributor. John Box had already started work on preliminary designs (some sets would actually be built for the film and then later destroyed). Unfortunately, the normally healthy Lean was beset by a series of illnesses, to the point that he had to agree that, should he die, another director of his choosing should be waiting in the wings (this had also been the case when the 78-year-old Ealing veteran Charles Crichton returned to the screen to make *A Fish Called Wanda* in 1988). From a list that included Robert Altman, Hugh Hudson, Kevin Costner and Peter Yates, Lean chose Guy Hamilton, whose successes included *An Inspector Calls*, *The Colditz Story* and *Goldfinger*. He'd also begun his career as an assistant to Carol Reed.

It was during this period that Lean flew to America to receive the American Film Institute's Lifetime Achievement Award, which he accepted on 8 Thursday March 1990, despite the fact that his illness had left him in a wheelchair. Gradually, over the year, his health began slowly to improve. His spirits rising, he proposed to Sandra, and the two were married in France on Thursday 15 December. Joy soon turned to pain, however, for it was not long after that Lean was diagnosed as having a tumour at the back of his mouth. Radiation therapy followed, and Lean's health fluctuated alarmingly, from death's door to recovery, hindered by bouts of pneumonia. Despite his strong will, he finally lost the battle and died on Tuesday 16 April 1991.

Lean was cremated six days later at Putney Vale Crematorium. Later that year, on Thursday 3 October, a memorial service was held at St Paul's Cathedral, and the echo of the (now restored) scenes from *Lawrence of Arabia* can't have been lost on those who attended.

Nostromo did eventually get made, appearing in 1995 as a BBC serial, although the script was by John Hale, not Christopher Hampton or Robert Bolt, while the director was Alistair Reid. Reception by both critics and audiences was luke warm at best. George Corraface didn't even get to star. Instead, he found himself cast as the lead in the dismal *Christopher Columbus: The Discovery*, which certainly did his burgeoning film career no good.

Those who had read the *Nostromo* script invariably described it as superb. Perhaps had Lean not spent so many years in the wilderness, we might have had both *Nostromo* and *Mutiny on the Bounty*, plus a couple more. But we do have the sinking of The Torrin, Celia Johnson with grit in her eye, Pip's dash across the marshes, Oliver asking for more, Charles Laughton's moonwalk, Katharine Hepburn falling into a canal, the POWs whistling Colonel Bogey, Omar Sharif emerging from a mirage, a charge across a frozen lake, the greatest storm ever filmed and a strange echo that simply won't go away. David Lean is responsible for some of the most memorable moments in film history. The gentleman filmmaker may no longer be with us, but his work will live forever.

Sixteen

FILMOGRAPHY

The following is a chronological filmography of every film worked on by Lean as either director, producer, writer, editor or assistant. All the key cast and technical credits for each film are listed where available, along with running times and the year of release. However, in the case of Lean's early films as an assistant, etc., it must be noted that very little information is available, as many of these films are either lost or unavailable for review. Oscar wins are noted AA, while Oscar nominations are noted AAN following the applicable credit.

THE QUINNEYS

GB 1927 B&W

Studio	Gaumont
Director	Maurice Elvey
Clapper boy/assistant	David Lean
Cast	Alma Taylor, John Longden

SAILOR'S DON'T CARE

GB 1927 B&W

Director	Will Kellino
Director of photography	Baron Ventimiglia
Camera assistant	David Lean
Cast	Alf Goddard, John Stuart

THE PHYSICIAN

GB 1928 B&W

Studio	Gaumont
Director	George Jacoby
Camera assistant	David Lean
Cast	Lissi Arna

PALAIS DE DANSE

GB 1928 B&W

Studio	Gaumont
Writers	John Longden, Jean Jay
Director	Maurice Elvey
Director of photography	Percy Strong
Assistant	David Lean
Cast	John Longden, Mabel Poulton

BALACLAVA

GB 1928 B&W

Studio	Gaumont
Director	Maurice Elvey
Wardrobe	David Lean, Geoff Boothby

WHAT MONEY CAN'T BUY

GB 1929 B&W

Studio	Gaumont
Director	Edwin Greenwood
Camera assistant	David Lean
Cast	Madeleine Carroll, John Longden, David Lean

HIGH TREASON

GB 1929 90m B&W

Studio	Gaumont
Writers	L'Estrange Fawcett based on the play by Noel Pemberton-Billing
Director	Maurice Elvey
Director of photography	Percy Strong
Assistant	David Lean
Cast	Jameson Thomas, Basil Gill, Benita Hume, Humbertson Wright, Raymond Massey

THE NIGHT PORTER

GB 1929 20m B&W

Studio	Gaumont
Director	Sewell Collins
Sound editor	David Lean
Cast	Donald Calthrop

GAUMONT NEWSREELS

1929–32

Editor and narrator	David Lean

THESE CHARMING PEOPLE

GB 1931 B&W

Producer	Walter Morosco for B&D
Playwright	Michael Arlen
Director	Louis Mercanton
Editor	David Lean
Cast	Nora Swinburne, Cyril Maude, Ann Todd, Godfrey Tearle

INSULT

GB 1932 B&W

Studio	B&D
Director	Harry Lachman
Editor	David Lean
Cast	John Gielgud, Sam Livesey, Elizabeth Allan

MONEY FOR SPEED

GB 1933 B&W

Studio	Wembley
Director	Bernard Vorhaus
Director of photography	Eric Cross
Editor	David Lean
Cast	Cyril McLaglen, Ida Lupino, John Loder

THE GHOST CAMERA

GB 1933 62m B&W

Studio	Real Art/H&S
Writer	H Fowler Mear based on the novel by Jefferson Farjeon
Director	Bernard Vorhaus
Director of photography	Enest Palmer
Composer	no credit given
Editor	David Lean
Art director	James A Carter
Sound	Carlisle Mounteney
Cast	Henry Kendall, Ida Lupino, John Mills, S Victor Stanley, George Merritt

TIGER BAY

GB 1933 B&W

Studio	Ealing
Director	J Elder Wills
Art director	J Elder Wills
Co-story	J Elder Wills
Director of photography	Robin G Martin
Editors	David Lean, Ian Thomson
Cast	Anna May Wong, Henry Victor

SONG OF THE PLOUGH

GB 1933 B&W

Studio	B&D
Director	John Baxter
Editor	David Lean
Cast	Rosalinde Fuller, Stewart Rome

DANGEROUS GROUND

GB 1934 B&W

Director	Norman Walker
Editor	David Lean
Cast	Joyce Kennedy, Malcolm Keen

SECRET OF THE LOCH

GB 1934 80m B&W

Producer	Bray Wyndham for ABFD
Writers	Charles Bennett, Billie Bristow
Director	Milton Rosmer
Director of photography	Jimmy Wilson
Composer	Peter Mendoza
Editor	David Lean
Art director	J Elder Wills
Cast	Seymour Hicks, Nancy O'Neil, Rosamund John, Gibson Gowland, Frederick Peisley, Ben Field

NELL GWYN

GB 1933 84m B&W

Producer	Herbert Wilcox for B&D
Writer	Miles Malleson
Director	Herbert Wilcox
Director of photography	Frederick A Young
Composer	Philip Braham
Editor	Merrill White
Assistant editor	David Lean (unaccredited)
Art director	LP Williams
Costume designer	Doris Zinkeisen
Sound	LE Overton
Cast	Anna Neagle, Cedric Hardwicke, Jeanne de Casalis, Muriel George, Miles Malleson, Esme Percy, Moore Marriott, Dorothy Robinson, Craighall Cherry, Lawrence Anderson, Helena Pickard

BREWSTER'S MILLIONS

GB 1935 84m B&W

Producer	Herbert Wilcox for B&D
Writers	Arthur Wimperis, Paul Gangelin, Douglas Furber, Donovan Pedelty, Wolfgang Wilhelm based on the novel by George Barry McCutcheon
Director	Thornton Freeland
Directors of photography	Henry Harris, Barney McGill
Composer	Ray Noble
Editor	Merrill White
Assistant editor	David Lean (unaccredited)
Art director	LP Williams
Cast	Jack Buchanan, Lili Damita, Fred Emney, Nancy O'Neil, Amy Veness, Sydney Fairbrother, Sebastian Shaw

JAVA HEAD

GB 1934 85m B&W

Producer	Basil Dean for ATP
Writers	Gordon Wellesley, Martin Brown based on the novel by Joseph Hergesheimer
Director	J Walter Ruben
Director of photography	Robert Martin
Musical director	Ernest Irving
Editor	Thorold Dickinson
Co-editor	David Lean (unaccredited)
Art director	Edward Carrick
Cast	Anna May Wong, John Loder, George Curzon, Elizabeth Allan, Ralph Richardson, Edmund Gwenn, Herbert Lomas, Roy Emerton

TURN OF THE TIDE

GB 1935 80m B&W

Producer	John Corfield for British National
Writers	JOC Orton, L DuGarde Peach based on the novel *Three Fevers* by Leo Walmsley
Director	Norman Walker
Director of photography	Franz Planer
Composer	Arthur Benjamin
Co-editor	David Lean (unaccredited)
Cast	John Garrick, Geraldine Fitzgerald, Niall MacGinnis, Joan Maude, Wilfred Lawson, Moore Marriott, J Fisher White, Sam Livesey

ESCAPE ME NEVER

GB 1935 95m B&W

Producers	Herbert Wilcox, Dallas Bower for B&D
Writers	Carl Zuckerman, Robert Cullen based on the play by Margaret Kennedy
Director	Paul Czinner
Director of photography	Georges Perinal
Composer	William Walton
Editors	Merrill G White, David Lean
Art directors	Andre Andrejev, Wilfred Arnold
Cast	Elisabeth Bergner (AAN), Hugh Sinclair, Penelope Dudley Ward, Griffith Jones, Lyn Harding, Irene Vanbrugh, Leon Quartermaine

BALL AT THE SAVOY

GB 1936 B&W

Director	Victor Hanbury
Editor	David Lean
Cast	Conrad Nagel, Marta Labarr

AS YOU LIKE IT

GB/USA 1936 96m B&W

Producers	Joseph M Schenck, Paul Czinner for Twentieth Century Fox/Inter-Allied
Writers	JM Barrie, Robert Cullen based on the play by William Shakespeare
Director	Paul Czinner
Director of photography	Harold Rosson
Composer	William Walton
Editor	David Lean
Cast	Elisabeth Bergner, Laurence Olivier, Henry Ainley, Richard Ainley, Leon Quartermaine, Sophie Stewart, Mackenzie Ward, Aubrey Mather, Peter Bull, John Laurie

DREAMING LIPS

GB 1937 94m B&W

Producers	Max Schach, Paul Czinner for Trafalgar
Writers	Lady Cynthia Asquith, Margaret Kennedy, Carl Mayer based on the play *Melo* by Henry Bernstein
Director	Paul Czinner
Directors of photography	Roy Clark, Lee Garmes
Composer	William Walton
Editor	David Lean
Art directors	Tom Morahan, Andrei Andrejev
Cast	Elisabeth Bergner, Romney Brent, Felix Aylmer, Raymond Massey, Donald Calthrop, Sydney Fairbrother, Joyce Bland

THE LAST ADVENTURERS

GB 1937 77m B&W

Producer	H Fraser-Passmore for Conway
Writer	Denison Clift
Director	Roy Kellino
Director of photography	Eric Cross
Composer	Eric Ansell
Editor	David Lean
Art director	WR Brinton
Cast	Niall MacGinnis, Kay Walsh, Peter Gawthorne, Katie Johnson, Linden Travers, Roy Emerton

PYGMALION

GB 1938 96m B&W

Producer	Gabriel Pascal (AAN best picture) for Pascal Film Productions
Writer	George Bernard Shaw (AA) from his play
Adaptation	WP Lipscomb, Cecil Lewis, Ian Dalrymple (AA)
Directors	Gabriel Pascal, Leslie Howard
Director of photography	Harry Stradling
Composer	Arthur Hoenegger
Musical director	Louis Levy
Editor	David Lean
Art directors	Laurence Irving, John Bryan
Costume designer	L Czettel
Sound	Alex Fisher
Camera operator	Jack Hildyard
Cast	Leslie Howard (AAN), Wendy Hiller (AAN), Wilfred Lawson, Marie Lohr, Scott Sunderland, Jean Cadell, David Tree, Everley Gregg, Iris Hoey, Leo Genn, OB Clarence, Esme Percy, Leueen MacGrath, Anthony Quayle (unaccredited)

SPIES OF THE AIR

GB 1939 77m B&W

Producer	John Cirfield for British National
Writers	AR Rawlinson, Bridget Boland based on the play *Official Secrets* by Jeffrey Dell
Director	David MacDonald
Editor	David Lean
Cast	Barry K Barnes, Joan Marion, Roger Livesey, Basil Radford, John Turnbull, Henry Oscar, Felix Aylmer

FRENCH WITHOUT TEARS

GB 1939 87m B&W

Producers	David E Rose, Mario Zampi for Paramount/Two Cities
Writers	Anatole de Grunwald, Terence Rattigan based on the play by Terence Rattigan
Director	Anthony Asquith
Director of photography	Bernard Knowles
Composer	Nikolaus Brodsky
Editor	David Lean
Art director	Paul Sheriff
Costume designer	Worth
Sound	Alex Fisher
Camera operator	Jack Hildyard
Cast	Ray Milland, Ellen Drew, Guy Middleton, Roland Culver, David Tree, Jim Gerald, Janine Darcy, Kenneth Morgan

SPY FOR A DAY

GB 1940 71m B&W

Producer	Mario Zampi for Two Cities
Writers	Anatole de Grunwald, Tommy Thompson, Emeric Pressburger, Ralph Block, Hans Wilhelm
Story	Stacy Aumonier
Director	Mario Zampi
Director of photography	Bernard Knowles
Composer	Nikolaus Brodsky
Editor	David Lean
Cast	Duggie Wakefield, Paddy Browne, Jack Allen, Gibb McLaughlin, Nicholas Hannen, Albert Lieven

MAJOR BARBARA

GB 1941 121m B&W

Producer	Gabriel Pascal
Writers	Anatole de Grunwald, Gabriel Pascal from the play by George Bernard Shaw
Director	Gabriel Pascal
Assistants in direction	Harold French, David Lean
Directors of photography	Ronald Neame (Freddie Young)
Composer	William Walton
Musical director	Muir Mathieson
Editor	Charles Frend
Montage	David Lean
Art directors	Vincent Korda, John Bryan
Costume designer	Cecil Beaton
Sound	Martin Paggi
Cast	Wendy Hiller, Rex Harrison, Robert Morley, Emlyn Williams, Robert Newton, Deborah Kerr, Sybil Thorndike, Marie Lohr, David Tree, Penelope Dudley Ward, Miles Malleson, Felix Aylmer, Walter Hudd, Donald Calthrop, Marie Ault, Kathleen Harrison, Joe Gladwyn

THE 49TH PARALLEL (AKA THE INVADERS)

GB/Canada 1941 123m B&W

Producers	Michael Powell, John Sutro for GFD/Ortus
Writers	Emeric Pressburger, Rodney Ackland (AAN)
Story	Emeric Pressburger (AA)
Director	Michael Powell
Director of photography	Frederick Young
Composer	Ralph Vaughan Williams
Editors	David Lean, Hugh Stewart
Art directors	David Rawnsley, Sydney S Streeter, Frederick Pusey
Sound	AW Watkins, CC Stevens, Walter Darling
Camera operators	Skeets Kelley, Henry Henty-Creer
Special photography	Osmond Borrowdaille
Cast	Eric Portman, Laurence Olivier, Anton Walbrook, Raymond Massey, Leslie Howard, Niall Macginnis, Finlay Currie, John Chandos, Raymond Lovell, Glynis Johns

ONE OF OUR AIRCRAFT IS MISSING

GB 1941 102m B&W

Producers	Michael Powell, Emeric Pressburger for British Lion/The Archer
Writers	Michael Powell, Emeric Pressburger (AAN)
Directors	Michael Powell, Emeric Pressburger
Directors of photography	Robert Neame (and Robert Krasker)
Composer	none
Editor	David Lean
Art director	David Rawnsley
Special effects	Ronald Neame, CC Stevs (AAN)
Cast	Eric Portman, Godfrey Tearle, Hugh Williams, Bernard Miles, Hugh Burden, Emrys Jones, Peter Ustinov, Googie Withers, Pamela Brown, Joyce Redman, Hay Petrie, Robert Helpmann, Alec Clunes, Roland Culver

IN WHICH WE SERVE

GB 1942 114m B&W

Producer	Noel Coward (AAN best picture) for Two Cities/Rank
Writer	Noel Coward (AAN)
Directors	Noel Coward, David Lean
Director of photography	Ronald Neame
Composer	Noel Coward
Musical director	Muir Mathieson
Editors	Thelma Myers (David Lean)
Art directors	David Rawnsley (Gladys Calthrop)
Special effects	Douglas Woolsey
Sound	CC Stevens, Desmond Dew
Camera operator	Guy Green
Cast	Noel Coward, John Mills, Bernard Miles, Celia Johnson, Kay Walsh, Joyce Carey, Michael Wilding Penelope Dudley Ward, Philip Friend, Derek Elphinstone, Frederick Piper, Geoffrey Hibbert, Kathleen Harrison, George Carney, James Donald, Richard Attenborough, Daniel Massey, Hubert Gregg, Johnnie Schofield, Juliett Mills, Wally Patch, Leslie Dwyer, Kay Young

*Special AA to Noel Coward for outstanding achievement in production

THIS HAPPY BREED

GB 1944 114m Technicolor

Producer	Noel Coward for GFD/Two Cities
Writer	Noel Coward from his play
Director	David Lean
Director of photography	Ronald Neame
Composer	Noel Coward
Musical director	Muir Mathieson
Editor	Jack Harris
Art directors	CP Williams (Gladys Calthrop)
Costume designer	Hilda Collins
Special effects	Percy Day
Sound	CC Stevens, John Cooke, Desmond Dew
Cast	Robert Newton, Celia Johnson, John Mills, Kay Walsh, Amy Veness, Alison Leggatt, Eileen Erskine, John Blythe, Stanley Holloway, Guy Verney, Merle Tottenham, Betty Fleetwood

FAILURE OF A STRATEGY

GB 1944 10m B&W

Producer	Arthur Calder-Marshall for Cineguild
Executive producer	Sidney Bernstein
Director	David Lean
Editor	Peter Tanner

FAILURE OF THE GENERALS

GB 1944 10m B&W

Executive producer	Sidney Bernstein for Cineguild
Editor	Peter Tanner

BLITHE SPIRIT

GB 1945 96m Technicolor

Producer	Anthony Havelock-Allan for Two Cities/Cineguild
Writer	Noel Coward from his play
Adaptation	David Lean, Anthony Havelock-Allan, Ronald Neame
Director	David Lean
Director of photography	Ronald Neame
Composer	Richard Addinsell
Musical director	Muir Mathieson
Editor	Jack Harris
Art directors	CP Norman, Gladys Calthrop
Costume designers	Hilda Collins, Rahuis
Special effects	Tom Howard (AA)
Sound	John Cooke, Desmond
Assistant director	George Pollack
Narrator	Noel Coward
Cast	Rex Harrison, Kay Hammond, Constance Cummings, Margaret Rutherford Joyce Carey, Hugh Wakefield, Jacqueline Clark

BRIEF ENCOUNTER

GB 1945 86m B&W

Producers	Noel Coward, Ronald Neame, Anthony Havelock-Allan for Eagle-Lion/Cineguild
Writers	Noel Coward, David Lean, Anthony Havelock-Allan, Ronald Neame (AAN) from the play Still Life by Noel Coward
Director	David Lean (AAN)
Director of photography	Robert Krasker
Composer	Rachmaninov
Musical director	Muir Mathieson
Piano solos	Eileen Joyce
Editors	Jack Harris, Margery Saunders
Art directors	LP Williams, Gladys Calthrop
Sound	Stanley Lambourne, Desmond Dew
Assistant director	George Pollack
Cast	Celia Johnson (AAN), Trevor Howard, Stanley Holloway, Joyce Carey, Cyril Raymond, Everly Gregg, Marjorie Mars, Margaret Barton, Valentine Dyall, Dennis Harkin, Irene Handl

GREAT EXPECTATIONS

GB 1946 118m B&W

Producer	Ronald Neame (AAN best picture) for Cineguild
Executive producer	Anthony Havelock-Allan
Writers	Ronald Neame, Anthony Havelock-Allan, David Lean (AAN), Kay Walsh, Cecil McGivern from the novel by Charles Dickens
Director	David Lean (AAN)
Director of photography	Guy Green (AA)
Composer	Walter Goehr
Editor	Jack Harris
Art directors	Wilfred Shingleton, John Bryan (AA)
Costume designers	Sophia Harris, Margaret Furse
Sound	Stanley Lambourne, Gordon K McCallum
Sound	Winston Ryder
Assistant director	George Pollock
Cast	John Mills, Alec Guinness, Finlay Currie, Valerie Hobson, Bernard Miles, Martita Hunt, Jean Simmons, Francis L Sullivan, Anthony Wager, George Hayes, Freda Jackson, Ivor Barnard, Hay Petrie, Torin Thatcher, Ob Clarence, Eileen Erskine, Edie Martin, Everly Gregg

OLIVER TWIST

GB 1948 116m B&W

Producer	Ronald Neame for GFD/Cineguild/Independent
Writers	David Lean, Stanley Haynes from the novel by Charles Dickens
Director	David Lean
Director of photography	Guy Green
Composer	Arnold Bax
Musical director	Muir Mathieson
Editor	Jack Harris
Art director	John Bryan
Costume designer	Margaret Furse
Special effects	John Suttie, Stanley Grant
Sound	Stanley Lambourne, Gordon K McCallum
Assistant director	George Pollack
Camera operator	Oswald Morris
Cast	Alec Guinness, Robert Newton, Francis L Sullivan, John Howard Davies, Kay Walsh, Anthony Newley, Henry Stephenson, Mary Clare, Gibb McLaughlin, Diana Dors, Peter Bull, Hattie Jacques, Edie Martin

THE PASSIONATE FRIENDS
(AKA ONE WOMAN'S STORY)

GB 1948 91m B&W

Producer	Ronald Neame for Cineguild
Writers	Eric Ambler, David Lean, Stanley Haynes from the novel by HG Wells
Director	David Lean
Director of photography	Guy Green
Composer	Richard Addinsell
Musical director	Muir Mathieson
Editor	Geoffrey Foot
Art director	John Bryan
Costume designer	Margaret Furse
Sound	Stanley Lambourne, Gordon K McCallum
Assistant director	George Pollack
Camera operator	Oswald Morris
Cast	Ann Todd, Trevor Howard, Claude Rains, Isabel Dean, Ann Davies, Arthur Howard, Wilfred Hyde-White

MADELEINE

GB 1949 114m B&W

Producer	Stanley Haynes for GFD/Cineguild
Writers	Stanley Haynes, Nicholas Phipps
Director	David Lean
Director of photography	Guy Green
Composer	William Alwyn
Musical director	Muir Mathieson
Editor	Geoffrey Foot
Art director	John Bryan
Costume designer	Margaret Furse
Sound	No credit
Assistant director	George Pollack
Narrator	James McKechnie
Cast	Ann Todd, Leslie Banks, Elizabeth Sellars, Ivor Barnard, Ivan Desny, Norman Woolland, Edward Chapman, Barbara Everest, Andre Morell, Barry Jones, Jean Cadell, John Laurie, Susan Stranks, Eugene Deckers, Moira Fraser, Amy Veness, Kynaston Reeves

THE SOUND BARRIER (AKA BREAKING THE SOUND BARRIER)

GB 1952 118m B&W

Producer	David Lean for London Films
Executive producer	Alexander Korda
Associate producer	Norman Spencer
Writer	Terence Rattigan (AAN)
Director	David Lean
Director of photography	Jack Hildyard
Composer	Malcolm Arnold
Musical director	Muir Mathieson
Editor	Geoffrey Foot
Art directors	Vincent Korda, Joseph Bato, John Hawkesworth
Sound	John Cox (AA)
Second unit director	Anthony Squire
Cast	Ralph Richardson, Nigel Patrick, Ann Todd, John Justin, Dinah Sheridan, Joseph Tomelty, Denholm Elliott, Leslie Phillips, Jack Allen

HOBSON'S CHOICE

GB 1953 107m B&W

Producers	David Lean, Norman Spencer for London Films/British Lion
Writers	David Lean, Norman Spencer from the play by Harold Brighouse
Director	David Lean
Director of photography	Jack Hildyard
Composer	Malcolm Arnold
Musical director	Muir Mathieson
Editor	Peter Taylor
Art director	Wilfred Shingleton
Costume designers	John Armstrong, Julia Squire
Sound	John Cox, Buster Ambler, Red Law
Cast	Charles Laughton, John Mills, Brenda De Banzie, Prunella Scales, Richard Wattis, Helen Haye, John Laurie, Daphne Anderson, Jack Howarth, Edie Martin, Raymond Huntley, Joseph Tomelty, Gibb McLaughlin, Derek Blomfield, Dorothy Gordon, Madge Brindley

SUMMER MADNESS (AKA SUMMERTIME)

GB 1955 99m Eastmancolor

Producer	Ilya Lopert for London Films/Lopert
Writers	David Lean, HE Bates from the play *The Time of the Cuckoo* by Arthur Laurents
Director	David Lean (AAN)
Director of photography	Jack Hildyard
Composer	Sandro Cicogini
Editor	Peter Taylor
Production designer	Vincent Korda
Costume designer	no credit given
Sound	Peter Handford, John Cox
Camera operator	Peter Newbrook
Cast	Katharine Hepburn (AAN), Rossano Brazzi, Isa Miranda, Darren McGavin, Andre Morell, Mari Aldon, Jeremy Spenser, Gaetano Audiero

THE BRIDGE ON THE RIVER KWAI

GB/US 1957 161m Technicolor Cinemascope

Producer	Sam Spiegel (AA best picture) for Columbia/Horizon
Writers	Michael Wilson, Carl Foreman (AA) (and David Lean) from the novel by Pierre Boulle
Director	David Lean (AA)
Director of photography	Jack Hildyard (AA)
Composer	Malcolm Arnold (AA)
Editor	Peter Taylor (AA)
Art directors	Donald M Ashton, Geoffrey Drake
Costume designer	John Apperson
Sound	John Cox, John Mitchell
Sound editor	Winston Ryder
Camera operator	Peter Newbrook
Cast	William Holden, Jack Hawkins, Alec Guinness (AA), Sessue Hayakawa (AAN), Percy Herbert, Geoffrey Horne, James Donald, Andre Morell, Ann Sears, Harold Goodwin

LAWRENCE OF ARABIA

GB/US 1962 222m Technicolor Super Panavision 70

Producer	Sam Spiegel (AA) for Columbia/Horizon
Writers	Robert Bolt (AAN) (and Michael Wilson) from *The Seven Pillars of Wisdom* by TE Lawrence
Director	David Lean (AA)
Director of photography	Frederick A Young (AA)
Composer	Maurice Jarre (AA)
Editor	Anne V Coates (AA)
Production designers	John Box, John Stoll, Dario Simoni (AA)
Costume designer	Phyllis Dalton
Special effects	Cliff Richardson
Sound	Paddy Cunningham, John Cox, Winston Ryder (AA)
Second unit directors	Andre Smagghe, Noel Howard (and Andre de Toth)
Second unit photography	Skeets Kelly, Nicolas Roeg, Peter Newbrook
Camera operator	Ernest Day
Cast	Peter O'Toole (AAN), Omar Sharif (AAN), Arthur Kenney, Jack Hawkins, Claude Rains, Anthony Quayle, Anthony Quinn, Donald Wolfit, Jose Ferrer, Alec Guinness, IS Johar, Michael Ray, Zia

Mohyeddin, Brian
Pringle, Harry
Fowler, Howard
Marion Crawford,
Jack Gwillim

* 1988 restoration

Producers Robert A Harris,
Jim Painten

Restoration Robert A Harris

Editors Anne V Coates,
David Lean

Sound Richard L
Anderson, Greg
Landaker

THE GREATEST STORY EVER TOLD

USA 1965 198m Technicolor Super Panavision 70

Producers George Stevens Jr,
Frank I Davis,
Antonioni Vellari
for UA

Executive producer George Stevens

Writers George Stevens,
James Lee Barrett

Director George Stevens

Directors of photography William C Mellor,
Loyal Griggs (AAN)

Composer Alfred Newman
(AAN)

Editors Harold F Kress,
Argyle Nelson Jr,
Frank O'Neill

Art directors Richard Day,
William Creberm
David Hall

Costume designers Vittoria Nino
Novarese, Marjorie
Best

Special effects J McMillam
Johnson, Clarence
Slifer, A Arnold
Gillespie, Robert R
Hoag

Sound Charles Wallace,
Franklin Milton,
William Steinkamp

Second unit directors Richard Talmadge,
William Hale,
David Lean
(unaccredited), Jean
Negulesco
(unaccredited)

Cast Max Von Sydow,
Claude Rains,
Charlton Heston,
Dorothy McGuire,
Jose Ferrer, David
McCallum, Sidney
Poitier, Donald
Pleasence, Telly
Savalas, Roddy
McDowell, Gary
Raymond, Carroll
Baker, Pat Boone,
Van Heflin, Sal
Mineo, Shelley
Winters, Ed Wynn,
John Wayne, Angela
Lansbury, Victor
Buono, Joseph
Schildkraut,
Nehemiah Persoff

DOCTOR ZHIVAGO

USA 1965 192m Metrocolor Panavision (filmed in 35mm, blown up to 70mm)

Producer	Carlo Ponti (AAN best picture) for MGM
Executive producer	Arvid L Griffen
Writer	Robert Bolt (AA) from the novel by Boris Pasternak
Director	David Lean (AAN)
Director of photography	Frederick A Young (AA)
Composer	Maurice Jarre (AA)
Editor	Norman Savage (AAN)
Ad/set decoration	John Box, Terry Marsh, Dario Simoni (AA)
Costume designer	Phyllis Dalton
Special effects	Eddie Fowlie
Second unit director	Roy Rissotti
Second unit photography	Manuel Berenguer
Sound	AW Watkins, Franklin E Milton (AAN), Paddy Cunningham, Franklin Milton, William Steinkamp
Cast	Omar Sharif, Julie Christie, Geraldine Chaplin, Rod Steiger, Alec Guinness, Rita Tushingham, Ralph Richardson, Tom Courtnay (AAN), Siobhan McKenna, Adrienne Corri, Geoffrey Keen, Eric Chitty, Klaus Kinski, Tarek Sharif, Mark Eden, Noel Willman, Gwen Nelson

RYAN'S DAUGHTER

GB 1970 206m Metrocolor Panavision

Producer	Anthony Havelock-Allan for MGM/Faraway
Writer	Robert Bolt
Director	David Lean
Director of photography	Frederick A Young (AA)
Composer	Maurice Jarre
Editor	Norman Savage
Production designer	Stephen Grimes
Art director	Roy Walker
Costume designer	Jocelyn Rickards
Special effects	Robert McDonald
Sound	John Bramall, Gordon K McCallum (AAN)
Second unit directors	Roy Stevens, Charles Frend
Second unit photography	Denys Coop, Bob Huke
Camera operator	Ernest Day
Cast	Sarah Miles (AAN), Robert Mitchum, Christopher Jones (dubbed by Julian Holloway), John Mills (AA), Trevor Howard, Leo McKern, Barry Foster, Marie Kean, Evin Crowley, Arthur O'Sullivan, Douglas Sheldon, Gerald Sim, Barry Jackson

LOST AND FOUND: THE STORY OF AN ANCHOR

NZ 1979 40m Colour TV documentary

Producer	George Andrews for South Pacific TV
Writers	George Andrews, Wayne Tourell (and David Lean, Robert Bolt)
Directors	Wayne Tourell, David Lean
Directors of photography	Ken Dorman, Lynton Diggle
Narrator	David Lean

A PASSAGE TO INDIA

GB 1984 163m Technicolor Dolby Stereo

Producers	John Brabourne, Richard Goodwin (AAN best picture) for Thorn-EMI
Executive producers	John Heyman, Edward Sand
Writer	David Lean (AAN) from the novel by EM Forster and the play by Santha Rama Rau
Director	David Lean (AAN)
Director of photography	Ernest Day (AAN)
Composer	Maurice Jarre (AA)
Editor	David Lean (AAN)
Production designers	John Box, Leslie Tomkins, Hugh Scaife (AAN)
Costume designer	Judy Moorcroft (AAN)
Special effects	Robin Browne
Second unit director	Robin Browne
Sound	John Mitchell, Michael A Carter, Nicholas Le Messurier, Graham V Hartsone (AAN)
Cast	Judy Davis (AAN), Peggy Ashcroft (AA), James Fox, Victor Banerjee, Alec Guinness, Nigel Havers, Clive Swift, Michael Culver, Saeed Jaffrey, Richard Wilson, Art Malik, Ann Firbank, Sandra Hotz, Antonia Pemberton, Ann Firbank, Peter Hughes

All photos supplied by The Joel Finler Archive.
Copyright is attributed to the studios that produced the various films